DICTIONARY OF ECONOMICS

C.S. NAGPAL

ANMOL PUBLICATIONS PVT. LTD.
NEW DELHI - 110 002 (INDIA)

ANMOL PUBLICATIONS PVT. LTD.
Regd. Office: 4360/4, Ansari Road, Daryaganj,
New Delhi-110002 (India)
Tel.: 23278000, 23261597, 23286875, 23255577
Fax: 91-11-23280289
Email: anmolpub@gmail.com
Visit us at: www.anmolpublications.com

Branch Office: No. 1015, Ist Main Road, BSK IIIrd Stage
IIIrd Phase, IIIrd Block, Bengaluru-560 085 (India)
Tel.: 080-41723429 • Fax: 080-26723604
Email: anmolpublicationsbangalore@gmail.com

Dictionary of Economics

First Edition 1989
Reprint 1990, 1991, 1992, 1993
Second Edition 1994
Reprint 1995, 1997, 1998, 2000, 2001, 2002, 2003, 2004, 2006, 2007, 2008, 2011, 2014

PRINTED IN INDIA

Printed at Harnam Offset Press, Delhi

Preface

It is a matter of great saftisfaction that the first edition of this dictionary got exhausted within a short period. Now I am presenting the new revised edition. This has been revised to make it uptodate.

This dictionary has been carefully compiled and edited to provide students of economics at all levels with a handy and reliable source for definitions of economic and financial institutions.

Every effort has been carefully made to write the entries in a clear and lucid style to provide both straight forward definitions and invaluable background information. At some appropriate places, line drawings have been incorporated whenever the meaning of a word can be best understood by means of a diagram.

The dictionary will be of immense value to undergraduate and postgraduate students and to those appearing for competitive examinations, research scholars, teachers, economic administrators, planners, journalists, business managers and the general reader.

In compiling a dictionary of this kind, it become essential to draw upon the work of many authorities and seek the advice of colleagues to all of whom the editor is deeply indebted.

C. S. Nagpal

A

A.A.A. Refers to a rating classification which is given by Standard and Poor in respect of the credit standing of outstanding corporations and companies; in this example, an indication of considerable commercial integrity, with minimal risk of default. The concept is also applicable to countries and public institutions.

Abandoned Option. Means a share option not exercised because the price is against the buyer (or taker) on declaration day, i.e. the situation has unprofitable.

Abatement Cost. Means the cost of abating a nuisance like pollution or congestion.

Ability-To-Pay. A principle which is most commonly associated with the theory of taxation. This principle states that the burden of taxation should be carried by the individual in accordance whit his ability-to-pay, and not in accordance with the benefits he may receive because of public expenditure. Adam Smith (1723-1790) gave this principle that citizens should contribute 'in proportion to their respective abilities: that is in proportion to the revenue which they respectively enjoy under the protection of the state.'

Abscissa. Refers to the value on the horizontal (or X) axis of a point on a two dimensional graph.

Absenteeism. Refers to the failure to report for work although the terms of the labour contract need the worker to do so and the contract has been still operational. The overemployed worker will resort to this where control of the terms of the labour contract has been lax or where sanctions for non-compliance are negligible. In particular employers who are currently experiencing labour shortage might have been reluctant to use the ultimate sanction of sacking.

Absolute Income Hypothesis. According to this hypothesis, consumption expenditures (C) have been a function solely of current personal disposable income (Y_d): $C=C(Y_d)$. This view of the determinants of consumption was discussed in the general theory by Keynes who postulated that consumption would be functionally related to income in the following way. First for any change in income the corresponding change in consumption would be in the same direction but of a smaller magnitude, the marginal propensity to consume would be less than l;

$$0<\Delta C/\Delta y\&Y<1$$

Where Δ represents 'small change in'. Second the marginal propensity to consume would be less than the average propensity to consume;

$$\frac{\Delta C}{\Delta Y}<\frac{C}{Y}$$

Finally the rate of change of the marginal propensity to consume would be negative; that is that the slope of the consumption function will become flatter as income rises.

Absolute Monopoly. Means the control of the entire output of a commodity or service, for which there exists no substitute, by a single producer or supplier. This kind of situation rarely arises in real life. It is also known as pure monopoly or perfect monopoly. The central idea is that the demand curve has been perfectly inelastic.

Abstinence. Refers to, the sacrifice of current consumption to increase future consumption usually by enabling resources to get directed to the production of capital goods. As this means that in the long run the flow of consumer goods will get increased, abstinence may be considered to be as the sacrifice of some current consumption in favour of greater future consumption.

Abstinence or Agio Theory of Interest. A theory which states that interest is a payment for abstaining from current consumption. This is but a partial explanation as there have been other reasons for saving.

Acclerating Inflation. Means increasingly sharp rise in the rate of inflation. If government tries to hold unemployment below the natural rate of unemployment this will cause accelerating inflation.

Accelerator Principle. The theory which states that the level of aggregate net investment has been found to depend on the expected change in output. In its native form it can be put as follows:

$$l_t—a\Delta Y_{f-1}+b$$

where *'a'* denotes the accelerator coefficient, 'Δ' means 'small change in', and $'\Delta'_{t-1}$ implies the change in the level of output in the previous year. $'\Delta'_{t-1}$ thus becomes a proxy for the expected change in output, and b is replacement investment. The theory hypothesizes that firms try to maintain a fixed ratio of desired capital stock to expected output. In the native version there is nor role for the interest rate and it therefore becomes an extreme Keynesian view of the determinants of investment.

Acceptance Credit. Also termed as a 'letter of acceptance'. It is a method of payment which is widely used in inland and international trade. If the credit of a foreign import merchant is regarded satisfactory an accepting house may open an acceptance credit for him in a bank. A purchase from an exporter may then be financed by means of a bill of exchange drawn on the accepting house. The exporter can then obtain his money quickly as the bill can be easily discounted in the bank.

Accepting House. A financial institution which has been accepting bills of exchange, with such backing the bills command a higher price.

Accessions Tax. In many countries, it is a tax which is levied on gifts and inherited property. Such receipts have been not usually classified as income but as they confer spending power they are arguably a legitimate subject of taxation. An accession tax has been levied on the recipient and, as it is related to his economic circumstances, is superior from an equity view-point to the capital transfer tax where liability has been on the donor.

Accommodating Credit. A term which is frequently used for referring to the 'automatic financing' of deficits, e.g., when an exporter provides credit to the importer.

Accommodating Movements. Mean transfers of gold and convertible currency abroad to over come deficits in the total balance of payments of a country.

Accommodation Bill. A bill which is drawn, accepted or endorsed for the sole purpose of discounting it, no goods being given or received for it, thus offering short-term cash accommodation.

Account. Refers to a running record of transactions which is taking place between two transactors, who may be two departments of one business and a basic element in all systems of recording business transactions. In retail trading it refers to the credit facility which is automatically extended to a customer with whom an account is operated.

Accountant. A Person who is qualified in book keeping and allied subjects.

Accounting Costs. Bosts regarded as recorded costs only; economic costs might be larger or smaller when alternative costs or opportunity costs and external effects have been taken into account.

A.C.P. Countries. The 63 African, Caribbean, and Pacific countries that had signed the Lome Convention with the European Economic Community. Most of these had been former colonial territories of the EEC countries.

Active Balance. In monetary theory, there are some models which postulate a division of the money supply into active balances, which are money stocks that turn over actively within periods determined by the intervals between payments; and idle balances, which are money stocks not used in the circuit of regular payments. In the quantity theory of money, changes in the velocity of circulation, in conditions other than hyperinflation, have been conceived to occur mainly through transfers between active and idle balances, and only to lesser extent through changes in the rate at which money moves round the payments circuit. Empirically, the distinction between active and idle balances has been clusive because the 'activity' of money is a matter of degree. But for practical purposes active, balances are frequently defined as currency in circulation plus current account deposits in banks.

Active Circulation. That part of the note issue of the Reserve Bank in circulation at any given time.

Activists. Refer to the descriptive of economist who believe in the use of monetary and fiscal policies for controlling the economy, and who tend to recognise and favour a large role for government in the economy. In particular, activists believe in the possibility of successful fine-tuning.

Additional Worker Hypothesis. On this argument, the fall in family labour force in the hope of finding a job so as to maintain family income. Hence labour force participation rates will move counter-cyclically. In fact, the evidence reveals that on balance labourforce participation rates move pro-cyclically. However, the added worker effect has been discernible among certain low income groups for whom need has been more important than price.

Address Principle. In a planned economy such as the USSR each target possesses an organization or 'address' which has been responsible for carrying it out.

Adjustment Process. Refers to the adjustment mechanisms which operate in the international economy for removing imbalances in foreign payments.

Ad Valorem. 'According to value', i.e., as a percentage.

Ad Valorem Tax. A duty which has been imposed on commodities in proportion to their value, i.e., a duty which is expressed as percentage and not a flat amount. It has been commonly used in respect of import tariffs.

Advanced Countries. The dividing line between advanced countries and developing countries has been know from per capita income. Those with per capita incomes of less than one-fifth of the level of those in the US are regarded 'underdeveloped'. However, it is not an absolutely clear definition because there are some countries, for example, Middle East oil producing countries which on this criteria would be advanced countries, but when the income distribution and availability of various services has been taken into consideration, they have been obviously not very advanced.

African Development Bank Group. Refers to a group of development financing institutions comprising the African Development Bank (A.D.B) and its affiliates, the African Development Fund (A. D. F) and the Nigeria Trust Fund (N.T.F). The A.D.B. established by African independent states in 1963 has been a collective instrument for promoting economic and social development in its member states. The A.D.B. provides financial and technical assistance to projects of proven economic, financial and technical feasibility. The A.D.F. and the N.T.F possess similar objectives. The A.D.F. got established with non-regional states in 1972, and the N.T.F. by the Federal Government of Nigeria in 1976. The 1982 memberships of A.D.B. include 50 independent African states, although membership has to be extended to non-regional states real incomes during a cyclical down-turn will make an income effect: additional workers from the family will try to enter the in order to mobilise funds on a more permanent basis. By far the largest portion of A.D.B. Group loans have gone into agriculture and physical infra-structure. Over 80 per cent of the softer loans from A.D.F. and N.T.F went to the poorer members of A.D.B.

Age Earnings Profile. Refer to the relationship between earnings and age. The simplest age earnings profile is expected to be horizontal line which is stepping up from zero at the age of leaving school with the size of step being determined by the quantity of schooling. In fact the typical post-school age-earnings profile has been found to be more complex than this; the pattern for annual earnings has been for a steep increase on leaving school followed by a lower increase until a plateau is reached in the mid-forties, after which a slow and then a faster decent takes place.

Agglomeration Economies. Cost savings in an economic activity which arise from enterprises or activities locating near one another. Examples of such savings have been the clustering of retail establishments which permit consumers to make price comparisons without multiple journeys, the efficient use of information where contact between buyers and sellers gets facilitated, the spreading of costs of public services and the development of specialized input suppliers serving a number of consumers on the surrounding area. In the last case, cost reductions arise through economies of scale and specialization in the supplying firms, thus they are said to be internal to the firms. Agglomeration economies have been an example of external economies where one firm's activities confer benefits on other firms.

Aggregate Demand Curve. Means the schedule which details the quantity of net national product that would be purchased at each general price level as shown below. The combinations of output and the price level at which the commodity and money markets have been simultaneously in equilibrium. In contrast to the individual demand curve the aggregate curve is not able to reflect the ordinary substitution effect of a rising price reducing demand. Rather in this case the rising price will tend to reduce the equilibrium level of output demand by reducing the real money supply and thereby raising interest rates and lowering investment.

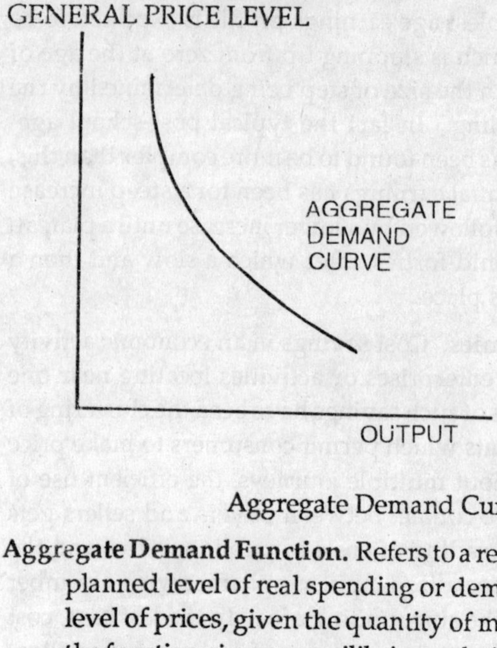

Aggregate Demand Curve

Aggregate Demand Function. Refers to a relationship between the planned level of real spending or demand for goods and the level of prices, given the quantity of money and fiscal policy; the function gives an equilibrium relationship between aggregate spending and the price level.

Aggregate Expenditure. (also known as aggregate demand). Refers to the sum total of (nominal expenditures on goods and services in the economy i.e., consumption (C), investment (I) and government Expenditure (G) together with exports, less imports. Thus,

$$Y=C+I+G(X-M)$$

In the simple income-expenditure model the volume of aggregate expenditure ascertains the volume of output and employment. The volume of these expenditures could vary systematically with changes in the general prices level.

Aggregate Supply. Means the total supply of goods and services in an economy which is available to meet aggregate demand. The stream of goods and services comprises domestic production together with imports.

Aggregate Supply Curve. Refers to the schedule which is detailing the quantity of net national product that would be supplied at each general price level given constant price expectations as shown below. In the short run the positive slope is derived from the hypothesis that workers are unable to adjust their expectations about the future level of prices to take account of the current movement in prices. In consequence the rise in nominal wages that accompanies the rise in prices would be mistaken for a rise in real wages and hence more labour will be offered and more output produced. The rise in nominal wages follows from the increase in the marginal revenue product of output due to the rise in prices which encourages employers to increase output. In the short run the only way this can be carried out is by employing more labour and hence they offer higher wages to secure this. The rise in wages does not of course match the rise in prices and the real wage has therefore fallen, a necessary condition on this view for increased employment. In the long run, however, increased labour will only be forthcoming if the real wage rises-labour supply is assumed to be a function of the real wage and therefore this situation cannot be sustained. Workers revise their expectations to take account of the movement in prices and the aggregate supply curve moves upwards with output and employment falling back to their previous levels. In the long-run the aggregate supply curve is vertical above the full employment level of output which corresponds to the natural rate of unemployment.

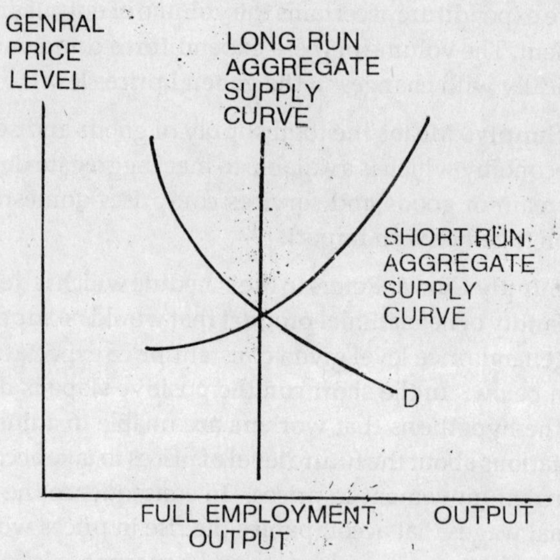

Aggregation. Refers to the bringing together or summing of primary data. For example, the national income has been an aggregate, in contrast with the income of an individual.

Aggregative Index. The term used for an index number which has been constructed by aggregating a number of items, e.g. Laspeyers' Index and Paasche's Index

Aggregative Model. Refers to an econometric model in which the variables have been themselves constructed from groups of individual variables, as when a price index number gets substituted for a set of prices.

Agio. Means a charge for changing one currency into another, or for changing paper money into coin; the excess value of one currency over another at the prevailing official rate of exchange. Agiotage has been exchange business such as stock-jobbing and speculation in stocks.

Agio Theory of Interest. See abstinence or agio theory of interest; interest, theories of.

Agriculture Bank. A bank which is especially established to assist the agricultural development by providing loans to a larger duration.

Allocation Function. Refers to the part of government tax and expenditure policy which deals with influencing the provision of goods and services in the economy.

Annual Financial Statement. Refers to an annual estimate of all anticipated revenue and expenditure. (See budget)

Analysis of Variance. (Also known as ANOVA. Refers to the breakdown of the total variation in a dependent variable (with total variation defined as the sum of squared deviations from its mean) into the proportions which have been accounted for by variation in individual, or groups of explanatory variables, and the unexplained or residual variation. This can offer the basis for testing hypotheses about the significance of either individual or subsets of explanatory variables in regression analysis.

Alienation. A term which was used by Karl Marx for describing the mental condition of workers in a capitalist system. Marx postulated that an industrial society characterized by capitalist ownership and organization of the tools of production would inevitably in still in workers a sense of isolation, self-estrangement and apathy. This aspect of Marx's theory has been greatly emphasized by a number of modern Marxists especially Marcuse, Paul Baran and Paul Sweetly.

Anarchy. Refers to the theory which states that social and economic affairs of individuals ought not to be restricted by any government interference. It is a more extreme view than that of laissez-faire or liberalism.

Andean Pact. A pact agreed to in 1969 forming a common market between Chile, Peru, Bolivia, Colombia, and Ecuador; Venezuela joined the pact in 1973, while Chile terminated her agreements in 1976. The aim of the group has been to set up a common external tariff and establish free trade between member countries.

Applied Economics. Branch of economic science which is devoted to the study of practical problems, utilising the principles and tools of economic analysis offered by theoretical economics.

Appraiser. A professional valuer of property.

Appreciation. Refers to an increase in the value of an asset. For example, an increase in; (a) the value of property in relation to other assets during a period of growing demand; (b) the value of stocks held by merchants and manufacturers during a period of rising prices; (c) the value of a currency when its value increases in relation to the value of other currencies; (d) the value of stocks and shares in general, or particular categories, on the stock exchange.

A Priori. Relates to speculation or reasoning which has been prior to actual experience. As reasoning it proceeds deductively from cause to effect; such speculation or reasoning stands in contrast to an appeal in evidence. The term is often used as a synonym for 'on theoretical grounds'.

Asian Development Bank. Founded in 1966, a bank to further development investment in Asia, to help prepare and co-ordinate development and provide technical aid. It has twenty regional members and thirteen non-regional members. The bank is having its headquarters in the Philippines.

Assets. Refers to the property of a business; they may be classified as:

(a) Current Assets, consisting of cash, stock and book debts;

(b) Fixed Assets, consisting of buildings, plant and machinery;

(c) Intangible Assets, being the value of goodwill or patents.

Assets/Employee Ratio. Refers to a ratio which is used as an indication of the capital intensity of a company; the ratio has been found to be useful for comparing the capital of companies within an industry group.

Association of South East Asian Nations (ASEAN). An association of the south east Asian nations of Singapore, Malaysia, Indonesia, Thailand, and the Philippines for security, diplomatic, and economic purposes. In November, 1982, the economic ministers of the member countries approved an agreement on joint industrial ventures which included 50 per cent tariff reductions for approved products.

At a Discount. At a price which is lower than par value, or lower than normal, because of special circumstances.

At a Premium. At a price which is higher than par value, or higher than normal, because of special circumstances.

Attrition. In labour economics it refers to the wastage of a labour force that occurs naturally because of voluntary quits, retirements, discharges for cause, and deaths. This is one method of dealing with excessive manpower levels which result from labour-saving technological change without unduly exacerbating the unemployment position.

Autarky. Refers to a situation where a country tries to isolate itself from international trade by restrictions like tariffs in an attempt to be self-sufficient usually for reasons of employment or politics.

Automated Policy. Refers to a reliance on fixed rates of change in money and tax rates, rather than frequent discretionary changes in monetary or fiscal policy to influence the level of economic activity. An example of automated policy has been the setting of a growth rate for the money supply to get adhered to over a long period independent of current economic conditions.

Automatic Saving. If a person's net income has been too large to spend, the unspent income is known as automatic saving.

Automatic Stabilisers. Refer to those elements of the economic system, both private and public, which tend to correct recessionary or inflationary tendencies. An example is that direct taxes on inflating money incomes, being progressive, try to curb excessive aggregate demand in inflationary conditions; in another instance, a tendency of people to maintain a customary level of consumption even by drawing of savings tends to retard a decline in aggregate demand in a recession.

Autonomous Expenditures. Refer to expenditure exogenous to a model which are used to forecast Gross National Product.

Autonomous Investment. Investment which is not influencedby such economiC factors as the rate of interest, the rate of growth of sales, or the rate of return on investment.

Autonomous Spending. Refers to the spending that has been found to be independent of the level of income and interest rates.

Average Cost. Means cost per unit of output, where the cost of all inputs (factors of production) have been included. Thus, average (total) cost (ATC) may be put as follows:

$$ATC = \frac{TC}{X}$$

where X denotes output and TC total cost. Average total cost will be comprised of Average Fixed Costs (AFC) and Average Variable Cots (AVC). Hence

$$ATC = AFC + AVC$$

In the short run the average cost curve will tend to possess the shape shown in the diagram. Thus 'U' shape is attributed to the fact that AFC declines as output exponds and initally more than out weights the rise in AVE. AFC falls because fixed total cost is being spread over a larger and larger output. AVC rise due to the operation0of the law of diminishing returns. Eventually the rise in AVE more than outweighs the fall in AFC and ATC starts to rise. In the long run the shape is decided by the existence or otherwise of economic of scale.

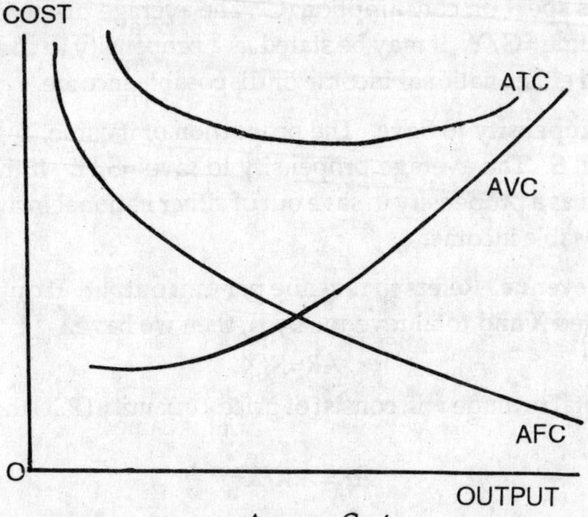

Average Cost

Average Cost Pricing. A pricing rule according to which firms add a mark-up onto Average Variable Costs (AVC) so as to cover its average total costs. Hence price (P) may be put as follows:

$$P=AVC+GPM=AC$$

where GPM denotes the gross profit margin make-up and is comprised of an overhead element and a fixed net profit margin thought 'normal' or 'fair' for industry. Given adoption of this rule supply considerations will be the predominant consideration in th-- price setting process.

Average Fixed Costs. Refers to the fixed cost per unit output. In the short run, some cost will not get changed regardless of the level of output. These fixed costs expressed peR unit of output will then be declining as outpuT expands. Hence.

$$AFC=TFC/X$$

whure AFC denotes qverage fixed coSt, TFC total fixed cost and X output. As TFC has been a consta~t amount and X has been variable, the equation vor AFC will be That of a rectangular hyperbla. (See Average Cost.)

Average Propensity to Sonsume. The proportion of income, Y, that is spent on consumption, C. The average propensity to consume =C/Y. It may be stated as a propensity to consume out of either national income or disposable income.

Average Propensity to Save. The proportion of income, Y, that is saved, S. The average propensity to save =S/Y. It may be stated as a propensity to save out of either national income or disposable income.

Average Revenue. Refers to revenue per unit output. If output is denoted X and total revenue by R, then we have.

$$AR=R/X$$

As Total revenue will consist of price x quantity (P.X) then we have

$$AR=A.X/X=P$$

That is, average revenue equals price. It implies that any curve relating average revenue to output has been the same as the demand curve which is relating price to output.

Average Revenue Product. Refers to the average physical product of an input (factor of production) multiplied by the average revenue. As average revenue equals price, it become possible to write.

$$ARP=P.APP$$

where P denotes the price of the product and APP denotes the average physical product.

Average Variable Costs. Refers to the variable cost per unit output Thus, if TVC has been total variable costs, average variable costs, AVC, may be put as follows:

$$AVC=TVC/X$$

Average Rate of Tax (also known as effective rate of tax). Usually taken to mean total income tax payments as a proportion of income. The definition of income normally means the gross income, i.e., before allowances. With regard to company taxation the effective tax has been most usefully stated as tax payments as a proportion of resources generated (i.e., revenue minus capital and operating costs).

B

Back-to-Back. A reference to offsetting loans, generally made in one currency in one country against a loan in another currency in another country; it is involving two parties, matching assets and liabilities in opposite directions. In the futures market, back-to-back describes an equal number of bought and sold contracts held by one trader in the same month.

Backward Bending Supply Curve of Labour. Refers to a negative relation between the supply of labour, however defined, and the real wage. The outcome may be understood as signifying the dominance of the negative income effect over the positive substitution effect (with respect to the particular supply measure).

Backward Linkage. Refers to the relationship between an industry or firm and the suppliers of its inputs. A change in the output of the industry will get transmitted backwards to the supplier of its inputs by changing in demand for inputs.

Backward Vertical Operations. Means the securing and exploiting of raw materials by a company which would otherwise have to buy such materials.

Backwash Effects. These are considered to operate where the economic growth in one region of an economy possesses adverse effects on the growth of other regions. These effects are said to have principally of flows of factors of production (usually labour and capital) from slow growing to fast growing regions.

Bad. Means a commodity or product which produces disutility for its consumer.

Balanced Budget. A budget is said to be a balanced budget when current income exactly equals current expenditure.

Balanced-budget Multiplier. Refers to the ratio of the change in real income to the change in government expenditure if government expenditure and tax revenues get changed by equal amounts.

Balanced Economic Development. Means the idea that all sectors of an economy should get developed simultaneously to attain a balanced type of development.

Balanced Growth. In growth theory it refers to a dynamic condition of an economy where all real variables have been growing at the same constant proportional rate (which have been zero or negative).

Balance of Payments. Refers to the relation between the payments of all kinds made from one country to the rest of the world and its receipts from all other countries. For the world as a whole, imports have to be equal to exports.

Balance of Trade. Refers to the relationship between the values of a country's imports and its exports, i.e., the 'visible' balance. These items are only forming part of the balance of payments which get also influenced by

(a) 'invisible' items and

(b) movements of capital.

Balance Principle. The basic method of Soviet planning, which involves double entry book-keeping in physical or price units.

Balance of Trade. Means the balance on 'visible' trade, this is trade in goods, over a given period. Thus if exports of goods becomes greater than imports the trade balance is said to be 'favourable' while an excess of imports over exports yields an 'unfavourable' trade balance.

Balance Sheet. An ordered statement of:

(a) The economic resources or assets of a company or other business organisation, each item having a value set upon it;

(b) The financial claims of persons or organisations upon the value of these assets.

Balancing Item. An item which gets entered in the balance of payments accounts to make the account balance; it is the net total of the errors and omissions in other items.

Bancor. The name assigned by Keynes to an international currency which he proposed has to be created by an international bank, used for setting international debts and which would constitute part of international liquidity.

Bandwagon Effect. Refers to the effect whereby as the price of a good falls and demand by some sections or individuals in the community expands other individuals or sections 'imitate' the reaction and expand their demand also.

Bank. Refers to a financial intermediary which accepts funds, principally as deposits repayable on demand or at short notice, and which it to make advances by overdrafts and loans, and by discounting bills, and to hold other, mainly financial assets like marketable securities. An important banking function has to maintain a money transmission system by accepting deposits on current account and operating a system of transferring funds by cheque or giro transfer. Other important banking activities include providing foreign exchange services for customers, financing foreign trade, operating in wholesale money markets and offering a wide range of financial advisory services.

Bank Advance. A general term for any form of bank lending.

Bank Bill. A bill which has been accepted by an accepting house, a clearing bank, or one of banks on behalf of a customer for whom an acceptance credit has been opened.

Bank Credit. Refers to the lending by the banking system, by whatever means: bank advances, discounting bills or purchasing securities.

Bank Deposits. The funds deposited in bank accounts. In reality they have been simply records of indebtedness of a bank to the depositor, and they arise from the character of banks as financial intermediaries.

Banking Panic. The terms used for an episode in which a failure of confidence in one or more banks produced a sudden and wide-spread 'run' by the public on banks in general, to withdraw deposits, or in times when private banknote issues had been common to demand payment of such notes in another medium.

Banking System. Refers to a network of commercial banks co-ordinated, influenced and controlled by statutory regulation and a central bank.

Bank Loan. Any advance by a bank, but there is a distinction in bank lending between overdraft terms and loan terms. A bank advance specifically in the form of a loan gets credited in full to the borrower's account at the outset and the interest liability might be a fixed sum calculated on the initial loan and its duration. In some cases, e.g., personal and term loans, there occurs provision for repayment by regular instalments.

Bank Note. Refers to a form of currency issued by a bank, and in essence a 'negotiable' evidence of the bank's indebtedness to the value of the note.

Bank of Issue. A bank, authorised to issue bank notes.

Bank Overdraft. A widely used type of short-term finance. It is particularly used to offer short-term working capital to tide over the production cycle, finance for seasonal requirements; and bridging loans for the purchase of property of plant with repayment coming from the realisation of another asset.

Bankruptcy. A legal proceeding under which the property of an insolvent debtor is taken for the benefit of his creditors generally.

Bargaining Tariff. The term used for the tariff imposed by a country to strengthen its position in trade negotiations with other countries, when it may be using the promise of reductions in the traffic to obtain trade concessions.

Bargaining Theory of Wages. Wages have been commonly fixed in a collective bargaining process; and arrangement that differs mechanically from the orthodox demand-supply adjustment process. The bargaining theory of wages is referred to model building exercises of the bargaining process applicable to union management relations that seek to proceed beyond the bilateral monopoly model in which the final outcome of bargaining has been indeterminate.

Barriers to Entry. Refer to the factors which place new entrants at a cost disadvantage relative to established firms within an industry.

Barter. Refers to a method of exchanging goods and services directly for other goods and services without employing a separate unit of account or medium of exchange.

Barter Agreements. Agreements between countries, usually with balance of payments troubles, for the direct exchange of agreed quantities of goods without the mediation of international finance.

Barter Economy. Refers to an economy where the exchange of goods and services is realised by the method of barter, which would give rise to very little specialization or division of labour due to the requirement of double-concidence of wants.

Base Drift. The term used for a problem when the money supply of a country grows beyond nominated ceiling.

Base Rate. Usually, the basic rate for lending by a bank.

'Basic' Balance of Payments. Refers to that part of a nation's balance of payments which covers the balance on current account and long-term capital flows.

Basic Export. Refers to the name given to the primary products which are produced by underdeveloped countries for export; it includes basic raw materials, like copper, tin, cotton, timber, tea, coffee, etc.

Basing-point System. Refers to a type of pricing in which the various sellers in a marketing agree that the price to be charged for a good has to be calculated by the sum of a fixed price, and an agreed transport charge which gets related to the distance between the consumer and the nearest of a number of agreed locations known as 'basic points'.

Bayesian Techniques. The term used for the methods of statistical analysis (including estimation and statistical inference) in which prior information has been formally combined with sample data to produce estimates, or test hypotheses. The techniques offer a way of including subjective impressions and or theoretical elements in quantitative analyses.

Beggar-my-neighbour Policies. The economic measures which are taken by one country to improve its domestic economic conditions, normally to reduce unemployment, and which have adverse effects on other economies.

Behavioural Equation. Refers to a mathematically specified relationship in an economic or econometric model which is able to reflect the reaction of an individual or set of individuals to economic stimuli (e.g., a consumption function).

Behavioural Expectations. A view on the formation of expectations which are based on social and psychological factors. It emphasizes the role of interpersonal contacts and of mass communications.

Benefit Principle. A traditional theory of taxation which may be stated as that tax burdens should be allocated among tax payers in accordance with the benefits they receive from the provision of public goods.

Benelux. Refers to a customs union established between Belgium. Luxembourg and the Netherlands in successive stages between 1944 and 1948. The purpose of the union had been to abolish tariff duties within the union and to apply a common tariff to imports from other countries.

Bertrand's Duopoly Model. Refers to a model of a two firm market developed by J. Bertrand in 1883. The model is different from the Cournot duopoly model in that each firm has been assumed to maximize profits on the presumption that the other firm will not change its price. Bertrand's model results in a stable equilibrium for the two firms. This is shown in a diagram illustrating the reaction curves of the two firms. For *A* we may plot a locus of points of maximum profits which it can get by charging various prices P_A, given the price which firms *B*. A similar process yields the reaction curve for firm P_B. A stable equilibrium is reached at point *E* where the two reaction curves cross and each firm charges the same price for the product. The model may be criticized on the grounds of its native assumptions concerning conjectural behaviour, that it does not take into account production costs, and does not permit entry of new firms.

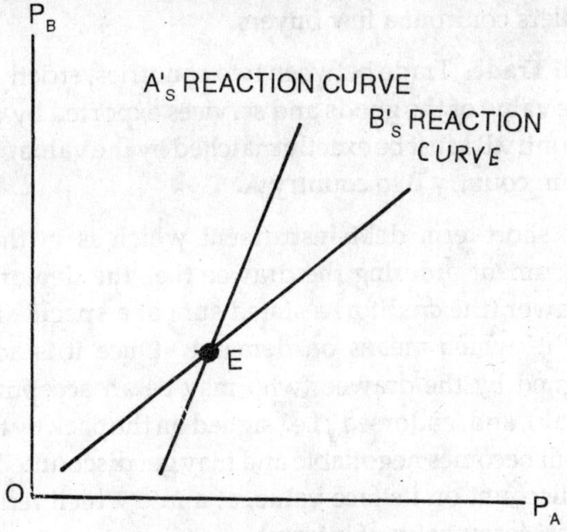

Bertrand's Duopoly Model

Bid. The term used for an offer of payment which an individual or organization makes for possession or control of assets, input, goods or services.

Bid-rent Function. The term used for a relationship which indicates the amount a household or firm will be able to pay for the use of a given quantity of land (the bid-rent) at varying distances from the centre of an urban area while maintaining a constant level of utility or profit.

Bilateral Assistance. Assistance or aid based on a direct arrangement between two countries; it is different from multilateral aid which can come from a group of countries or an international organization.

Bilateral Exchange Rate. The term used for a conventional concept of a currency exchange rate, such as the dollar price of sterling, yen, or Deutsche marks.

Bilateral Monopoly. Refers to a market structure in which single seller faces a single buyer.

Bilateral Oligopoly. Refers to a market situation in which a few sellers confront a few buyers.

Bilateral Trade. Trade between two countries, strictly interpreted the value of the goods and services exported by country A to country B Must be exactly matched by the value of the exports from country B to country A.

Bill. A short-term debt instrument which is in the form of a document ordering the drawee (i.e., the debtor) to pay the drawer (the creditor) a stated sum at a specified date, or 'at sight' which means on demand. Once it is accepted, i.e., signed by the drawee (who may be an accepting house or bank), and 'endorsed', i.e., signed on the back by the acceptor, a bill becomes negotiable and may get discounted, i.e., sold at a discount on its face value, at a rate which reflects current short terms rates of interest.

Bill Broker. The term used for person who specializes in bringing together, for a commission, buyers and sellers of bills.

Binary Variable. Refers to a variable which can only take two value (e.g. 0 and 1), normally used to account for qualitative, or quantifiable influences in regression analysis.

Biological Interest Rate. Refers to a value for the interest rate in growth theory where amongst all balanced growth paths the highest per capita consumption has been achieved and sustained by the path on which the marginal productivity of capital (equal to the rate or profit under perfect competition) has been equal to the constant exogenously determined rate of growth of the labour force.

Birth Rate. The average number of live births per 1,000 of population, per year.

B.I.S. The Bank for International Settlements.

Bivariate Analysis. An analysis which is involving only two variables.

Black Market. Any illegal market which has been established in a context where prices have been fixed at minimum or maximum level, usually by government. Thus, when maximum prices have been fixed, trading may occur at prices above the maximum. Black markets have been common in times of rationing or national crises as with the occurrence of war.

Bliss Point. A consumer equilibrium in which the consumer experiences total statction with respect to the goods consumed and which point of satiation has been within his budget constraint. Such a point can only take place if the consumer is not acting in accordance with the axiom of dominance -- i.e., if he does not always prefer more and more of all goods. In such circumstances the relevant indifference curves cease to have their usual (convex) shape and become complete circles.

'Blown up' Price. Descriptive of the final price of a good following a rise in the price of basic materials and fuel.

Blue Chip Rate. Refers to the lowest interest rate payable by borrowers having the highest credit rating.

Bodgies. Individuals and teams who engage in work contracts on a cash only basis; they may work under 'bodgie' or false names.

Body Hire. The terms used for a system in which workers, particularly labourers, have been recruited at unofficial pick-up points in the early hours of the morning by labour supply firms which deliver them to various sites; the workers have been paid in cash only without records or tax payments, and are encouraged to stay on unemployment relief. No provision will be made for workers' compensation, sick pay, vacation pay, annual loading long-service leave, public holidays, or wet weather.

Bonded Warehouse. Warehouse in which dutiable articles are stored without previously paying duty. Thus, if the goods will be re-exported, the duty need not be paid at all. On the other hand, if goods have been removed to be consumed in the country, i.e., taken out of bond, duties have been then payable.

Boom. Refers to a period of expansion of business activity. It is opposite of slump or recession. A boom reaches a peak when the economy has been working at full capacity.

Boulwarism. The process of collective bargaining over terms and conditions of employment has been normally one of compromise and concession; the two parties bargain and approach one another until a point somewhere between their original or opening positions is realised that is mutually satisfactory to them.

Bounded Rationality. Refers to the cognitive limits of human agents in relation to the complexity of the problems with which they get confronted. In essence, economic agents have been rational up to a limit because of their limited capacity for computation and information processing. Rules and institutions emerged to reduce the amount of complexity faced by economic agents. These are to be seen as devices that economize on bounded rationality.

Bourgeoisie. Refers to that section of industrial society which came into prominence in the course of the industrial Revolution as entrepreneurs and professional persons. Generally used for describing the property-owning middle classes, and since Karl Marx's discussion of their role the term has often been employed in a pejorative sense.

Box-Jenkins. A forecasting method which is based on ARIMA time series models. The technique does not take casual factors into account, as would forecasts based on regression analysis for example, but relies on being able to capture the trend, cyclic and other systematic characteristics of the time series statistically.

Brain Drain. Means the migration of educated and skilled labour from poorer to richer countries.

Branch Banking. Refers to the provisions of banking services through a network of branch offices which are owned by a single banking company.

Break-even Analysis. The costs of producing a good have been splitted into two main parts. Fixed costs have been those that remain the same for the firm however many goods are produced, i.e., rates, rent etc. Variable costs very with the number of items produced, i.e., raw materials for the goods labour to produce them, etc. From the cost accountant's point of view, the break-even sales volume may be defined as that which ensures that all fixed and variable costs are covered, given a particular selling price.

$$\text{Break-even volume} = \frac{\text{Fixed costs}}{\text{Selling price minus variable cost per unit}}$$

This can also be illustrated graphically.

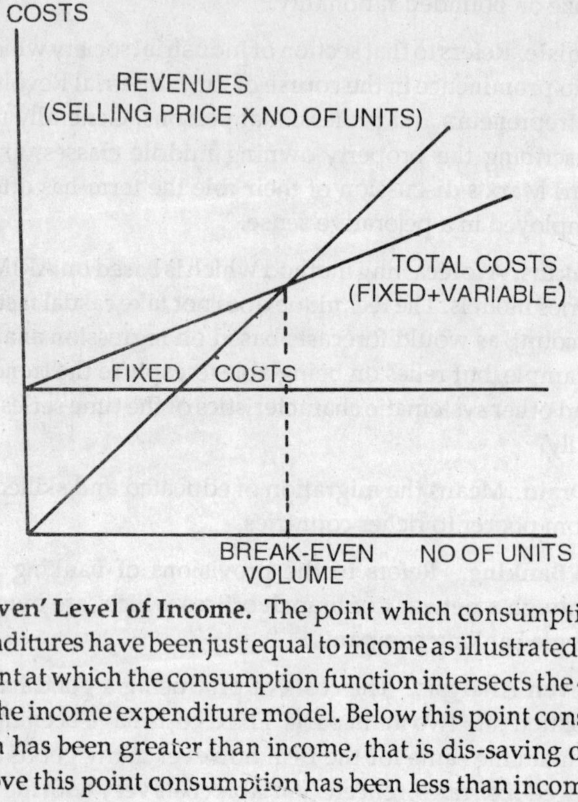

'Break-even' Level of Income. The point which consumption expenditures have been just equal to income as illustrated by the point at which the consumption function intersects the 45 line in the income expenditure model. Below this point consumption has been greater than income, that is dis-saving occurs, above this point consumption has been less than income that is saving occurs.

Broker. One who buys sand sells bonds and other financial assets.

Brokerage. A fixed cost which is charged by the broker for cash act of investment or encashment of bonds and other financial assets.

Buddy Gangs. Self-employed workers who work from home but operate in groups, e.g. as building sub-contractors or subbies.

Budget. In India Government presents a major budget every year. Traditionally the Budget was the occasion when the Government made changes to the level and structure of taxation.

Budgetary Control. Refers to a system whereby checks have been made on expenditure and revenue flow against targets which have been set out in a budget. The purpose is to discover to what extent practice is actually deviating from targets so that action can be taken in reasonable time to bring the flows into line with the desired objective.

Budget Deficit. An excess of government expenditures over revenues; a negative budget surplus.

Budget Line. Refers to a line commodity space which indicates what combinations of goods the consumer is able to buy with a given income. The slope and location of the line have been determined by the prices of the goods in question. Thus, if all

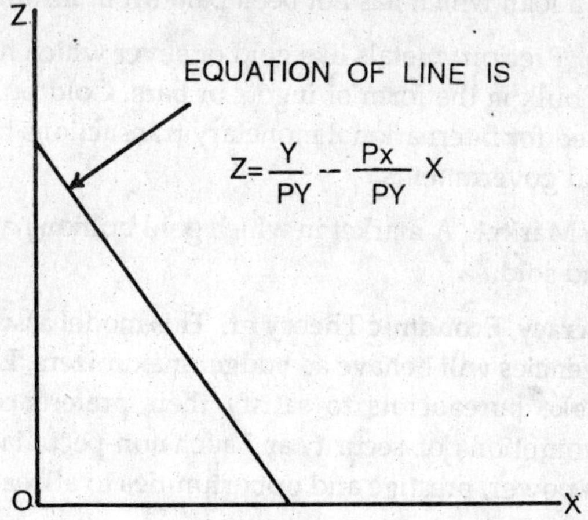

income, Y, has been spent on two goods X and Z with prices p_x and p_z then

$$Y = p_x . X + p_z . Z$$

which on rearrangement becomes as follows :

$$Z = \frac{Y - P_x}{P_Z \quad P_Z}$$

so that the slope of the budget line is the ratio of the two prices. The budget line has been also known as the income line, consumer possibility line, budget constraint, wealth constrant and even price line.

Budget Surplus. Current income in excess of current expenditures.

Bufferstock Facility. Refers to a facility extended by the International Monetary Fund for the purposes of providing loans for countries wanting to finance commodity stocks.

Bullet Loan. A single-repayment loan having no amortisation; that is, a loan which has not been paid off in instalments.

Bullion. Precious metals like gold or sliver which have been held in bulk in the form of ingots or bars. Gold bullion has been used for international monetary transactions between banks and governments.

Bullion Market. A market in which gold bullion has been bought and sold.

Bureaucracy, Economic Theory of. This model assumes that state agencies will behave as budget maximizers. Larger budgets make bureaucrats to satisfy their preference for salaries, promotion, job security and such non-pecuniary advantages as power, prestige and opportunities to allocate contracts.

Bureaux. Non-profit organizations that have been financed , at least in part, from a periodic appropriation or grant and which provide a total output in exchange for a budget as opposed to units of production at a price.

Business Behaviour. Refers to those actions or policy strategies pursued by firms with the aim of favourably changing the business conditions they face. Examples of such behaviour have been research and development and advertising.

Business Finance. Refers to the provision of funds at the time they are needed to assist a business during an adverse period of identity between payment and receipts; a situation particularly acute during the setting--up of a business when there may be no receipts for a considerable period of time.

Business Performance. Refers to extent to which an industry achieves the goals or objectives its member firms pursue. Performance is then multi-dimensional and can cover aspect such as profitability, innovation, product design and quality and growth.

Bue Back. An offsetting purchase to cover or liquidate a short sale.

Buyer Concentration. The extant to which total transaction within a market get dominated by the largest few buyers. Two extremes have been monopsony i.e., the single buyer, and the many buyers of perfect competition where there have been a sufficiently large number in relation to total market size for all buyer to be price takers.

Buyers Market. A market characterized by excess supply in which sellers consequently experience difficulty at selling all their output at anticipated prices.

Buy in. To cover, offset, or close out a short position.

Buying-in. In respect of currency, the buying by a government of its own currency in order to maintain its international value.

C

Call Loan. A loan which may be terminated or called at any time by the lender or borrower.

Call Money. Funds borrowed by discount houses from the clearing and other banks in many countries, and which they employ in holding a portfolio of assets. A high proportion of these funds are borrowed literally 'at call'.

Call-option. Refers to a contract giving the option for burying shares at a future date within a prearranged time limit.

Call, to. To buy.

Callable. Refers to a bond issue, all or part of which may be redeemed by the issuing corporation under specified conditions before maturity; the term is also applicable to preferred shares that may get redeemed by the issuing corporation.

Cambridge School. A view of economics, which had derived from two main intellectual influences.

1. J.M. Keynes who has been regarded as the originator of the Cambridge School.

2. Ricardo and Marx of the classical tradition.

It has been particularly critical of neoclassical economics and of the work of P. Samuelson and R. Solow of the Massachusetts Institute of Technology (MIT) of Cambridge, USA, who have been seeen as its main representatives. This antagonism results in a debate between the two Cambridges that has been continuing from the 1930s to the present with the participants scarcely agreeing on the importance of topics considered or on the techniques of the discussion.

The Cambridge School (England) considers an economic model as encompassing, historical, sociological and psychological notions and facts as well as the purely economic. In its attack on neoclassical economics, a principal target involves the use of the aggregate production function, especially in growth theory. Some of the more noteworthy members of the school have been Mrs., J. Robinson. N. Kaldor, Lord Kahn, L. Pasinetti and P. Sraffa. The influence is also to Italy where P. Garenguani, D.M. Nuti and L. Spavanta have been associated with the work of the school.

Cambridge Theory of Money. It is a 'cash balance' from of the quantity theory of money. It has been developed by Cambridge economists like Marshall. Pigou and Robertson (the early Cambridge School) and contained in the equation:

$$M = kPT$$

where M represents the amount of money (bank deposits); k represents the reciprocal of the velocity of circulation; P represents the general price level; and T represents the value of output. If the velocity of circulation of money becomes four times in a given period, the k will be one-quarter of expenditure; k is the proportion of the community's expenditure on goods and services which on average is held as cash during the period.

CAP. Abbreviation of common agricultural policy.

Capacity. The term used for the estimated maximum level of production from a plant on a sustained basis, permitting all necessary shut-downs, holidays, etc.

Capacity Utilization. Refers to the ratio of actual to potential output. It refers to firms, industries or whole economies and gives a measure of the amount of the total capacity that is being used.

Capital. Refers to one of the factors of production. It may be defined as 'wealth which is used for the production of further wealth; or simply a commodity which is used in the production or other goods and services, e.g., such as plant or equipment. It represents current consumption forgone in order to obtain future production and future consumption; it enhances the productivity of labour and land. Capital is called 'real' when it is having machines, factories, railways, stocks of raw materials, etc. Real capital may be subdivided into:

(a) *Fixed capital.* It includes factories, warehouses, offices, shops and other builidng used in industry and trade; plant and machinery and equipment; means of transport and communication;

(b) *Floating or circulating capital.* It includes raw materials, fuel, goods in process of manufacture, stocks held by producers or traders. Alfred Marshall described circulating capital as 'fulfilling the whole of its office in the production in which it is engaged by a single use.

(c) *Specific capital.* It includes equipment which cannot normally be used for any other purpose than that for which it was originally designed and constructed.

(d) *Non-specific capital.* It includes equipment which can be used in a variety of processes.

The term 'capital' is generally used for the money subscribed by shareholders or stockholders, or lent by banks, for use in a business. This is more correctly described as business finance, although Adam Smith argued that 'a person's capital has been that part of his stock from which he expects to derive an income.'.

Capital Accumulation. Means an increase in manmade equipment like machinery, tools, buildings and other structures, and stocks of goods, used for or capable of being used for the production of goods and services.

Capital Allowances. Refer to the dedications from gross business profits for the purpose of covering the depreciation of assets which are allowed by the tax authorities when calculating taxable income.

Capital Asset. The term used for an asset, which is not bought or sold as part of the everyday running of a business. Examples include property, land, or shares in another company.

Capital-Authorised, Nominal or Registered. Synonymous terms for capital fixed by the Memorandum of Association of a company.

Capital Budgeting. The process of allocating investible funds to capital projects. Many techniques are used for this purpose. There are traditional accountants' methods like payback period and rate of return on capital employed. These are not highly appreciated by economists who have suggested techniques like net present value and internal rate of return based on discounted cash flow analysis. The traditional accountants' methods have not been favoured because they fail to highlight the timing of cash flows from projects. Capital budgeting is used by all types of organizations but a variety of techniques giving different answers -- is used.

Capital Charges. The charges which companies and individuals are making in their accounts for interest payments on capital borrowed, depreciation of assets and loan repayments.

Capital Coefficients. It is another name for the capital-output ratio.

Capital Controversy. The term used for a debate between the Cambridge School (centered in Cambridge University, England) and the Neoclassical School, of the Massachusetts Institute of Technology, Cambridge, Massachusetts; about the validity or otherwise of the neoclassical approach to economics. Debate has centered mainly on the correct concept of capital to use and its place, if any, in an aggregate production function. The possibility of a reswitching of techniques argued forcefully by the Cambridge School has been sufficient to render invalid many of the assumptions of neoclassical economic theory (especially neoclassical growth theory). The debates some what ceased because the Cambridge School (England) consider their view as proved.

The neoclassical school while accepting that reswitching weakens economic theories derived from assumpations which are unsustainable, do not accept that neoclassical theory should be abandoned in totality.

Capital Cost Component. In relation to the total production cost of each unit of output, the capital cost component is given by :

$$\frac{\text{Capital Charges}}{\text{Units of Output}}$$

where the capital charges have been the sum of the annual interest charges on capital employed and the annual depreciation charges, and the units of output relate to the year under consideration.

Capital Cost of. The cost of obtaining the total capital employed by a business, expressed as a rate of interest.

Capital Deepening. Refers to the process of accumulating capital at a faster rate than the growth of the labour force. The capital labour ratio has been rising.

Capital Employed. The term used for the capital in use in a business; it consists of the total assets minus the current liabilities.

Capital Employed, Return on. The relating of profit to the estimate of estimate of average capital employed to yield a ratio, commonly called the primary ratio, as follows:

$$\frac{\text{Profit}}{\text{Capital}}$$

Capital Expenditure. Expenditure of a non-recurrent nature resulting in the acquisition of assets.

Capital Formation and Depreciation. Capital formation in a given time period has been the expenditure on fixed capital assets (buildings, plant and machinery, vehicles, etc.) either for replacing or adding to the stock of fixed assets. Expenditure on repairs and maintenance has been excluded. During a year fixed capital resources are also used up, or 'consumed', due to wear and tear obsolescence, etc. Thus from the value of gross capital formation, there must be deducted the value of capital consumption or depreciation thereby leaving a value for net capital formation.

Capital Gain. Refers to the difference between the purchase price of an asset and its resale price at some later date, where that difference has been positive.

Capital Gains Tax. A tax which is levied on the capital appreciation of property. In most countries capital gains are not classed as income but they confer purchasing power and so have been fit subject of taxation. In practice it is only realized income which is taxed rather than accrued income. Generally it is monetary gains which are liable rather than real gains.

Capital Gearing. Refers to the ratio of fixed interest capital including prior charges to ordinary share capital.

Capital Goods. Goods which are made for the purpose of producing consumer goods and other capital goods, e.g., machinery of all kinds. This term is synonymous with 'producer goods'.

Capital Intensity. The ratio of capital to labour employed in production.

Capital Intensive. A technique of production A is regarded to be more capital intensive than some other equivalent technique B if the ratio of other factors of production is greater in A than in B.

Capital-intensive Economy. Refers to an economy in which the majority of production techniques have been capital-intensive. Most advanced countries have this property.

Capital-intensive Industry. Refers to industry in which the ratio of capital input to labour input has been higher than the average ratio for industry as a whole. The capital input could be found out by the depreciation costs of plant and equipment. Examples of capital intensive industries have been petroleum refineries, chemical works, primary metal smelters, and open-cut mining.

Capital-intensive Sector. Refers to a sector in an economy where the majority of production techniques have been capital-intensive in nature. The industrial sectors in less developed countries have been usually capital-intensive.

Capital-intensive Techniques. The term used for a production technique which is having a higher proportion of capital than any other factor of production.

Capitalized Value. The value which would be placed on an asset if it were to produce its existing earnings at current market rates of interest.

Capitalism. Refers to a political, social and economic system in which property including capital assets have been owned controlled to a large extent by private persons. It differs from socialism principally in its prevalence of private ownership as opposed to social ownership of the elements of production.

Capitalist Development, Schumpeter's Theory of. A theory developed by Professor J.A. Schumpeter (1883-1950). This theory starts from the circular flow of economic life where producers and consumers all function in a state of equilibrium, all adjustments and adaptations having been made, into this circular flow Schumpeter introduces a shift in the production function which generates a sequence of alterations in the behaviour of economic actors--bank credit expands and eventually a secondary wave of investment activity gets imposed on top of the primary wave as the expectations of the enlarged business community have been influenced by the evidence and by the consequences of business expansion.

Capitalist Ethic. Refers to the sustaining drives of industrial development which are based upon private ownership of the means of production, distribution and exchange.

Capital Labour Ratio. Refers to the ratio at which labour and capital have been combined whithin the production process. Generally labour and capital have been measured as flows per unit of time.

Capital Labour Substitution. The term used for the process of changing the factor proportions of capital and labour in a production technique, if one factor costs less than the other, there will exist a tendency for the expensive factor to get substitute by the cheaper one in a free market situation.

Capital Levies. Once-for-all capital taxes. Death duties are a form of capital levy.

Capital Market. A market comprising institutions which are involved in the purchase and sale of securities, e.g., the new issue market and the stock exchange.

Capital Market Instruments. Financial instruments like company shares and bonds, long-term government bonds, and local government bonds.

Capital Movements. Refer to international flows of funds which may be undertaken by either private individuals or governments. An important element in the Balance of Payments.

Capital Output Ratio. Means the ratio of the amount of capital to the amount of output produced by that capital. A constant capital output ratio is forming the basis of the accelerator principle.

Capital-output Ratio, Incremental. For a given industrial technique, it refers to the ratio of the capital cost of the technique to the value added by the additional output.

Capital Rationing. A situation where there has been a budgetary constraint on the amount of funds available for investment in project over and above the normal market constrain determined by the relationship between cost of capital and expected returns.

Capital Recovery. Refers to the process by which the original investment in a physical asset has been recovered over its economic life. In the absence of inflation, capital recovery has been achieved through depreciation allowances.

Capital Stock. The aggregate or sum of capital goods in an economy. This implies that the stock of capital can be measured by a single number, and needs the heroic assumption that the diverse constituents of this stock (factors, roads, tools, etc.) can be reduced to a common unit and summed to get on unambiguous measure of society's physical stock of capital. Karl Marx argued that capital consists merely of past embodied labour and thus can be reduced to the common unit of labour time.

Capital, Theory of. An area of economic theory concerned with the analysis of the formation of capital, the role of inputs, the role of time and intertemporal planning, and the mechanism of resource allocation between consumption and investment.

Capital Transactions. The leading or borrowing of sums of money, or the transfer of assets accumulated in the past.

Capital Turnover Criterion. An early investment criterion which was suggested for use in developing countries. The suggestion is that projects be selected in accordance to their incremental capital output ratio and that priority be given to those with the lowest ratio. The argument was that in capital scarce countries a high rate of capital turnover would give rise to an efficient allocation of resources. The use of the criterion would also give rise to the utilization of labour-intensive production techniques which would be appropriate in developing countries.

Capital Widening. Refers to the process of accumulating capital at the same rate as the growth of the labour force so that the capital--labour ratio remains constant.

Capitation Tax. Also known as a poll tax. It is a tax which is levied on each member of the community equally irrespective of wealth or income.

Captive Market. The term used for a market in which the supplier of a good or service has been in a monopolistic position, the consumer being unable to get suitable substitutes or to do without. For many years, the gas industry, using no other raw material cave coal, was a captive market.

Capture Theory. A theory of regulation which was developed by George Stigler. Basically, an industry, that is regulated can benefit from its regulation by 'capturing' the regulatory agency involved. This can take place because of political influence; superior technical knowledge that forces the regulatory agency to depend on the industry; appointees being selected from the regulated industry or the possibility of future positions in the industry; and the agency's need for recognition and informal co-operation from the industry.

Cardinalism. Refers to the doctrine that utility has been measurable in cardinal units.

Cardinal Utility

1. The utility attached to a bundle of goods is capable of absolute measurement in terms of some units like 'utils' (a term used for example by Jevons in his Theory of Political Economy in 1871) which would be comparable to the units used for height, weight and distance. That is, absolute numbers would be kept on the utility level and those members would be related to a 'real' origin of zero (we do not speak of minus weights or distances).
2. It relates only to the intervals between utility levels. Thus, faced with four situations 1, 2, 3 and 4, if a consumer can say that the difference between the utility levels of 1 and 2 is some multiple or fraction of the difference between the utility levels of 3 and 4, he can be said to have scaled his utility levels in cardinal terms.

Now few economist believe that utility is measurable in cardinal terms in either of the senses above. Indeed, it was the reaction against the unreality of cardinal measurement that gave rise to ordinalism.

Carrying. A general term which is used for both borrowing and lending which is on commodity futures markets.

Carrying Charge. Charge which are associated with the storage of a commodity, e.g., warehouse charges insurance and other incidentals often including an interest charge and estimated values in respect of the loss or gain in weight.

Cartel. Means the formal agreement between firms in an oligopolistic market to co-operate with regard to agreed procedures on such variables as price and output. The result will be diminished competition and co-operation over objectives as, for example, joint profit maximization or avoidance of new entry.

Cartel Sanctions. Refer to the penalties which are imposed by members of a cartel to induce adherence to the joint goals of the group.

Cash Crops. This term is used for crops grown by peasant farmers specifically for sale in the market as opposed to crops directly consumed for subsistence purposes.

Cash Economy. Refers to a sector of the economy in which individual tradesmen, trade terms, or small builders, deal directly with customers for cash or cash cheques; customers may include other tradesmen, builders or subcontractors.

Cash Flow. Refers to the sum of retained earnings and depreciation provision made by firms. As such it has been the source of internally generated long--term funds available to the company.

Cash Generation. Means the net cash flow which is arising from an investment by a business enterprise, assuming this to be positive.

Cash in Hand System. Refers to a system in which workers have not been paid on, say, an hourly basis for labour only, receiving cash in payment on which income tax has not or will not be paid; such payments may get received in conjunction with tax-free dole payments.

Cashless Society. Refers to a society either so primitive that exchanges through barter alone, or so controlled that goods and services are provided on vouchers only, or sophisticated through the used of credit cards and instant debiting that bank notes and cash become redundant.

Cash Management Systems. Refer to sophisticated systems which are aiming to reduce the amount of money companies and corporations leave idly floating in low-earning accounts.

Cash Market. The term used for a market for the immediate delivery of, and payment for, commodity.

Cash Price. Refers to the price in the market place for a cash commodity (or spot commodity) to get delivered through normal market channels.

Cash Ratio. Refers to the ratio which banks maintain between their holdings of cash and their deposit liabilities, and sometimes referred to as the cash reserve ratio.

Cash Settlement. Refers to a procedure for settlement of contracts by automatic close-out at a cash price which is designed by the clearing house in futures markets which make no provision for delivery, e.g. U.S. dollars.

Casual Employment. Refers to the state of being employed on an *ad hoc* basis without regular hours or a wage contract.

Ceiling. Refers to the limit upward growth of output in trade cycle theory. The ceiling will be reached when all factors of production have been utilized at their full capacity output levels.

Census of Population. An enumeration of inhabitants. A census of the population of the has been taken every tenth year.

Central Bank. The institution which is charged primarily with controlling a country's money and banking system, though with other functions depending on the financial structure and environment.

Central Business District. Refers to the area at the centre of most cities and large towns which gets dominated, in terms of land use, by commercial activities. The central business district has been generally the area of highest land values and rents in the city since commercial and financial activities are willing to pay high rents so as to get the advantages of a central, and thus highly accessible, location.

Centralization of Reserves. The name which is given to plants proposing the location of reserves of currency and gold with a central international institution. It has been based on the idea that currency holdings should be used only for working balances, with the majority of reserves kept as credit money controlled by a central institution which would act as a central bank to central banks. This would resemble a widely expanded International Monetary Find, and the establishment of special drawing rights (SDRs) has been a step in this direction.

Central Limit Theory. It states that the sum (and mean) of a set of random variables will follow a normal distribution if the sample has been sufficiently large, regardless of the distribution from which the individual variables come. The theorem has been often used to justify the assumption of normality of the error term in econometric work, which permits the use of the usual t-statistics for hypothesis testing, since this error term is supposedly composed of the sum of a set random omitted factors.

Certificate of Deposit. A document which is issued by a bank acknowledging a deposit of money with it and constituting a promise to repay that sum, to the bearer, at a specified future date. Certificates of deposit (CDs as they are called) are negotiable, i.e., may get transferred by simple delivery, which given an active market, makes, them highly liquid for the holder while securing the funds to the bank for a fixed period. Interest is paid on certificates of deposit.

Ceteris Paribus. A Latin expression which means 'other things being equal', Economic analysis, frequently takes place by considering the effect of varying one or a few independent variables while other things remain uncharged. To indicate that this is being done, the term ceteris paribus is used.

Characteristics Theory. Generally it is associated with consumer demand theory and the work of K. Lancaster. The basis idea has been that consumers do not demand products but the characteristics of products. Thus demand has been not for housing but for accessibility to shops and schools, clean air, peace and quiet, a garage, room for the children to play and so that the procedure has been than analogous to indifference curre analysis but preferences have been expressed across characteristics rather than products.

Charge Account. Refers to a credit facility which is extended by retail traders to customers. Conditions normally call for settlement within a given period though until recently failure to meet this rarely incurred a penalty.

Charter Party. Refers to a contract to convey goods by sea to a special place for a state sum.

Cheap Money. Refers to a phase in which loans have been available at low rates of interest or a policy which creates this situation.

Check-off. Refers to the direct deduction by the employer of union dues from the employee's wage, which charge is then paid over to the union. Check-off arrangements, need the written assignment of the employee.

Check Trading. Refers to a method of consumer credit financing whereby a company sells a voucher or cheque on credit. The purchaser will be able to repay the debt by agreed regular installments and with interest. The check gets exchanged for goods at specified shops.

Cheque. Refers to a document which is normally supplied in printed form by an bank, ordering the bank to transfer funds from the drawer's current account to a named payee. If the payee signs the reverse side of a cheque it becomes 'negotiable', i.e., he may assign his claim in it to someone else simple by handing it over. A cheque 'crossed' with two lines and bearing the words 'and Co' effectively can be paid only by being credited to a bank account; it should not get paid in cash over a bank's counter.

Cheque Card. Cards which are issued by banks to current account customers, and guarantee the payment of cheques drawn by these customers up to specified limits. Such cards also allow the holder to get cash up to this limit; on demand, from any branch of the issuing bank.

Chervonets. A quarter-ounce coin of Russian gold which is effected by the Soviet Union and advertised in capitalist countries. Chervonets have been offered as a 'personal gold reserve', or even as a 'contribution to a lover one's nest-egg', it has been argued that gold is not longer the 'privilege of the privileged few'. The coin carries the slogan, in Russian, 'Proletarians of all countries unite!'

Chicago School. Name assigned to a group of economist who, among other things, believe that changes in the money supply have been a major determinant of short-run changes in the level of economic activity, and the most important of the policy instruments available to a federal or national government for affecting short-run changes in economic activity. The members of this school generally advocate reliance on automated policy. The school emphasizes the desirability of individual freedom and competitive markets.

Choice. A fundamental principle which is underlying all market activity. The individual must decide on the distribution of his/her income between expenditure and saving and the distribution of expenditure between different goods and services; the business person must decide on what it has been intended to produce, the method of production to be adopted the location of production facilities, and the methods of marketing; the State must decide how the resources of the nation are to be best deployed. All these decisions often involve difficult choices between alternatives.

C.I.F. Cost, insurance and freight. Term used of goods shipped where the price includes shipping and insurance charges. A C.I.F. quotation implies that the seller must ship the goods, meeting all charges up to 'on board' and paying freight, insurance, etc. The seller must supply the buyer with all the documents required to enable the goods to be imported. The buyer must pay all expenses, customes duties, etc., on arrival of the goods at the port of destination.

Circular Flow of Income. Refers to the flow of payments and receipts between domestic firms and domestic households. Money will pass from households to firms in return of goods and services produced by firms and money passes from firms to household in return for the factor services provided by households. The simple notion that the money value of the income of household must equal the money value of output of firms and the money value of household expenditures for purchasing this output offers the basis for national income accounting.

Classical Dichotomy. Means the separate and independent determination of relative and absolute prices in classical and neoclassical economics.

Classical Economics. Deals the economic thought of the period from the mid eighteen to the mid–nineteenth century, of which the great bulk emerged from the UK. The major practitioners were Smith, Ricardo, Malthus, Say, Serion and J.S. Mill.

Classical Real Wage Doctrine. Refers to a doctrine which holds that, in the long-run, there exists no trade-off between unemployment and price increases as is implied by the Phillips Curve: it has been taken to indicate that a rising price level will not affect permanently the level unemployment.

Classical Techniques. A term which is normally used to describe standard statistical techniques, so as to distinguish them particularly from Bayesian techniques. The feature of classical methods has been that no information other than the sample data has been used to make statistical inferences, or in the estimation of parameters of regression equations.

Clay-Clay. Refers to an aspect of the production function in growth theory which does not permit the capital-labour ratio to be varied either before or after investment is carried out. The term 'clay' referring in particular to capital, has been used due to that substance's assumed lack of malleability when compared with 'putty'.

Clean Float. Means completely free floating exchange rate with which monetary authorities never interfere. This rarely occurs in practice.

Closed Economy. A concept which is used mainly in theoretical models to describe an economy having no external trade, which will be completely self-sufficient and insulated from external forces.

Closed Shop. A condition imposed by trade unions or employers that all employees of a firms shall be members of the appropriate trade unions.

Clubs Good. Refers to an intermediate case between purely public goods and private goods. With the club good exclusion has been feasible but the optimal size of the club has been in general larger than one individual.

Clubs, Theory of. The theory of clubs has been part of theory of impure public goods. A club goods has been excludable (i.e., it is possible to prevent its consumption by whole groups of people, in contrast with public goods) but non-rival in that the consumption of the good by one person does not reduce the consumption of the same good by other persons.

'Coase' Theorem. A theorem which is based upon the argument that externalities do not give rise to a misallocation of resources provided that there occur no transaction costs and given property rights that are well defined and enforceable. Here the parties--the producer and consumer of the externally--would we having a market incentive to negotiate a mutually beneficial trade; that is, to interalize the externality. The neutrality theorem states, that the outcome of this trading process would be the same irrespective of whether it was the producer or consumer of the externality who held the property right of veto over the use resource.

Cobwed Theorem. Refers to the simplest form of a dynamic model in which the supply of a good in *t* has been a function of the goods price in year *t* - I and where, in any period, price is adjusted so as to clear the market'. Such examples may take place in agriculture where the decision to grow a crop or breed certain in animals for food may be based on conditions in previous years. The effect could be to generate a process of fluctuating prices, with the fluctuations being 'damped' so as to coverage on an equilibrium of prices or 'antidamped' so as to continue fluctuating from one period to the next.

The diagram gives an example of a convergent cobweb process. For convergence to take place the slope of the demand curve must be less than the slope of the supply curve (Measured in absolute terms--i.e., ignoring the sign of the slope). At P_0a supply of S_1 takes place in the next period (since supply in period 1 has been dependent upon price in the previous period 0). But supply now exceeds demand in period 1 so price falls to P_1. Price in period 2 has been now based on P_1 and is S_2. Supply is now less than demand so that price moves to P_3 and so on.

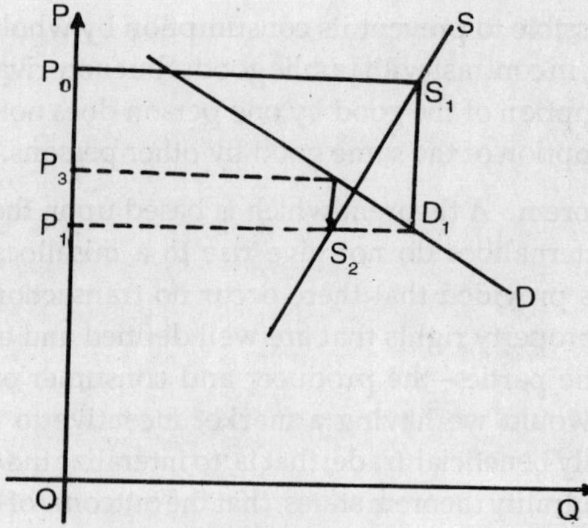

Cobwed Theorem

Coercive Comparisons. Refer to the comparisons which are drawn between the pay of different groups of workers and used by the representatives of employees as justification for a pay increase. Such comparisons may occur from formal or informal comparability exercise or may be drawn between jobs with a widely differing content.

Coinage. Refers to that part of the hand-to-hand currency that is having metallic coins. Coins have been pieces of metal, normally shaped and stamped which a device which is evidence of their value and of their legal status as money.

COLA. Cost of living adjustment.

Collective Good or Service. A good or service like defence, from which the benefit accure to all or none.

Collateral Security. Means any security (other than personal security such as a guarantee) taken by a bank when it tends to make an advance to a borrowing customer and which it is entitled to claim in the event of default.

Collective Choice. Sometimes also known as social choice. It is a decision made by or on behalf of group. The study of market economies has been largely concerned with choices made by individuals but in all economies many decisions concerning resource allotation have been made by governments or other groups.

Collective Bargaining. Negotiations which are taking place between employees and employers about the establishment of procedures and rules to cover conditions of work and rates of pay. Such arrangements usually are involving the joint regulation of agreed procedures.

Collusion. Means an agreement between firms to co-operate so as to avoid mutually damaging rivalry.

Collusive Tendering. Refers to a restrictive practice in which firms tendering for a particular job agree to submit a common price, or to permit one of their number to submit a lower tender, thus allocating orders between themselves.

Coming out Price. Refers of the price at which new shares are issued.

Colombo Plan for Co-operative Economic Development in South and South East Asia. It is an inter governmental organization, which was established in 1950 following a meeting of Commonwealth foreign ministers in Colombo, Sri Lanka, which encourages economic growth and co-operation in the South and South-East Asian region. The plan supports development projects by offering technical assistance and capital aid in the form of direct grants and loans or commodities (e.g., food grains, fertilizers, transport equipment). Since the inception of the plan regional members have already received more than $50 billion in capital aid and technical assistance from the major donor countries of Australia, Canada, India, Japan, New Zealand, UK and US.

Command Economy. An economic system which is dominated by central planning, as distinct from a free enterprise economy with a minimum of state interference. Command economy characteristics are not restricted to socialist economies; systems which encourage free enterprise maintain a powerful apparatus of central control and influence although much of it may be of an indirect character through the use of monetary and fiscal policies.

Commercial Banks. A general, term denoting those banks, which conduct a general rather than a specialized type of business. They accept deposits on varying terms, but including demand deposits; and their lending to private sector business for non-fixed capital purposes, generally accounts for the greater part of their assets.

Commercial Bill. A bill which is drawn to finance trade or other commercial or production activities. It has been distinguished from a Treasury Bill or local government bill which have been instruments of public financial operations.

Commercial Paper. A collective term for commercial bills.

Commercial Paper Market. A non-bank short-term money market in which corporations lend their surplus cash directly to each other, cutting out intermediate financial institutions.

Commercial Policy. The rules which are adopted by a country for the conduct or regulation of its foreign trade and payments. At one extreme a country may be able to adopt a policy of free trade and at the other one of autarky, while in between there would be policies of varying degrees of protection by traffic, quotas, exchange control etc.

Commodities. Objects which are produced because of the process of production, Goods and services.

Commodity Exchange. Refers to a market for the open, competitive, bulk sale and purchase of commodities including financial instruments, for immediate and forward delivery often in the form of a futures contract.

Commodity Futures Contract. Refers to a legally binding commitment to buy or sell a precisely defined quantity and quality of a commodity in a given month, the price of which is determined by the participants at the time of transaction.

Commodity Money. Refers to an object used as money which has been also a saleable commodity in its own right: the obvious example has been gold. This differs from fiat money which has in itself no real value.

Common External Tariff. A tariff which is applied by members of customs union, common market or economic commodity at an agreed, similar rate on imports from non-members. While the rate for any given imported goods has been identical in all members countries, different rates of duty have been applied to different goods.

Common Facility Co-operatives. A policy measure which has been designed to facilitate the growth of progressive technology, by forming co-operatives which are using common facilities or joint production workshops to raise productivity of local artisans and craft industries.

Common Market. In addition to the common external tariff and the concerned commercial policy of the customs union, a common market is aiming at a unified market area with the free movement of goods, services and factors of distributions.

Common Pricing. Means the fixing of identical prices for goods by agreement between otherwise competing firms selling through wholesale or retail channels of distribution.

Communism. In the strict sense it refers to a stage of economic development which is said to take place when all classes in society have been absorbed into the proletariat. In this ideal society the state would have withered away and each person would contribute according to ability and receive according to needs. This utopia envisaged by Marx has been seen to be the stage of economic development which follows on from capitalism and socialism. The term is however generally used to denote the planned economic system operated in the Comeon countries, China and elsewhere where the government is having centralized economic decisions and taken control of productive activity.

Community Indifference Curves. Each point along such a curve is representing a bundle of commodities which could be distributed among individuals so as to yield a particular distribution of utility within the community. Community indifference curves (unlike individual indifference curves) can intersect. As many indifference curves will pass through any point in commodity space as there have been different ways of distributing that commodity bundle.

Company. A joint stock company, which has been a legal entity set up for the purpose of conducting commercial or industrial operations, and with a capital divided into shares that have been held by its members. In principle, the shareholders are able to control the company through their right to vote at annual meetings and to elect the board of directors, whose function has been to observe the running of the company. The formation and conditions of operation of companies have been regulated by the Companies Acts, which confer rights as well as apply restrictions.

Company Savings. Refers to that part of firms profits which has been neither paid out in taxes or distributed to shareholders as dividends

Company Taxation, the Economist's Canons of. The Economist's criteria for a good company tax have been as follows:

(a) It should be easy and cheap to administer and to comply with:

(b) It should not distort firms' investment and fund-raising decisions;

(c) The burden of the tax should be eased according to companies' ability to pay; and

(d) Tax liabilities should be clear-out

Comparability. Refers to the formal and informal comparisons which are drawn by work groups between their pay and the pay of other workers. Such comparisons are able to influence the wages determination process.

Comparability Argument. Refers to the belief that workers doing similar jobs and producing the same amounts must be paid, the same wage.

Comparative Advantage. Credit for the discovery of the doctrine of comparative advantage, which has been the basis of the case for specialization on the part of nations or individuals and for freedom of trade, is given to David Ricardo.

Comparative Advantage, Theory of. In international trade it refers to a statement that countries tend to specialise in the production of those goods and services which they are able to make or provide most profitably. Let us assume that Country A can produce two commodities more cheaply that Country B. Country A will still specialise in that commodity in which it has the greater comparative advantage and let country B specialise in the other. It is a mutually profitable arrangement.

Comparative Cost Method. Refers to a method of comparing the profitability of alternative projects. The method takes into consideration the initial cost of alternative projects only; it is possible to use this method only where the output and life of each competing scheme is the same.

Comparative Dynamics. The term used for a method employed in dynamic economics with a special feature that the rates of change in the values of the parameters and in the equilibrium values of the variables have been constant.

Comparative Statics. Refers to the comparison of a new equilibrium position with an old one after some change in the variables, without reference to the way in which the new position gets reached, and generally without quantitative aspects. Simply, the determination of the direction in which variable will alter consequent upon some disturbance to the original equilibrium.

Compensated Demand Curves. Refers to a demand curve in which the income effect of a price change has been netted out so that, along the demand curve real income has been held constant. The demand curve then exhibits the shape it does because of the substitution effect only. The Marshallian demand curve is including both income and substitution effects. The method of taking the income effect out depends on how that effect is measured. The two procedures have been those of Hicks and Slutzky. For normal goods, the compensated demand curve will be steeper in slope than the Marshallian curve.

Compensation Tests. Such tests will be able to ask the question whether the losers from some particular change could be compensated for their losses while still leaving the gainers better off than they were before the change. The compensation has been hypothetical and not needed to take place. The most famous one has been the Kaldor-Hicks test.

Competitive Market. Refers to a market in which a very large number of small buyers and sellers trade independently, and as such no one trader is able to significantly influence price.

Complement. Refers to a good which tends to be purchased when another good gets purchased because it 'complements' the first good. Favourite examples have been cups and saucers, cars and petrol etc. Complementary goods have a negative cross elasticity of demand. The indifference curve for perfect complements has been shown in the diagram.

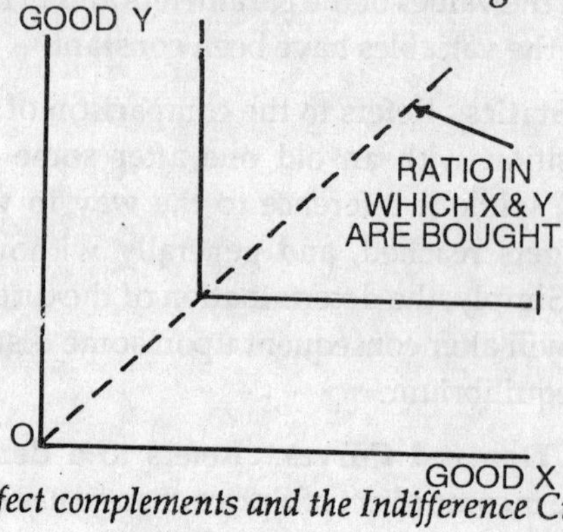

Perfect complements and the Indifference Curve

Composite Commodity Theorem. This theorem states that if there exists a set of goods whose relative prices (i.e., the price of any one relative to the price of another) do not change then those goods can be treated as if they had been one commodity, the so-called composite commodity'.

Compound Interest. The procedure whereby future interest has been paid on past interest earned. Thus if a sum of Rs. 1 is invested at a rate of interest r, its value after one year will be Rs. (1+r). If the interest gained is now removed, the Rs. 1 will remain and will gather r per cent again in the following year. If however the Rs. (1+r) is left to secure interest, then it will secure interest in the second year of Rs. (1+r) r, and the original Rs. (1+r) will remain. The total investement at the end of the second year will therefore be

$$\text{Rs. }(1+r)+\text{Rs.}(1+r)r$$

which reduces to

$$\text{Rs. }(1+r)\,(1+r)=\text{Rs. }(1+r)^2$$

At the end of year t, the investment will have a value of

$$\text{Rs. }(1+r)^t.$$

Concentration

1. A term which indicates the state of competitive conditions prevailing in an industry. Two extremes have been Perfect Competition and Monopoly with market structures in between representing various degrees of imperfect competition.

2. A concept which is used either in connection with the size distribution of firms in an industry or economy, or with reference to the location of industry. In its former use concentration means the extent to which a market' or an economy's total output has been accounted for by the few largest member firms. When used in the context of industrial location. Concentration implies the degree to which an industry has become localized within a particular area.

Concentration Ratio. Refers to the percentage of total industry size accounted for by the few largest firms in the industry. The measure may be considered as a proxy for one dimension of market structure, i.e., the degree to which and industry has been centralized.

Concertina Method of Tariff Reduction. Refers to a procedure of tariff reduction, which involves cutting the higher tariff rates, while leaving lower rates unchanged, so that the gap between tariffs gets diminished.

Conciliation. Refers to the intervention in an industrial dispute at the request of the parties to the dispute by an independent and impartial third party in an attempt for reconciling the views of the two parties.

Condorcet Criterion. Refers to a system of collective choice in which the chozen alternative has been that which defeats all other alternative in a series of pairwise (one to one) contests using majority rule. The procedure has been named after the Marqius de Condorect who discussed it in 1785. While the Condorect approach may be said to provide a more complete reflection of voters alternative than simple majority rule, it can, like majority rule fail to yield an unambiguous 'winner'. Consider the preferences of a three person community shown below concerning alternatives X, Y and Z.

		Voter	
Ranking	A	B	C
1	X	Z	Y
2	Y	X	Z
3	Z	Y	X

With these preferences, x will defeat y but not z, y will deal z but not x and z will defeat x but not y. There has been not a Condorect winner.

Constant Capital. In the Marxian scheme refers to that part of capital which has been represented by the means of production raw materials and instruments of labour. It may be defined as constant because it can add no more to the value of output than its own value; value being defined as hours of embodied, socially necessary labour.

Confidence Problem. Refers to one of the problems of the international monetary system which arises when there has been an expectation that a currency has been about to be devalued, such that short-term capital has been then withdrawn from that country and there has been a loss of confidence in that particular national currency. To maintain a pegged value for the currency will need a high level of international reserves capacity if this takes place often and or has been particularly severe.

Connected Lending. Loans to companies or persons connected with the institution lending the funds, its managers, director or controllers.

Conscious Parallelism. Firms which are co-ordinating sales and output policies one with another without formal or indeed informal understanding or agreement.

Consistency. Refers to a desirable properly of econometric estimators. A consistent estimator has been one whose mean tends to the true value of the parameters and whose variance tends to zero as the sample size becomes very large. The Ordinary, Least Squares estimator has been a consistent estimator if there had been no econometric problems.

Consols. Funded Government securities or stock which the Government need not repay until it wishes. The terms has been an abbreviation for 'consolidated annuities'.

Consortium Bank. A type of international bank which is formed by groupings of existing banks usually drawn from different countries. These banks appeared in the 1960s and have now established in several financial centres. They are mainly involved in medium-term lending, frequently to multinational companies; they get the greater part of their funds in the eurocurrency market; but they also arrange 'syndicated' loans (i.e., loans raised among a group of lenders) frequently bringing in lenders outside the consortium members.

Constant Elasticity of Substitution Production Function. The CES production function has been a linearly homogeneous production function having a constant elasticity of input substitution. This elasticity is able to take on values other than unity. The actual form of the CES production function has been

$$Q=A[aK^{-b}+(l-c)L^{-b}]^{-1/b}$$

where Q represent output, K and L represent capital and labour, and a,b,c care constants.

Constant Market Share Demand Curve. The term used for the relation between quantity sold and price which faces the firm if all its competitors exactly match any price change made by this firm. It has been therefore more inelastic than the conventional demand curve, as each point will represent an equal share of the market. This concept finds use analytically in the kinked curve model of oligopoly and the theory of monopolistic competitions.

Constant Returns. Description of a situation in which all the productive services can get increased in a given proportion, the amount of product being increased in the same proportion. Factor substitutions and qualitative changes have been not introduced.

Constrained Optimization. Refers to the maximization or minimization of an objective function where the choice variables have been subject to some constraint. Examples include the maximization of utility subject to a budget constraint. Mathematical methods to deal with this sort of problem have been Lagrangean Techniques.

Consumer. Refers to any economic agent which is responsible for the act of consuming final goods and services.

Consumer Behaviour, Principles Governing. The generalisation which are made in economic analysis relating to the behaviour of a consumer in distributing a limited personal income amongst an infinite variety of goods and services available. It is assumed that:

(a) the consumer will so arrange expenditure that the relative marginal utility of all the goods consumed will be in the same proportion to their relative price;

(b) a fall in the price of a good or service, other things being equal, will increase consumption of it, while a rise in its price will have the opposite effect; and

(c) a rise in real income will normally result in an increased consumption of goods and services, a fall in real income having the opposite effect.

Consumer Credit. Refers to a loan which is given to the consumer for a short period of time, for the purchase of a specific commodity.

Consumer Demand Theory. Refers to that area of economic which defines testable theories of how consumers behave in response to change in variables like price, other prices, income changes and so on. The two main schools of thought have been those based on indifference curve analysis and revealed preference theory, but considerable attention is also given to the theories which are based on the characteristic goods.

Consumer Durable. A commodity of responsible long life, like a refrigerator or piece of furniture; as distinct form, say foodstuffs.

Consumer Equilibrium. Refers to the situation in which the consumer is able to maximize utility subject to a given budget constraint. In terms of an indifference map this situation has been achieved when the consumer reaches the highest possible indifference curve given the limitations imposed by his budget line. This will give rise to a situation where the indifference curve has been tangential to the budget line--i.e., their slopes are equal. Formally, the marginal rate of substitution has been equal to the price ratio of two goods--i.e.

$$MRS_{xy} = \frac{px}{py}$$

for two goods X and Y

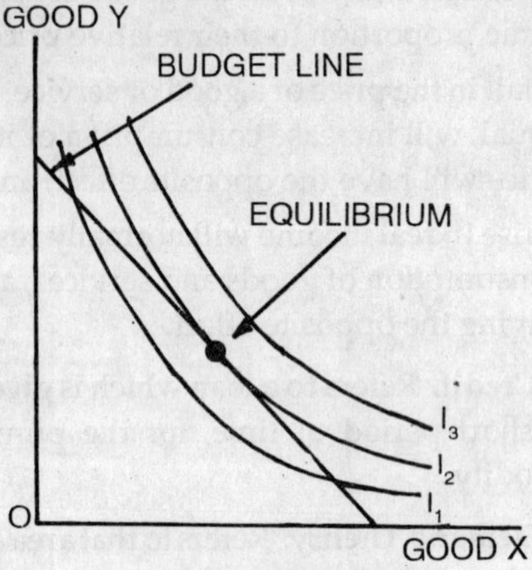

Consumer equilibrium

Consumer Goods. Products in the actual form in which they will reach domestic consumers.

Consumer Goods and Services. Tangible and intangible commodities which get consumed for their own sake for satisfying current wants.

Consumerism. A widespread movement which is concerned with the quality and safety of consumer goods, with harmful advertising and the conduct of business in a manner harmful to the consumer.

Consumer Preference, Theory of. Refers to a theory of consumer has been asked if he/she 'prefers' one set of goods to another, or is 'indifferent' between them. The theory has been not concerned with by how much the consumer prefers one set of good to another.

Consumers' Sovereignty. Refers to influence of consumers exercising freedom of choice in a free market over the activities of producers of goods and services.

Consumers' Surplus. Means the excess of the price which a person would be willing to pay rather than go without an articles, over that which he/one actually does pay; it may be termed as consumer's rent.

Consumption. Means the act of using goods and services to satisfy current wants. While theoretically precise there have been practical problems in meeting consumption. The main problem arises in the treatment of consumer durables.

Consumption Expenditure. Refers to aggregate expenditures on goods and services to satisfy current wants.

Contigency Reserve. Refers to the unallocated reserve for contingencies and other requirements which cannot be quantified.

Contact. An agreement which is either oral or in writing, whereby one party undertakes to do something for the other party to the contract. It is also a term of reference describing a unit of trading for a commodity futures contract.

Contract Curve. In the context of two consumers it represents the locus of points where the marginal rate of substitution between the pair of gocus has been the same for both individuals.

Contract Unit. Refers to the actual amount of a commodity which is designated in a given futures contract.

Contractual Savings Institutions. Institutions like life insurance companies and pension funds, whose schemes and policies have been characterised by regular contributor payments and by defined obligations for future payments in respect of such events as retirement or death. With liabilities that have been predictable, these institutions are able to invest in longer-term securities than ordinary deposit-type financial intermediaries.

Convenient Social Virtue. Refers to a description by Professor John Kenneth Galbraith of virtues which have been held up as eternally desirable yet serve the ends of the more powerful members of the community. Merit has been ascribed to any pattern of behaviour, however, uncomfortable and unnatural for the individual involved, that serves the comfort or well-being of, or has been otherwise advantageous for, the more powerful and influential members of the community.

Convergence Thesis. An idea that socialist and capitalist economies have been departing from their respective 'ideal' forms and are evolving increasingly similar modes of behaviour and thinking, institutions and methods.

Convertibility. Refers to the freedom to exchange any currency for another currency at the ruling rate of exchange.

Cooling Off Period. Refers to a period of legally enforced delay before strike activity can commence so as to allow a de-escalation or cooling off of emotions and thus, it has been assumed, a more rational evaluation of matters in dispute.

Co-operative Banks. Small local institutions, which are generally organised by a group of individuals with a common bond or purpose. Designed to give members easier and cheaper access to credit, these institutions tend to remain small.

Co-ownership Firm. Refers to a firm in which control and ownership have been largely in the hands of the employees of that firm.

Co-partnership Industry. Schemes which are introduced by individual firms to provide employees a bigger stake in the prosperity of the firms they work for.

Coreper. A group which comprises of the ten ambassadors of the European Economic Community.

Corner Solution. In an optimization problem it refers to a situation in which one or more of the choice variables is having zero value at the optimum.

Corporate Capitalism. The term used for a contemporary view of modern developed western economies in which the productive sector has been dominated by large corporations characterized by a separation of ownership from control.

Corporate Paper. Notes which are sold by large corporations in the money market as a means of getting funds; such notes are secured by the general credit standing of the corporation.

Corporate Planning. Refers to an approach to top level management problems which emphasises :

(a) the need for an organisation to decide exactly what its objectives are; and

(b) the need for long-term planning in every part of the organisation to achieve these objectives.

Corporate Risk. The total risk involved in a business is termed as corporate risk. It comprises two main types of risk. Financial risk which is arising out of debt finance, and business risk which has been the basic risk involved in the firm's day to day operations.

Corporate State. Refers to an economic and political system where the major sectors of the economy have been organized into single large corporations and administered through the collaboration of government, workers' organizations and organized employers' associations. The corporation is an umbrella organization which is used for determining the running of individual firms-input and output prices and quantities.

Corporation. The term used for a contemporary form of business organisation in the United States of America and elsewhere, having two distinct characteristics : it is a legal entity separated from its owners, the stockholders; and it has been usually on a scale much too large for the sole proprietor or partnership to manage or fund.

Correspondent Banks. A bank which is acting as agent for another bank in a Place where the latter is having no office, or for some reason is unable to conduct certain operations for itself.

Cost. Means the amount of expenditure incurred in obtaining the services of a factor of a production.

Cost-benefit Analysis. Refers to a systematic comparison between the cost of carrying out a service or activity and the value of that service or activity, quantifying, as far as possible, all costs and benefits whether direct or indirect, financial or social.

Cost-benefit Ratio. A ratio calculated:

$$\frac{\text{Gross Benefit (present value)}}{\text{Gross Cost (present value)}}$$

The gross costs and benefits have been discounted over the life of the project by a selected annual rate of interest. The difference between the two amounts has been the present value of net benefits. The ratio of the two amounts is the gross cost-benefit ratio. Both considerations are relevant in choosing between projects.

Cost Co-efficient. Refers to the cost of a unit of output, e.g., the cost of processing a kilogram of material or the cost of mining a ton of coal. A concept useful in comparisons between process of a similar character.

Cost Control. Refers to the procedure by which the management accountant evaluates the actual cost of a capital project or a manufacturing operation for the purpose of comparison with the authorised estimates or cost standard.

Cost Curve. A graph which shows by means of a curve the expenses which a firm will incur in attaining any given volume of output.

Cost-effectiveness Analysis. A technique which is closely related to cost-benefit analysis. It thus aids choice between options but cannot answer the question whether or not any of the options are worth doing. It has been utilized when there have been difficulties in associating monetary values with the outcomes of projects but where the outcomes can be quantified along some non-monetary dimension.

Cost-inflation. Refers to a type of inflation, sometimes called costpush inflation, in which powerful unions have been blamed for making large wage demands in the absence of excess demand in the labour market. The employers give in to these demands and the extra costs, get passed on to consumers in the form of increased prices.

Cost Minimization. For any given level of output that choice of input combination which provides the smallest possible total cost. The choice of a cost minimizing firm facing fixed input prices and using the two factors inputs. Capital K and Labour L, can be illustrated using isocost lines and isoquants. The cost minimizing choice for output level Y_2 has been represented by the input combination A, where the isoquant labelled Y_2 has been tangent to the lowest possible isocost line I_2. Other input combinations lying on I_2, such as those represented by points B and C, will not be chosen because they yield the lower output level Y_1. On similar grounds, the firm will be able to reject input combinations lying upon isocost lines above or below I_2 as those above I_2 require a higher outlay, whereas those below I_2 represent outlays which purchase an insufficient amount of inputs to give rise to output level Y_2.

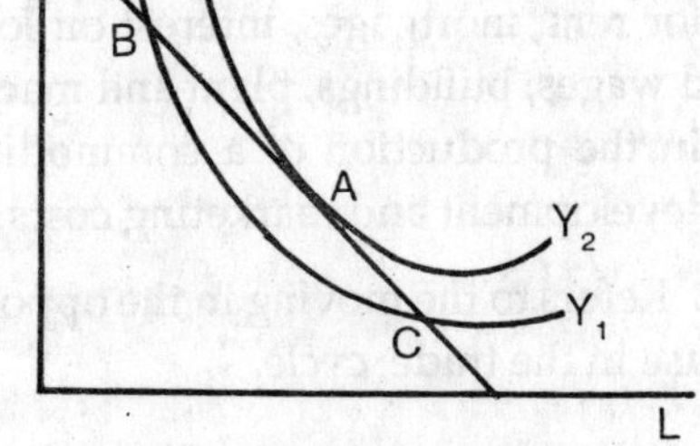

Cost Minimization

Cost of Capital. Refers to the cost which is measured as a percentage rate of the various sources of capital required to finance capital expenditure.

Cost of Protection. The protection of domestic industry by tariff, quota or other restriction normally puts a cost on the protected economy in the two forms of a misallocation of resources in production and of a distortion in the pattern of consumption. The former is involving a reduced marginal revenue product from factors of production and the latter a loss of consumer's surplus.

Cost of Sales. All cost which are incurred in a factory in converting raw materials into a finished product: such cost include raw materials, labour, and factory overheads.

Cost of Service Principle. Refers to a basis for charging for services, regard being had to the costs of producing a particular service rather than the value of the service to the consumer.

Cost-plus Pricing. Refers to a pricing whereby firms add a margin on to average variables cost so as to cover fixed costs and some reasonable level of profits.

Cost-push Inflation. Refers to a sustained rise in the general price level arising from an autonomous rise in costs. This may arise from either an autonomous decision by employees to demand higher real wages or by employers to raise their profit margins or it may arise from an autonomous increase in import prices.

Cost of Production. Expenditure which is incurred by way of payments for rent, mortgages, interest on loans, dividends, salaries and wages, buildings, plant and machinery and raw materials, in the production of a commodity or a service, including development and marketing costs.

Countercyclical. Refers to the moving in the opposite direction to a given phase in the trade cycle.

Countervailing Duty. Or matching duty. A situation achieved when an excise duty on an article produced at home becomes equal to the customs duty imposed on a similar article imported from abroad, neither the home-produced or imported product being given an advantage.

Countervailing Power. Countervailing power is considered to prevail when the market powers of firms(s) or economic agents (s) has been counterbalanced by market powers possessed by trader(s) who buy from or sell to the former. The concept of countervailing power was given by J.K. Galbraith, who argues that it can lead to a more workable and equitable economic and political system.

Coupon Bond. A bond having interest coupons attached to the coupons have been clipped as they become due and have been presented by the owner for the payment of interest.

Coupon Interest Rate. The interest rate attracted by the coupons attached to a bond.

Cournot's Duopoly Model. This model is based upon the behavioural assumption that each of the two firms will maximize profits assuming that its competitor's output remains constant.

Covering. Buying a security previously sold short.

Craft Unions. Trade Unions which organize all workers having a particular skill, or group of related skills, regardless of the industry in which they work.

Crawling Peg. Refers to a compromise arrangement between a fixed exchange rate and a floating exchange rate, where the exchange value of a currency has been allowed to alter over time but only by some agreed-upon percentage each year.

Credentialism. Means the problem of hiring standards that have been too severe for the limited skill requirements of the lower grade jobs in question.

Credit. A wide term which has been used in connection with operations or states involving lending, generally at short-term. To 'give credit' is to finance, directly or indirectly, the expenditures of others against future repayment.

Credit Card. A card which is issued to customers by a bank or group of bodies or other agency (*e.g.*, Diner's Club) which provides the holder direct access to credit, e.g., from a retailer, hotel etc., or, in the case of some cards issued by banks, to cash from the banks operating the particular scheme. When goods or services are purchased with a credit card, the supplier secures rapid reimbursement from the issuing bank(s) or agency which takes over the credit providing function.

Credit Ceiling. In monetar policy, refers to an announced limit on the amount of credit which may get extended by specified institutions, usually banks, during restrictive policy phases. The limit could be fixed in relation to lending outstanding in a base period and allow for increase at specified rates, and it may be able to discriminate between classes of borrowers.

Credit Control. The term which is denoting the set of measures used by the monetary authorities to control the volume of lending by certain groups of financial institutions*e.g*, bank credit, hire purchase credit.

Credit Creation. Refers to the process by which a group of deposit taking and lending institutions which are operating on fractional reserve ratios, can on the basis of an increase in their reserve assets, produce an increase in the volume of their lending, and the associated deposit liabilities, of an amount greater than the increase in reserves.

Credit Guarantee. Refers to a type of insurance whereby a credit guarantee association offers insurance against default.

Credit Multiplier. Refers to the ratio of the change in the volume of lending by a group of deposit-taking financial intermediaries (and especially banks) to the change in reserve assets which initiated the change.

Creditor Nation. A nation having a balance of payments surplus.

Credit Rating. Means an evaluation of the soundness of an individual or business firm as a credit risk. It has been usually based on the three 'Cs' of credit (a) character or inegrity; (b) capacity, or earning power, and (c) capital, or the overall financial status of the applicant.

Creditors. The individuals or institutions who are lending money in return for promises made by the recipient, to pay a certain sum of money each year by way of interest, and to repay the principal at some date in the future.

Credit Rationing. Refers to the act of rationing loan finance by non-price means in situations of excess demand for credit, by financial intermediaries.

Credit Restrictions. Refer to the measures which are taken or imposed by the monetar authorities, to limit or reduce the volume of credit extended by banks and other financial institutions.

Credit Sale. Refers to a procedure for purchasing goods under which the purchaser is paying deposit on receipt of the goods followed by a number of instalments until the debt gets cleared.

Credit Sales System. Refers to a credit sales system, which may be offered as an alternative to hire-purchases, under which ownership is obtained at the outset. The borrower must, of course, continue to make the agreed payments.

Credit Squeeze. Refers to a policy phase of credit restrictions.

Credit Transfer. Refers to the system by which funds can get transferred directly through the banking system to the account of a specified recipient. Such a transfer may get initiated simply by anybody, whether a customer or not, paying money into a bank office with the necessary credit slip.

Credit Union. Refers to a group of people engaging in organised self-help who are able to save their money together and make low-interest loans to each other. The loans have been usually short-term consumer loans, but may extend to loans for farm or small business enterprise purposes.

Creeping Inflation. Refers to a slow, but continuous inflation, which can result inter alia from increases in aggregate demand.

Cross. To buy and sell simultaneously in the same contract month for the same commodity.

Cross Elasticity of Demand. Refers to the responsiveness of quantity demanded of one good to a change in the price of another good. To avoid the measure being sensitive to the units being sensitive to the units being used, the measure may be expressed as follows :

Cross Elasticity of Demand =

$$\left(\frac{\Delta Q_i}{Q_i} \cdot 100\right) \div \left(\frac{\Delta P_i}{P_j} \cdot 100\right)$$

$$= \frac{\Delta Q_i \cdot P_i}{\Delta P_j Q_i}$$

where Q_i represents the quantity of good i, and P_i is the price of another good j. The symbol Δ refers to a change in the variable in question.

Cross-Entry. Refers to a category used with regard to new entrant firms who are already established firms in industries using similar technology to that in which entry has been taking place.

Cross-Section Analysis. Refers to the analysis of a series of records of economic data for different groups of people, firms or countries, at the same moment or in broadly the same period of time; it is contrasted with time series analysis which measures the changing situation at successive points in time.

Cross-Subsidization. With reference to multi-product firms, the funding of losses in one line of business from monopoly gains on other products sold by the firm.

Crowding Hypothesis. Refers to the argument that entry barriers and informational imperfections will be able to tend to crowd certain groups, chiefly women and blacks, into a limited range of occupations and in the process lower the relative wage of these occupations.

Crowding Out. Refers to a fall in either private consumption or investment because of a rise in government expenditure.

Cum All. With-all advantages. Refers to a description which may get attached to the sale of a security, implying that any dividend interest, rights, bonus or other benefit, just declared or current has been not being withheld.

Cum Bonus. With bonus just declared. Refers to a condition which may get attached to the sale of a security.

Cum Drawing. With benefit of the current drawing. If there exists no benefit, it means with the liability for loss of drawing. A condition that may get attached to the sale of a security.

Cum Interest. With current interest. A condition which may get attached to the sale of a security.

Cum Rights. With 'rights' recently issued. A condition which may get attached to the sale of a security.

Cummulative Preference Share. A preference share which entitles the holder to receive not only the current dividend but also any unpaid arrears, before any dividend has been paid to ordinary shareholders.

Currency-deposit Ratio. Refers to the ratio of the public's holdings of currency to its holdings of deposits at banks.

Currency Hedge Market. Refers to a currency market which provides hedging against future currency rates of exchange.

Current Assets and Liabilities. Current assets have been those assets of the company which have been reasonably expected to be realised in cash, or sold or consumed during the normal operating cycle of the business. Such assets include cash, bonds, inventories, and money due within 1 year. Current liabilities, one the other hand, have money owned and payable by a company, usually within one year.

Current Cost Accounting. Refers to a system of inflation accounting in which assets have been recorded in the accounts of a company at their 'value to the business', i.e., the loss the business would suffer if the asset get destroyed, in money terms.

Customs Duty. Refers to the revenue protective or preferential duty which is imposed on goods imported from abroad.

Cultural Change. One of the criticisms of certain types of economic development has been that it destroys the indigenous culture, but technological change and economic development can get achieved without profound cultural change; an example of this is the industrialization of Japan which occurred by transferring the feudal system directly from the farm to the factory.

Cumulative Causation Model. Refers to an approach to the analysis of regional economic growth, owing much to the work of G.Myrdal, which argues that market forces tend to increase economic inequalities between regions of the same economy.

Customs Union. Refer to a grouping of countries within which trade restrictions get abolished but which is having a concerted commercial policy towards non-members and a common external tariff on imports from them, though the tariff rate may be varying between commodities.

Cyclical Unemployment. Refers to short-run demand deficient unemployment. It reveals that during certain phases of the business cycle there will be insufficient jobs for the whole of the labour force no matter how it gets trained or deployed.

D

Daisy Chain Schemes. Commercial schemes in which the ownership of a commodity gets transferred through the hands of a chain of subsidiaries, tax-haven companies, affiliates, and other companies, a commodity may be sold at a low price for export and re-imported later for sale at a higher world price, leaving offshore a substantial untaxed make-up.

Damage Cost. Means the money cost of damage done by pollution. In economics, pollution is generally considered to be an instance of an externality. Placing money values on externalities is a complex and often dubious procedure as with valuing injuries, death, loss of recreational land, loss of wilderness, wildlife and so on. In other cases valuation may be more straightforward as with the loss of commercial fisheries due to say, oil population.

Damped Cycle. Refers to one of a series of cyclical fluctuations which exhibit a decreasing amplitude over time (also known as a convergent cycle).

Damping. Means a reducing effect. For example, at low levels of market demand some people may be able to withdraw from the labour market, thus damping the rise in unemployment figures.

Data. Means observations on the numerical magnitude of economic phenomena like national income, unemployment or the retail price level.

Dated Security. Refer to any security, like a bond, which has a stated redemption date. Such securities have been conventionally divided into short-dated, medium-dated and long-dated securities depending on the length of time which has to elapse before they 'mature' (*i.e.*, have been repaid).

DCF. Abbreviation of Discounted Cash Flow Analysis.

Dead Horse. Work which is paid for but is yet to be completed; a situation in which services and goods have been paid for in advance of performance or production.

Dear Money. Refer to phases when interest rates have been high compared with their historical average values.

Deadweight Debt. Means that part of the National Debt which is not covered by real assets, in contrast to Reproductive Debt. Most of the National Debt is of this type.

Death Duties. Duties which are payable when a property passes at death. Death duties have been often progressive, increasing in proportion with the value of the estate.

Debt. Refers to a sum of money, or quantity of goods or services, owed by one individual or body to another.

Debt Finance. It involves borrowing. It refers to the use of loans by companies to finance their operations, especially capital expenditure through long-term loans. The overall cost of capital may get reduced by the use of debt. Governments also borrow to finance their operations and to help regulate the volume of aggregate activity in the economy. Such borrowing involves the issues of short-term and/or long-term securities. In a recession a government may incur a budget deficit and increase its borrowing to stimulate the economy.

Debtor Nation. A nation having a balance of payments deficit.

Debtor's Repayment Period. Refers to a measure of the average length of time taken for debtors to pay their accounts.

Decausalisation. Means the abolition of the causal employment of workers.

Decimal Coinage. A system of currency which uses the base ten.

Decimal Currency. Metallic and paper currency in which each successive denomination is ten times the value of the next below it.

Decision Leg. Means the delay which occurs between the recognition of the need for action on an economic problem (in particular macro-economic) and a policy decision.

Decision Rule. A criterion which is used in making choices, such as whether or not to carry out a given project or how to price output. These rules are emerging from economic analysis; for example, economic theory yields the decision rule that a firm which wishes to maximize profit (or minimize losses) should produce the output level at which marginal cost equals marginal revenue. Economists are also attempted to produce decision rules for, among other things, the evaluation of projects and the pricing policies of state industries. The precise nature of a decision rule will be found to depend upon the objective pursued and the constraints on choice.

Decision Theory. Means the theory which is relating to the establishment of appropriate courses of action with the aim of achieving given objectives under specified circumstances, which might be subject to uncertainty. Decision analyses give rise to the selection of appropriate criteria by which a course of action may be judged.

Decreasing Cost Industry. Refers to an industry where the long-run supply curve has been downward sloping. This could take place if there were important economies external to the firm and internal to the industry.

Decreasing Costs, Law of. This law refers to the tendency towards falling average costs of production in taking advantage of the economies of scale, over the long period. Sir Roy Harrod (b. 1900) described the form of the long-period cost curve as the envelope of the short-period cost curves.

Decreasing Returns. See law of Diminishing Returns, Returns to Scale.

Decreasing Returns to Scale. Refers to a possible response of total output to change in the scale of the production process; when the employment of all factors of production gets doubled, total output will be less than doubled.

Dead of Transfer. Means a formal agreement under seal bearing a government revenue stamp and signed by both the buyer and the seller of.

Deficit. Refers to a situation where outgoings exceed income, on an ongoing basis, or where liabilities exceed assets at a specific point in time.

Deficit Blow-out. Means an unexpected and unplanned enlargement of a Government budget deficit due to a combination of unforseen and unforeseeable events.

Deficit Financing. Means situation where expenditure exceeds income such that a deficit is operated deliberately. Keynes was the first to suggest that governments should deliberately run a planned deficit as part of monetary policy. The term also refers to a planned deficit whether operated by a government in its domestic affairs or with reference to a balance of payments deficit.

Deficit Units. Means economic units who cannot meet their expenses in a given period from their incomes during that period, either from the sale of their labour, or their assets, such that they have been dependent on borrowing money or obtaining credit.

Deflation. Means situation in which prices and money incomes have been falling, accompanied by an increase in the value of the monetary unit.

Deflationary Gap. Aggregate expenditure runs short of that needed to produce a level of national income which would ensure full employment. In the income expenditure model it is shown by an aggregate expenditure function which cuts the 45 line, where E=Y, at less than the full employment level of national income. The diagram below demonstrates that an unemployment equilibrium exists at Y_1 and that there exists a corresponding deflationary gap of magnitude AB at full employment Y_f.

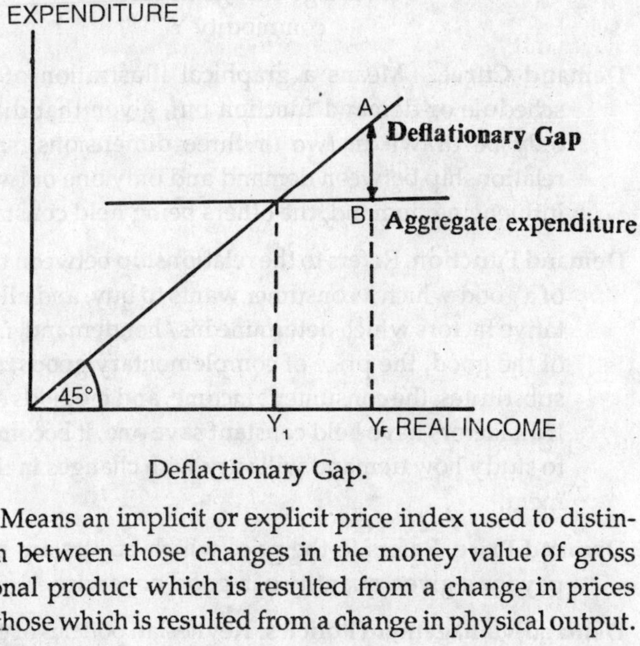

Deflactionary Gap.

Deflator. Means an implicit or explicit price index used to distinguish between those changes in the money value of gross national product which is resulted from a change in prices and those which is resulted from a change in physical output.

Deindustrialization. A trend in a national economy towards a large and larger share of the gross domestic product is taken up by services. For this to occur the rate of growth of the service sector must be greater than that of the manufacturing sector.

Demand. Refers to the amount of a commodity or service which will be bought at any given price per unit of time. In society, the two main components of demand have been consumption and investment. Aggregate demand curves slope down from left to right, with real income increasing as prices fall.

Demand, Cross-Elasticity of. Refers to the responsiveness of the demand for a commodity or service to changes in the prices of other commodities. It is calculated as follows:

$$\frac{\text{Percentage change in demand for commodity X}}{\text{Percentage change in price of commodity Y}}$$

Demand Curve. Means a graphical illustration of a demand schedule or demand function but, given that diagrams can only be drawn in two or three dimensions, showing the relationship between demand and only one or two variables influencing demand, the others being held constant.

Demand Function. Refers to the relationship between the quantity of a good which a consumer wants to buy, and all the quantitative factors which determine his/her demand, *i.e.*, the price of the good, the price of complementary goods, the price of substitutes, the consumer's income, and methods of payment. If all factors have held constant save one, it becomes possible to study how demand will vary with changes in that one element.

Demand Price. Refers to the price which buyers are prepared to pay for a given quantity of a good or service.

Demand Management Policies. Keynesian policies of purshing an activist, stabilization course by regulating aggregate demand so as to minimise unemployment and curb inflation.

The concept of demand management has been applicable to areas other than the economy as a whole.

Demand Schedule. Refers to a table giving the demand for a commodity or service at various prices, while all other factors determining demand get unchanged.

Demand, Theory of. Refers to a branch of economic theory which deals with analysing the determinants of a consumer's choice of a particular set of goods from all those that are available for purchase especially with how a consumer's tastes and income, and the prices of the goods influence his/her pattern of purchases.

Demographic Transition. Refers to a fundamental change in the characteristic trends of a population, e.g., a transition from high birth rates and high death rates to low birth rates and low death rates.

Demography. Means the study of population characteristics.

Demurrage Charges. Refers to the monetary penalty which is paid to compensate for the delaying of a ship or freight car due to a consignee's failure to load, unload or sail within an allotted amount of time.

Deposit Banks. Banks whose primary business has been the receipt, transfer and encashment of deposits.

Dependence Structure. The third world countries have been part of a wide structure of economic, social and political dependence between power groups in advanced countries, especially multinational companies; and key interest groups in the poor countries.

Demand-Shift Inflation. Means a theory which is combining elements of demand-pull and cost-push inflation which considers inflation to be a result of a change in the structure of aggregate demand.

Demand Management. Refers to the control of the aggregate level of demand in an economy through the use of monetary policy and/or fiscal policy.

Demand-pull Inflation. Refers to a sustained rise in aggregate demand beyond the full employment level of output which results in a sustained rise in the general price level.

Depletion Allowance. Refers to a tax advantage that permits the owner of natural resources to deduct against gross income; the depletion is value of a non-renewable asset such as oil or gas.

Deposit. Sums lent to certain financial institutions, e.g., banks, building societies and finance houses, on terms permitting withdrawal with or without notice, or providing for repayment after specified periods–such sums have been described as 'on deposit'. Current account deposits in banks are directly transferable by cheque, while those deposits for which certificates of deposit are issued are effectively transferable since the certificates of deposit themselves may be bought and sold.

Deposit Account. A type of account which is designed to attract customer's less active balances, and also as a savings medium.

Deposit Money. Money created by the commercial banks constituting the greater proportion of the supply of money.

Deposit-type Financial Institutions. Institutions which take deposits from the public; they may be bank or non-bank.

Depository or Warehouse Receipt. A document' which is issued by a bank or warehouse, or a clearing house, indicating ownership of a commodity stored in a depository or warehouse.

Depressed Area. Refers to a geographical area or region within a nation which experiences a significantly poorer economic performance than the nation as a whole. The index of 'depressed-ness' most frequently used has been the rate of unemployment.

Depression. Means prolonged and severe slowing-down of economic activity exemplified by mass unemployment and a level of national income well below its potential level. It is more severe and long-lasting than a recession.

Derived Demand. Refers to the demand for a commodity not needed for its own sake, but for its contribution to the manufacture of another commodity.

Detrending. Refers to the process by which a time trend is removed from data, often by prior estimation of a time trend, and the calculation of residuals.

Devaluation. Refers to a fall in the fixed exchange rate between one currency and others.

Developed Nations or Industrial Nations. Those countries which have achieved substantial manufacturing and service capability in addition to advanced techniques in agriculture and raw material extraction.

Developing Countries. This description of the poorer nations of the world came into current usage in the 1960s and started to replace the less complimentary expressions 'underdeveloped' or 'backward'. An attempt to quantify the definition has been in terms of those countries with a per capita income below one-fifth of that of the US.

Development. Means the application of human, financial, living and non-living resources to satisfy human needs and improve the quality of human life.

Development Strategy. Refers to the approach taken to the problem of underdevelopment, which will depend on which particular growth model is being used. There have been many different strategies, like industrial development, import substitution, balanced growth of urban and rural areas, expanding and supporting agriculture so as to support the surplus population involved in establishing industry or developing the export sector so as to earn foreign exchange.

Differential. Refers to the difference between physical price and futures price.

Differentiated Growth. Means an aspect of firm growth by diversification, referring to that growth stimulated by the introduction of products which are sufficiently different from others as to be perceived as new by both consumers and the firm alike. The effects arising from the introduction of such a product have been spread thinly over a large number of producers, in contrast to the impact produced by the introduction of initative growth.

Dillon Round. Refers to the popular name for the fifth round of trade negotiations which was held under the auspices of the General Agreement on Tariffs and Trade in Geneva (1960-61).

Diminishing Marginal Utility. Means the phenomenon whereby it is assumed that the marginal utility attached to an extra unit of any good diminishes as more and more of that good has been purchased . In the cardinal utility approach to demand theory, the existence of diminishing marginal utility is sufficient to explain the downward slope of the demand curve, other things being equal. The principle has been also widely used to explain the convexity of indifference curves since more and more of one good will be required to compensate for the surrender of extra units of any other good the less there is of the latter good. That this is not a strictly correct explanation of convexity is demonstrated in H.A.J. Green, consumer theory.

Diminishing Returns, Law of. Refers to a generalisation that while an increase in some inputs relative to other fixed inputs in a productive process may, in a given state of technology, cause total output to increase there will come a point where the extra output resulting from the same additions of extra inputs has been likely to diminish. This falling off in extra returns has been a consequence of the fact that the additional doses of the varying resources must work with smaller proportions of the fixed resources. In the extreme, the process of additions will become counter-productive.

Direct Debit. Refers to a system of recent development for making payments through the banking system. Under this, the bank of a transactor who is due to receive a payment issues a direct claim on the bank of the party liable to make the payment, which in turn debits the payer's account. The direct debit has been like the credit transfer, much used for the making of regular payment, e.g., insurance premiums and mortage loan repayments.

Direct Taxes. Traditionally direct taxes are those levied directly on individuals or firms such as income tax, profits tax and capital gains tax. The original idea was that the bodies on whom these taxes had been levied actually paid the tax. It is in contrast to indirect taxes.

Dirty Float. Refers to a type of floating exchange rate which is not completely freely floating because central banks interfere from time to time to alter from its free market level.

Disadvantaged Workers. The workers who in terms of the skills they bring to the market or the 'signals' they transmit to would be employers are at a relative disadvantage. They are alternatively be described as the working poor.

Disappreciation. Means a movement of prices which, while downward in direction, was merely a correction of a previously excessive rise.

Discharges. Refers to the total number of people which are involuntarily leaving employment in any single period. Those may take the form of sackings, redundancies temporary layoffs, or retirements.

Discount.

(a) Refers to a reduction in a previously determined price granted to a customer or class of customers;

(b) Also, refer to the difference between the price at which a security was issued and the price at which it now stands.

Discounted Cash Flow. Refers to a technique of appraising projects which has been based on the idea of discounting future costs and benefits to their present values. The essential idea has been future cash flows--both inwards and outwards--are worth less in today's terms. Income received now can be reinvested to produce additional income. The two best known techniques using the discounting procedure have been net present value and internal rate of return. They both involve discounting all future net cash flows and finding their sum.

Discounted Cash Flow Method. Refers to a method of comparing the profitability of alternative projects. This method may be sub-divided into (a) yield method, and (b) net present value method. Both of these techniques are using as a measure of the 'rating' of an investment the present cash value of a sum to be received at some future date, discounted at compound interest. The present value or worth of a sum to be received at some future date will be such an amount as will, with compound interest at a prescribed rate, equal the sum to be received in the future. The yield method has been based upon the assumption that the best investment is that from which the proceeds would yield the highest rate of compound interest in equating the present value of the investment with future proceeds. In the net present value method an appropriate percentage rate get stipulated, the present value of the cash inflow is determined using this percentage the original cost of the investment is subtracted therefrom, and the resulting surplus is the net present value of the investment. Both the yield and net present value methods provide reliable guidance to the profitability of alternative schemes, on the assumptions that may be used. However, errors of a serious nature may take place in the assumptions made regarding capital costs or trading returns.

Discount House. A business institution which will buy acceptances from their owners for less than their face value and hold them to maturity. The difference between the price paid and the face value, expressed as a percentage per annum, is called the discount rate. Discount houses borrow 'at call' from banks and other financial institutions, such funds may be called in by the banks at short notice.

Discount Market. Narrowly defined, the market in which treasury and commercial bills are traded.

Discount Yield Formula. A formula which has been used to discount bills of exchange (q.v), e.g., a bank accepted bill (q.v). The formula is

$$\frac{365 \times \text{Face Value}}{365 + \left(\frac{\text{Yield} \times \text{Days to Maturity}}{100}\right)}$$

By this formula the face value of a bill could be discounted to a price which is governed by two variables: The interest rate (yield) and the term to maturity.

Discouraged Worker Hypothesis. Deals with the responsiveness of labour force participation rates to cyclical changes in the economy. When the economy turns down it could be argued that there will occur a fall in the real wage and family incomes. The discouraged worker hypothesis argues that the rise in the cost of market work relative to non-market work and leisure will, on balance, induce a shrinkage in the labour force because of the dominance of the substitution effect. Some secondary workers will exit from the labour market and others will get deterred from entering it. A cruder version of the argument has been that secondary workers looking for employment in conditions of high unemployment will become so disheartened by fruitless search for employment that they give up the attempt and withdraw from the labour force.

Discretionary Stabilization. Refers to direct intervention by the government generally in the form of monetary or fiscal policy to stabilize the growth or level of national income. It is opposed to automatic stabilizers.

Disinflation. Refers to the removal of inflationary pressure from the economy so as to maintain the value of the monetary unit. If government measures to achieve this go too far, the result may be deflation.

Diseconomies of Growth. Means the dynamic constraints which set in beyond some high rate of growth and impair the efficiency of the firm's activities. On the supply side, organizational and financial constraints operate.

Disembodied Technical Progress. Refers to technical progress which appears costless completely independent of capital accumulation or any other variable in the economic system.

Disequilibrium. Refers to a state of not being in equilibrium . In such cases forces may exist which will automatically bring the system back into equilibrium , or it may be the case that the system will get diverged further from equilibrium.

Disinflation. Refers to the process of eliminating or reducing inflation.

Disintermediation. Means a process of cutting out the financial middle man, both in short-term money markets and long-term (capital) markets.

Displacement Effect. Means an observed tendency for Public Expenditure to rise during a war or other national crisis but not to fall to the original level after the crisis. In this way, such crises give rise to a permanent increase in government expenditure. This phenomenon has formed part of the explanation of public expenditure growth put forward part of the explanation of public expenditure growth put forward by A.T. Peacock and J. Wiseman.

Disposable Income. Income less tax payments.

Dissaving. Means consumption in excess of current income. Consumption financed out of wealth or out of anticipated future income by borrowing.

Distributed Profits. Refer to that portion of net profits which are released by firms in the form of dividen payments to the owners of equity capital.

Distribution. Branch of economics which deals with the determination of payments made to the factors of production for their share in the work of production, these being known as rent wages, interest and profits.

Distribution Theories of. Theories relating to the mechanism by which the national income has been distributed between individuals and groups in the economy. It is able to distinguish between the functional distribution of income which refers to the division of national product between the owners of different factors of production--land, labour and capital, and the personal distribution of income which refers to the determinants of individuals incomes regardless of the factor from which income in derived.

Distributional Equity. Refers to the Justice or fairness in the manner in which the economy's output gets distributed between individuals. It has been of interest to economists in that alternative economic arrangements, projects or polices generally have different effects on distribution, thus a concept of what has been desirable in terms of distributional equity facilitates the evaluation of alternatives. Distributional equity has been sometimes expressed in terms of the distribution of income , of wealth or, particularly in the case of theoretical welfare economics, in terms of utility.

Distribution Function. Means that part of government tax and expenditure policy which deals with altering the distribution of income or wealth within society. This function will be undertaken if the distribution of income or wealth which emerges in the absence of government action is deemed to be undesirable.

Distribution Marginal Theory of. A theory seeking to demonstrate that the price of each factor of production has been found to depend upon its marginal productivity.

Distribute Judgement. When economists have been evaluating policies or projects, they face the difficulty that, in general, policies will affect not only the total output of the economy but also the way in which that output and its benefits are distributed between individuals. Given this, in the formation of a policy recommendation some judgement have to be made which deals with the desirability or undesirability of a policy's distributional effects since any decision will have distributional consequences. This distributive judgement has been value judgement--a matter of ethics not facts.

Distributive Justice. Means a concept or principle by which alternative distributions of income or wealth between individuals have to be judged.

Disutility. Refers to dissatisfaction or unhappiness generated by a product, or 'bad'.

Divisions of Labour. Means the process whereby labour gets allocated to the activity in which it has been most productive- i.e., in which it can make best use of its skills. No one man therefore carries out all the tasks in the production of a good. Rather, one specializes in one process, another in another process, and so on. Division of labour has been therefore generally synonymous with the specialization of labour.

Domestion Credit Expansion. Referred to as DCE. It is an indicator of monetary change within an economy which was developed and strongly advocated by the IMF in the 1960s as a truer current measure of expansionary forces in the monetary system than measured changes in the money stock. Broadly, it measures the total change within a given period in those types of credit which lead directly to changes in the money supply, as conventionally defined.

Double-coincidence of Wants. If trade has to take place under a system of barter then it becomes necessary for there to be a double-coincidence of wants between the two parties to the transaction. That is, the set of goods or commodities one individual is willing to exchange must be exactly what is needed by the other party.

Double Counting. Refers to the counting of a single element of benefit or cost more than once in a cost benefit analysis. An example is that if the construction of a new bridge makes a particular location more attractive to live in, due to its increased accessibility, property values will increase. It should not be counted as part of the benefits because it represents simply the capitalized value of future time saving, improved job and shopping opportunities etc., which already will have or should have been included in the cost–benefit analysis. Double counting has been also a potential danger in the estimation of National Income.

Double Taxation and Double Taxation Relief. An individual or organization may get income in a foreign country and may be liable for taxation on that income in both the foreign country and the country of origin. A system of reliefs for such double taxation has been developed by most countries in the world. Sometimes the nature of the relief has been given on a unilateral basis.

Drawing. Refers to a method of determining the order in which creditors have to be paid off.

Dual Decision Hypothesis. In modern developments of Keynesian economics, it refers to the argument that conventional demand and supply functions do not offer the relevant signals for equilibrium to come about in markets. The argument has been that conventional demand and supply curves yield quantities that buyers and sellers wish to exchange given their planned receipts. If realized current receipts are different from these planned receipts, buyers and sellers have been accordingly constrained by their actual incomes and must therefore revise their plans. The 'duality' in question is related to the initial and revised demand and supply plans.

Dual Economy. Refers to a term descriptive of an economy undergoing important developments in say both primary and secondary industry. In the case of Japan, dualism refers mainly to the concomitance, in the same areas of the country and often within the same industry sector, of very advanced large-scale firms and small low-productivity establishments (not infrequently employed as subcontractors by the larger companies).

Dualism, Theory of. This theory was outlined originally by Malthus who saw an economy as having two major sectors, one industrial and one agricultural; breaking the economy into two sectors and looking at the interaction between them has been said to increase the understanding of the development process. The agricultural sector features subsistence farming often using primitive and inefficient techniques. Standards of living and wages have been low.

Dual Labour Market Hypothesis. On this view, the labour market has been dichotomized into primary and secondary sectors. 'Good' jobs make up the primary sector of the dual economy, while 'bad' jobs and the workers frozen out of the primary sector comprise the secondary sectors. In the latter, jobs have been sufficiently plentiful to employ all workers but are low paying, unstable and generally unattractive. Workers in that sector have been precluded from entering the primary sector not so much by their lack of human capital and trainability as by institutional restraints in the form of discrimination, the restrictive practices of unions, and a simple dearth of good jobs. Workers in the secondary sector have been thus subject to under-employment.

The policy prescription of the dual labour market hypothesis is the creation by the government of better jobs or more good jobs. This conflicts with the basic neo-classical analysis which would interpret labour market disadvantage as reflecting deficiencies in human capital investments.

Dummy Variable. Refers to a binary (off-on) variable which is designed to take account of exogenous shifts (shift dummy) or changes of slope (slope dummy) in an econometric relationship. For example, dummies can be used to account for seasonal influences in the data.

Dumping. Means the sale of a good on a foreign market at a price below its marginal cost.

Duopoly. Refers to a market situation in which there have been only two sellers, neither seller being able to ignore the actions and reactions of the other. Duopoly has been the simplest case of olligopoly (q.v.).

Duopsony. Refers to a market situation in which there have been only two buyers of a particular good or service.

Duration of Unemployment. Refers to the average period of time an individual spends on the unemployment register. The level of unemployment at any one time has been a function of both flows on to the register and the average duration.

Dynamic Economics (or Economic Dynamics). Refers to the intertemporal analysis of the economic system. The economy may be passing from one equilibrium point to the other (i.e., two comparative static equilibria) or it may be continuing through time without reaching a state of static equilibrium. The essence of such models has been the introduction of lags in the adjustment of variables, the current values of which depend on past values of themselves and/or other variables. Effectively any economic model which simultaneously has variables dated in more than one time period may be considered dynamic.

E

Early Warning System. Any technique adopted which gives an early indication of an economic problem likely to lie ahead.

Earmarking. Refers to the practice of linking particular elements of public expenditure to the revenue raised by specific taxes. This process of assigning certain revenues for specific purposes is also termed as hypothecation.

Earnings. The term is used in two ways :

1. In labour economics, earnings is used to describe the total payments an individual receives from his employment.
2. The earning of a business refers to the income of that business which may be either distributed to shareholders or retained.

Earnings Drift. A rise in earnings in excess of the rise in negotiated wage rates.

Easy Money. Refers to a general state of ease and cheapness of borrowing in the financial system. It may be resulting from policy action to reduce interest rates, increase liquidity of the banking system, relax any non-price restrictions on lending like credit ceilings and restrictive conditions on hire purchase contracts.

Econometric Models. Pioneered by Klein mathematical models which are designed to assist in forecasting the needs and demands of the national economy some years ahead. Models are constructed for static or dynamic economic situations, and the interaction of forces (i.e., the in-built economic assumptions) can be isolated and studied.

Economic Anthropology. Refers to the comparative study of the relations between the system of management and allocation of the economic resources of societies of various types, and the structure and values of those societies. It is a branch of social anthropology.

Economic Appraisal. Means the study of the economic implications of a project, as a first step in assessing its acceptability.

Economic Base. Refers to those economic activities whose growth and development has been said to determine the economic growth of a town or region. Other activities which are said to develop as a consequence of the area's growth are called 'non-basic' or 'residentiary' activities.

Economic Base Multiplier. The term used for a form of regional multiplier which is able to estimate the effect of changes in an area's economic base on the economy of the area as a whole.

Economic Behaviour. Refers to the way in which people pursue their material well-being, individually and collectively.

Economic Community. An economic community or economic union among countries is not only having a common external tariff and commercial policy and the removal of restrictions on trade within the community, but is also aiming at a harmonization of industrial and social policies, concerted monetary and exchange rate policies as a step to a common currency and other agreed policies like regulations governing transport.

Economic Development. Refers to the process of improving the standard of living and well–being of the population of developing countries by raising per capita income. This is usually realised by an increase in industrialization relative to reliance on the agricultural sector.

Economic Disturbances. Refers to the shifts in aggregate demand or aggregate supply, or shifts in money demand or supply, that make output, interest rates, or prices to fluctuate or diverge in such a manner as to move the economy off-course.

Economic Dynamics. A subject area defined by Sir Roy Harrod (b.1990). It is concerned with the determinants of rates of change of both traditional micro and macro variables; Harrod regarded the domain of economic dynamics as being narrower in scope than that of growth economics. He always distinguished sharply between statics (or the conditions of stationary equilibrium) and dynamics.

Economic Efficiency. Refers to the efficiency with which scarce resources have been used and organised to achieve stipulated economic ends.

Economic Ends. Means the objectives of economic activity. Ends have been both quantitative and qualitative, but with the nature of ends economics has no direct concern, economics deals only with the number of ends and with their degree of relative intensity.

Economic Friction. Influences, natural or deliberate, which tend to impede the full or rapid operation of economic laws.

Economic Growth. Means the growth per head of the population in the production of goods and services of all kinds which are available to meet final demands, e.g., goods and services for domestic consumption, capital goods for accumulation, export goods to pay for imports.

Economic Growth. Typically taken to mean an increase in the real level of net national product, although the measure will then be sensitive to the way in which national product has been measured. Thus, an economy having a large sector having bartered goods or unrecorded consumption of its own product (e.g., farmers' consumption of their own produce) may raise its actual level of national product without the recorded level showing an increase.

Economic Growth, Stages of. There are five stages of economic growth in society distinguished by Professor W.W. Rostov. All societies, in their economic dimensions, have been within one of these five categories; the traditional society, the preconditions for take-off, the take-off, the drive to maturity, and the age of high mass-consumption.

Economic Indicators. Statistics which are sensitive to changes in the state of industry, trade and commerce.

Economic Interpretation of Theory. A theory which was developed by Karl Marx (1818-1883). This theory asserted :

(a) The forms or conditions of production are the fundamental determinant of social structures which in turn breed attitudes, action and civilizations; and

(b) The forms of production themselves have a logic of their own, that is to say, they change in accordance to necessities inherent in them so as to produce their successors through their own working.

Economic Law. Refers to a statement of what will take place in the economic world under specified condition. George J. Stigler, in his 'Theory of Price' offers the following statement of an economic law; if :

(a) An entrepreneur seeks maximum profits.

(b) His marginal cost curve does not fall so fast as (or more rapidly than) his marginal revenue curve;

(c) The curves are continuous.

Then: He operates at the output where marginal revenue equals marginal cost.

Alfred Marshall's view of economic laws was that 'there have been no definite and universal propositions in economics which can compare with the Laws of Gravitation and of Conservation of Energy in physics. But there are many which rank with the secondary laws of those natural sciences which resemble economics in dealing with the complex actions of many heterogeneous and uncertain causes. An economic law is nothing but a general proposition, or statement of uniformity, more or less certain, more or less definite'.

Economic Liberalism. Refers to the doctrine which advocates the greatest possible use of markets and the forces of competition to co-ordinate economic activity. It allows to the state only those activities which the market cannot carry out, e.g., the provision of public goods–or those which have been necessary to establish the framework within which the private enterprise economy and markets can carry out efficiently, e.g., by the establishment of the legal framework on property and contract and the adoption of such policies as anti-monopoly legislation.

Economic Man. Refers to the name given to the 'construct' in economics whereby individuals have been assumed to behave as if they maximize utility, subject to a set of constraints of which the most obvious is income.

Economic Nationalism. Usually, a concomitant of political nationalism. It is also a reaction to the frustrations of multinational solutions to common trade problems resulting in unilateral measures for protecting the national interest, most narrowly defined.

Economic Planning. It could be classified as imperative or indicative. Imperative planning is applicable to a centralized macroeconomic plan in an economy which has been dominated by the public sector. As in a fully planned economy the government will take control of output, price and wage determination. Indicative planning refers to the indication of a series of goals by the government and indirect stimulation of certain economic activities through taxation or monetary policy to undertake planning by inducement.

Economic Problem. Refers to a problem of ensuring that all available resources have been used to the best possible effect, in the resolving of which decisions must be made as to which ends have to be satisfied first and perhaps which wants will have to get left unsatisfied.

Economic Quantities or Aggregates. The terms used for the subject-matter of macro-and micro-economic quantities or aggregates which include such diverse items as the amount of a commodity produced, stored and consumed; the volume of employment and unemployment; the price of butter; the interest on bank loans; the wages of brick-layers; the price of houses; taxes on tobacco or shirts, the surcharge on imported raw materials, etc. The man task of economic analysis has been the explanation of the magnitude of economic quantities.

Economic Rent. Refers to a payment to a factor in access of what has been necessary to keep it at its present occupation.

Economics. A social science which is concerned with how people, either individually or in groups try, to accommodate scarce resources to their wants through the process of production, substitution and exchange. It has been not as a science concerned with the problems of what ought to be, but with the explanation and understanding of what already exists. There have been many definitions of economics in the past.

Economic Surplus. Refers to the difference between the output of an economy and the necessary costs of producing this output whereby necessary costs have been meant wages, depreciation of capital and the cost of raw materials. The concept is used in development economics.

Economic System, Functions of an. Refers to the functions of an economic system which could be defined as follows:

(a) generally, to match supply to the effective demand for goods and services in an efficient manner;

(b) To determine what goods and services have to be produced and in what quantities;

(c) To distribute scarce resources among the industries producing goods and services;

(d) To distribute the products of industry among members of the community;

(e) To provide for maintenance and expansion of fixed capital investment;

(f) To fully utilise the resources of society.

In a free enterprise system, the fulfilment of these six economic functions has been left to the profit motive and the price mechanism working within a framework of social safeguards. In a socialist society all the operations needed consciously planned by salaried officials; there are no private investors.

Economic Welfare. Defined by A.C. Pigou as that part of social welfare that can be brought directly or indirectly into relation with the measuring rod of money.

Economies of Growth. At or below some rate of growth it can be argued that economies of growth are likely to dominate and provide the growing firm advantages over the stationary one.

Economies of Scale. Refers to the reductions in the average cost of a product in the long run, resulting from an expanded level of output. They are also known as long run increasing returns.

Economist. The term used for a social scientist who has become an expert in dealing with the economic aspects of social phenomena. He may specialise in theoretical or applied economics.

Edgeworth Box. Refers to a diagrammatic construct which in the case of consumption using the indifference maps of the two individuals A and B, one sited with origin in the 'south-west' corner of the box and the other in the 'north-east' demonstrates the opportunities for mutually beneficial exchange. The dimensions of the box are represented by the total quantity of the two goods 1 and 2 available. In the production case the dimensions of the box have been determined by the factor inputs available and two isoquant maps are combined to show output maximizing substitutions.

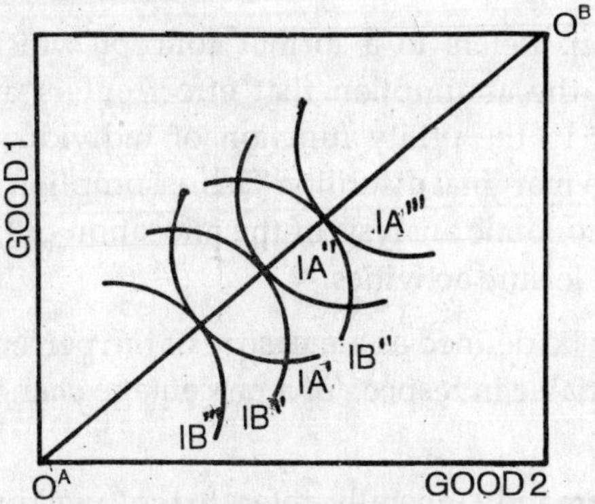

Edgeworth Box

Effective Demand. Demand which is measured by spending on consumption (goods and services more or less used up immediately); on investment (plant, buildings, equipment, stocks), and on the difference between exports (which adds to demand for output at home) and imports (which satisfies home demand without adding to home output).

Effective Rate of Protection. Defined as the increment in value added made possible by the tariff structure as a proportion of the free trade value added.

Efficiency Earnings. If economists take of the tendency of competition to equalize earnings in the same local labour market, they are implicitly referring to efficiency earnings.

Efficiency Units. Refer to a method of measuring the labour force in actual labour service inputs used, which distinguishes 'effective labour force' (i.e., that measured in efficiency units from that in natural units (i.e., number of employees). 'The effective labour force' or labour force in efficiency units will grow at a rate equal to the sum of the rate of growth of the labour force in employees plus the rate of Harrod Neutral Technical progress.

Effort Aversion. Refers to a formal concept which is used to represent the assumption that effort enters as a negative argument in the utility function of individuals i.e., effort provides a marginal disutility. This assumption is commonly used in economic analysis of the allocation of time between work and leisure activities.

Elasticity. May be defined as a measure of the percentage change in one variable in respect of a percentage change in another variable.,

Elasticity of Demand. Generally, refers to the (own) price elasticity of demand, but care should be taken to specify which elasticity of demand is being discussed.

Elasticity of Demand, Income. Refers to the response of the demand for a commodity to changes in the real income of consumers. Its computation has been as follows :

$$\frac{\text{Percentage change in quantity demanded}}{\text{Percentage change in income}}$$

For most commodities, increases in income lead to increases in demand, income elasticity being positive.

Elasticity of Demand, Price. Refers to the response of demand to a changes in the price of a commodity. It is measured :

$$\frac{\text{Percentage change in quantity demanded}}{\text{Percentage change in price}}$$

If the price gets lowered, the amount demanded will normally be increased.

Elasticity of Input Substitution. May be defined as a measure of the responsiveness of the optimal labour/capital combination to a change in the relative prices of the two inputs (or the term may be generalized to refer to any two inputs). As the detailed expression is somewhat unwieldy we present it here in its general form

$$e_A = \frac{\text{percentage change in } K^*/L^*}{\text{percentage change in } P_L/P_A}$$

where K^*/L^* represents the optimal capital/labour ratio and P_L and P_A represent the prices of labour and capital.

If the elasticity of substitution has been zero, then factors have been always used in fixed proportions. An elasticity of substitution greater than zero implies that the capital labour ratio will respond to changes in relative factor prices.

Elasticity of Substitution. Refers to a measure of the ease of difficulty of substituting between commodities (by consumers) or between factors of production (by producers). The elasticity of commodity substitution may be measured by the following relation :

$$\frac{\text{Percentage change in the ratio in which two commodities are combined}}{\text{Percentage change in the ratio of their marginal utilities}}$$

A high value, revealing that substantial changes in the proportions of commodities combined would make little change in relative marginal utilities, would indicate a high degree of substitutability, and *vice versa.* The elasticity of factor substitution may be measured as follows:

$$\frac{\text{Percentage change in the ratio in which two factors are combined}}{\text{Percentage change in the ratio of their marginal physical productivities}}$$

Again a high value indicates a high degree of technical substitutability between factors, and *vice versa.* The result reveals how far one, factor may be substituted for another (more expensive) factor before the benefits are nullified by changes in the relative productivities of the two factors.

Elasticity of Supply. Means the response of supply to a change in the price of commodity. If the price rises, the amount supplied will normally get increased. The elasticity may be calculated as follows :

$$\frac{\text{Percentage change in quantity supplied}}{\text{Percentage change in price}}$$

Eligible Margin. Means the cash or other collateral which a commodity exchange specifies that members may be able to accept from their customers for the purpose of satisfying initial and variation margin requirements.

Eligible Paper. Refers to the financial assets which the central bank is prepared to by (rediscount) or accept as security for loans, in particular circumstances and usually in dealings with defined institutions.

Embodied Technical Progress. Menas the technical progress which cannot occur unless it gets embodied in new capital.

Emoluments. Emoluments are defined as that portion of management's salary and non-pecuniary benefits which are not part of the entrepreneurial supply price. They characterize firms which possess monopoly powers sufficient to permit managers discretion over the distribution of returns.

Employment, Classical Theory of. It is a theory which is held by the Classical School of economist and based on two fundamental postulates :

(a) The wage will be equal to the marginal product of labour; and

(b) The utility of the wage when a given volume of labour is employed is equal to the marginal disutility of that amount of employment, i.e., the real wage is just sufficient for inducing the volume of labour actually employed to be forthcoming.

Postulate (a) represents the demand schedule for labour, and postulate (b) the supply schedule for labour.

Endogenous Income Hypothesis. A theory which states that utility has been a function of both consumption expenditure and of wealth. The implications are that once some optimum level of wealth has been achieved, all income will be spent while normally one would expect some saving still to take place. The approach is derived from a microeconomic approach to the consumption function.

Endogenous Money Supply. Refers to the situation where the level of the money supply will be determined by forces within the economy itself, like rates of interest, and the level of business activity.

Endogenous Variable. May be defined as a variable whose value has been determine within the framework of an economic or econometric model.

Energy Computer Models. Refer to the computer models of the energy sector of an economy, which are being developed largely in the United States of America and Europe; the models regard both the sector itself in detail and its relationship with the national economy.

Engagements (also known as new hires). Mean the total number of people that are entering employment in any single period.

Engel Curve. Refers to a line which plots the relationship between an individual's income and his consumption of a specified good. An Engel curve is illustrated in the diagram below. The slope of the curve at any point will give the individual's marginal propensity to consume the good and the ratio of change in consumption to change in income. The ratio of total consumption of the good to total income will give the average propensity to consume the good--this is equal to the slope of a line such as OA. The ratio of the marginal propensity to consume the good to the average propensity to consume has been the income elasticity of demand for the good.

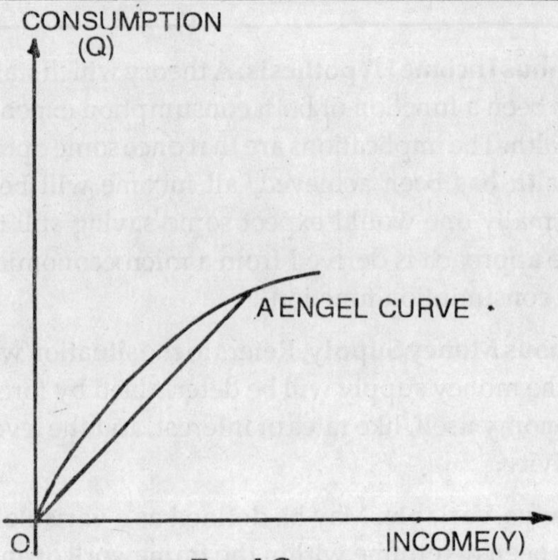

Engel Curve

Engel's Law. Refers to a generalisation that states that the proportion of income spent on food tends to decline as income grows, with given tastes, or preferences. This law or tendency was postulated by Ernst Engel (1821-96) in a paper published by him in 1857.

Entitlement Principle. Refers to a principle of distributive justice which holds that individuals are to be considered as 'entitled' to their possessions so long as these had been obtained by 'legitimate' means like voluntary exchange or gifts. The adoption of such a principle would severely limit the scope for redistribution by government.

Entrepreneur. The term, used for the organizing factor in production. Entrepreneurs have been responsible for such economic decisions as what to produce, how much to produce and what method of production to adopt.

Environmental Impact Analysis. Refers to an analysis which attempts to identify the effect on the whole environment of any investment project. This would include the forecasting of potential pollution emission, loss of visual amenity etc.

Equal Pay. This terms is used to refer to equality between the sexes as regards the terms and conditions of employment : a concept of equal pay of equal work, although the precise definition of 'equal pay' and 'equal work' differs by country.

Equal Sacrifice Theories. In the ability-to-pay theory each taxpayer tries to make the same sacrifice of utility which he gets from his income. There have been three definitions of equal sacrifice, namely equal absolute sacrifice, equal proportional sacrifice and equal marginal (or least aggregate) sacrifice.

Equilibrium. A term used to describe a situation of economic agents or of aggregates of economic agents such as markets. Applied to an individual agent, such as a consumer or firm, it is used to describe a situation in which the agent is under no pressures or incentives to alter current levels or states of economic action, because given his aspirations and the constraints he faiths he to improve his position in terms of any economic criteria. When applied to markets, equilibrium is used to denote a situation in which, in the aggregate, buyers and sellers get satisfied with the current combination of prices and quantities bought or sold, and so are under no incentive to change their present actions.

Equilibrium Level of National Income. Refers to that level of national income which exhibits no tendencies to alter. In the simple Keynesian income--expenditure model this would be where the level of injections equalled the level of withdrawals.

Equilibrium Price. Means the price at which a market has been in equilibrium.

Equivalence Scale. Refers to a ratio or 'weighting' factor which is employed in evaluating levels of income or consumption needed for households in different circumstances to reach a given 'standard of living.'

Equilibrium Rate of Inflation. Refers to the fully anticipated rate of inflation. Refers to that rate of price inflation at which expectations have been fully realized. Also, refers to that rate at which the expected inflation rate equals the actual inflation rate.

Equity Leasing. Lease under which the lessor contributes the entire capital cost, unlike leveraged leasing where the lessor contributes only a minor portion of the capital.

Equi-Marginal Returns, Law of. A basic theorem which describes the way in which consumers with limited resources divide their expenditure between the innumerable different goods and services they could enjoy, based on the assumptions that consumers wish to get the maximum utility (q.v.) from their income and that they act rationally in seeking that end.

Equities. Refers to the ordinary shares of a limited company. They have the right to the residue of a company's assets after it has paid all its creditors, and share in the distribution of profits, if any, after interest has been paid to preference share-holders and debenture holders each year.

Equity. Another name for ownership; often used to describe a share in a company.

Equivalent Commodity Scale. Refers to a numerical factor which is applied to the level of consumption of certain commodities by households in different circumstances in order to indicate levels of consumption needed for each type of household to reach a given standard of living.

Escalators. Offer a mechanism for periodic adjustments of wage rates based on movements in a specified price index. Escalators rarely fully compensate for price changes.

Essentialist Arguments. Arguments in economics which are concerned with correct definitions, labelling, and classification, rather than facts.

Estate Economy. A sector or whole economy in an under-developed country which is mainly used for large-scale production of export crops normally managed and owned by foreign powers; it was very prevalent during the colonial era.

Euro-currencies. The currencies of the European Economic Community together with euro-dollars (q.v.).

European Economic Community. Popularly known as the European Common Market. It is free trade organisation which was created by the Treaty of Rome, 1957. Its members comprised France, West Germany, Italy, Belgium, the Netherlands and Luxembourg, although the Treaty allows for the admission of other countries at a later date. With the signing of the Treaty, the 'Six' became combined in three distinct but interlocked functional communities; the European Coal and Steel Community formed in 1952, the European Atomic Energy Community ('Euroatom') and the European Economic Community. The total population of the Community, about 186 million, was only slightly less than that of the United States. Later, England and other countries also joined.

Evening Up. Buying or selling to offset an existing market position.

Ex. Without or minus.

Ex-all. Without everything that has just been declared payable or detachable from a security.

Ex Ante. Refers to the planned, desired or intended level of some activity. Thus ex-antê demand will be the planned level of demand. This contrasts with the ex-post level of demand which will be the realized or actual level of demand. Plans and their realization obviously need not be the same since expectations may not be fulfilled. Thus ex-post and ex-ante need not coincide.

Excess Capacity. Firm is said to be producing with excess capacity it its output level has been below that at which average costs are at a minimum. The more common usage prefers to firms operating plant at a rate of utilization below that regarded normal, e.g., at some percentage level of output that could be achieved.

Excess Capacity Theory. Refers to the monopolistic competition model's prediction that firms in long-run equilibrium will be producing on the downward sloping segment of their long-run average cost curves, therefore producing at more than minimum cost.

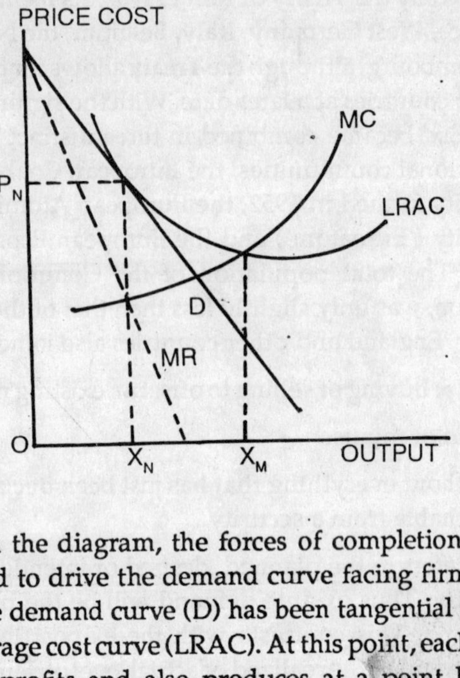

Thus, in the diagram, the forces of completion have been regarded to drive the demand curve facing firm to the left until the demand curve (D) has been tangential to the long-run average cost curve (LRAC). At this point, each firm earns normal profits and also produces at a point higher than minimum average cost (at X_N rather than X_M in the diagram).

Excess Demand. Refers to a state in which demand exceeds supply at some given price. The excess demand curve will slope down wards from left to right and will cut the vertical (price) axis at the equilibrium price. In order to construct the excess demand curve, subtract supply from demand at each given price. In the diagram, for example, demand level D_1 will be less than supply at that relevant price, P_1. Excess demand has been therefore negative, as shown. At P_2, supply and demand are equal, so that excess demand is zero. At P_3, there exists excess demand equal to D_3–S_3.

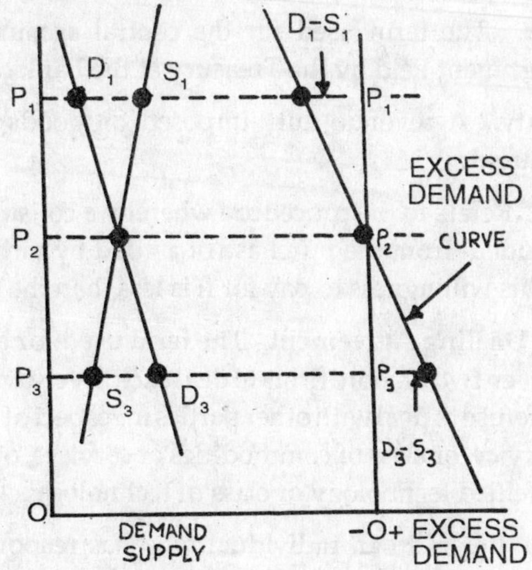

Excess Supply. Refers to a state in which supply exceeds demand at some given price.

Exchange. Means the act of accepting one thing for another. e.g., as in barter or in a transaction involving money.

Exchange Control. Refers to the system whereby the State exercises control over all or some transactions in foreign currencies and gold, undertaken by its nationals. Exchange controls has been applied for balance of payment reasons, and in the final analysis to avoid the depreciation of the exchange rate, which it is supposed, complete freedom in foreign transactions would produce.

Exchange Rate. Refers to the price of a currency in terms of another currency. Exchange rates have been regularly quoted between all major currencies, but frequently one important currency, e.g., the dollar, has been used as a standard in which to express and compare all rates. The exchange rate of all fully convertible currencies will be determined, like any price, by supply and demand conditions in the market in which it has been traded, i.e., the foreign exchange market.

Exchequer. The term used for the central account of the UK government held by the Treasury at the bank of England.

Excise Duty. A revenue duty imposed on goods and services produced.

Exclusion. Refers to the procedure whereby a consumer has been 'excluded' from the purchase of a good by virtue of the fact that his willingness to pay for it is less than the market price.

Exclusive Dealing Agreement. The term used for an agreement between two or more firms to deal exclusively with each other and refuse to deal with other parties in respect of a commodity or service, or class of commodities or services, or in respect of a specified technology or class of technology.

Executive. Refers to an individual who has responsibility with respect to some branch or aspect of a firm's activities.

Existence, Theorem of. Any theorem which seeks to establish, that there exists a set of equilibrium prices and quantities.

Exogenous. A term which describes anything pre-determined or given in a piece of economic analysis.

Exogenous Variable (also known as pre-determined variable). Refers to an explanatory variable (i.e., appears on the right hand side of an equation), but never appears as a dependent variable in the model. Exogenous variables can include lagged values of endogenous variables.

Expansionary Phase. Refers to the phase of the trade cycle which will be following a through or lower turning point, lasting to the next upper turning point or peak.

Expansion Path. With reference to the firm, this is the curve which is traced out by joining up the factor input choices at each output level as in the diagram below, i.e., the locus of the points of tangency between a set of isoquants and isocast lines. For given input prices, the curve reveals what the firm's chosen path of expansion will be in terms of factor input combinations. With a cost minimizing firm any point on this curve will satisfy the condition that the ratio of the marginal physical product of any two factor inputs will equal the ratio of their prices.

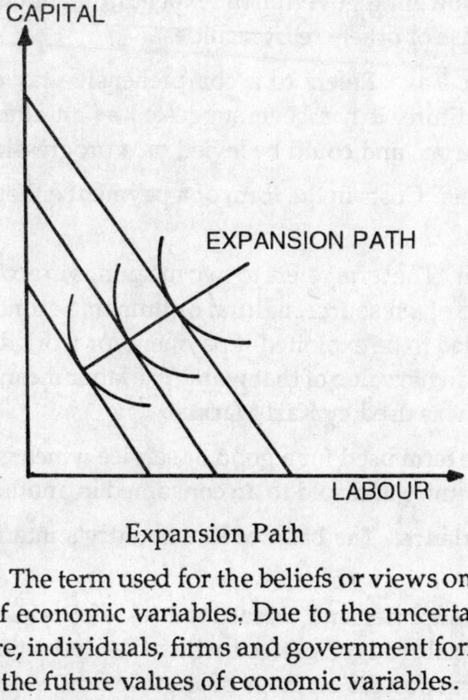

Expansion Path

Expectations. The term used for the beliefs or views on the future values of economic variables. Due to the uncertainty about the future, individuals, firms and government form expectations on the future values of economic variables.

Expectations, Augmented. Refers to modifications to an economic model to allow for an expectations effect. Probably the most widely known example has been the expectations augmented Phillips curve, where the expected price inflation rate has been included as explanatory variable augmenting the basic model.

Expected Inflation. Refers to anticipated inflation the rate of inflation which is expected to occur over some specified time in the future.

Expected Net Returns. Means the flow of expected gross revenue minus expected costs. i.e., the flow of expected profits, from an investment project.

Expenditure-depening Policies. Government measures which are designed to reduce the aggregate demand for goods and services in the community. The measure may involve raising taxes, lowering government expenditure, or curtailing hire-purchase or other credit facilities.

Expenditure Tax. Refers to a comprehensive tax on consumer expenditure. It has been suggested as an alternative to an income tax, and could be levied on a progressive basis.

Explicit Costs. Costs in the form of a payment either in cash or in kind.

Exploitation. The term refers to two meanings in economics. First, the use of a resource, natural or human. Second, a worker is regarded to be exploited if payment for work done has been less than the value of that work. The latter meaning of exploitation was used by Karl Marx.

Export. The term used for a good or service which is produced in one country and sold to an consumed in another.

External Balance. The balance in a country's international payments.

External Economies and Diseconomies of Scale. Refer to the beneficial or adverse effects which the production activities of one firm possess on those of another firm.

External Economy. Refers to a fall in the cost of any of the materials and services which a firm requires, which are obtained from outside source. These materials and services comparise raw materials, labour, fuel and power transport services, and the services of specialised firms and selling agencies. Where large quantities of, say, fuel and ores have been used then any change in their prices may have a marked effect on costs of production without any change in the internal economy of a firm. An external economy is external to a firm but internal to an industry.

Extrema. Also known as extreme points or extreme values. Refer to the highest and lowest values of functions.

F

Face Value. Means the nominal value, as distinct from the market value, of a security or share. Consols have a nominal value and a fixed rate of interest; the market value may vary considerably from the nominal value to give a yield comparable with other securities.

Factor Augmenting Technical Progress. Refers to the technical progress which raises the level of output even though the stock of capital and the labour force have not get changed.

Factor Cost. Refers to the price net of indirect taxes and subsidies. it is being the amount received by the factors of production during the manufacture of a good. National income has been equal to the incomes received in the economy valued at factor cost.

Factor Demand Curve. Refers to a curve which represents the quantities of a factor of production that business firms will want to purchase or hire at various hypothetical prices per unit of the factor.

Factor Endowment

1. Refers to the levels of availability of factors of production in an area, or country; these are usually defined as land, labour, capital and entrepreneurial skills.
2. Also, refers to the quantities of factors of production in a country. The different relative abundance of factors of

production has been made the basis for explaining comparative cost differences in the Heckscher. Ohlin approach to international trade.

Factors Incomes. Incomes accruing to the factors of production which are wages, salaries, profits, interest and rent. Such incomes has both transfer earnings and economic rent; in limiting cases all earnings may be either transfer earnings or economic rent.

Factoring. The term used for a method of disposing of trade debts where a company 'sells' these debts to a financial institution.

Factor Markets. Refer to the markets in which factors of production or inputs have been bought and sold, e.g., the labour market, the capital market.

Factor Mobility. Refers to the ease or difficulty with which factors of production can move between uses.

Factors Non-specific. Refers to factors of production which have been not specialised and can be put to alternative uses, e.g., most land, unskilled labour, raw materials.

Factor-price Differentials. Refers to the situation where a factor of production is having tow separate prices; for example, the price of labour between capitalistic wage-based production and family based production activities.

Factor-Price-Frontier. The term used for the name assigned by Paul Samuelson to the negatively sloped trade off between the wage rate and the rate of profit in growth theory. Cambridge School economists preferred the title 'wage/rate of profit frontier', where as John Hicks referred to the same notion as the wage frontier. In equilibrium the elasticity of the factor price frontier has been equal to the ratio of the shares of output going to the two factors.

Factors Proportions. Refers to the ratio in which factors of production have been combined.

Factor Reversals. One of the assumptions of the Heckscher Ohlin approach to international trade has been that the production functions for commodities are different in the ratios (intensities) in which they use factors of production and that a commodity which uses a higher ratio of, say, labour to capital than another will do so at all possible relative factor prices.

Factors of Production. The term used for the resources of society which are used in the process of production. These have been usually divided into three main groups land, labour, capital, but may also include entrepreneurship.

Factors, Specific. Factors of production of a specialised kind which cannot easily get adjusted to serve an alternative purpose. e.g., skilled labour, intricate machinery.

Factor Supply Curve. Curve which is representing the quantities of a factor of production that factor-owners will be willing to sell or hire to business firms at various hypothetical prices per unit of the factor.

Factor Utilizations. Refers to the amount of the available factors of production which are actually being utilized.

Fair Comparison. The term refers to the belief that workers doing roughly similar jobs should be paid the same wage. Frequently such beliefs are forming the basis of coercive comparisons but take no account of the differing levels of productivity in the two jobs. Because of this they can serve as a basis for inflationary wage claims.

False Trading. Refers to the trading at dis-equilibrium prices.

Father of Economics. Refers to a role and title assigned to Adam Smith (1723-1790) by the leading expositors of the English classical version of the history of political economy including McCulloch and John Stuart Mill; they considered Smith as the supreme founding father of the subject. Karl Marx (1818-1893) on the other hand regarded Sir William Petty (1623-1687) as 'the founder of modern political economy'.

Featherbedding. Refers to the make-work practices that encompass overmanning and/or rejection technologically advanced machinery. Featherbedding is having its origin in technical change and can thus be thought as the carrying forward of a set of practices appropriate for one technology to another where it is alien--more 'protective' than 'restrictive' practice.

Federal Budget. Refers to a centrally prepared national budget which is covering all the important activities of the executive branches of the United States Government, subject to direct presidential scrutiny and congressional review.

Feedback/Entrapment Effects. The arguments here is that entrapment in the secondary labour market makes workers to acquire bad work habits. Unstable employment relationship in the secondary labour market have been thus said to encourage workers who hold 'bad' jobs to become 'bad' workers. Note that once the worker has acquired such habits (or received feedback) he becomes less skilled and less trainable than his primary sector counterpart.

This phenomenon has been only one aspect of a larger system of feedback in which workers get influenced by many socio-economics factors, including family back ground.

Feudalisms. The terms ascribed to a type of political and economic system which had been dominant in Europe in the Middle Ages. It get characterized by the social pyramid extending from the dependent peasant through the 'fief' endowed lords and knights to the monarch. A rigid class or status structure linked to the land had been the basis of the society. The lord who was granted an estate in return for a military obligation to the monarch rented this land to serfs in return for a rent, in kind or money, and having his estate cultivated by these serfs. this decentralized economic system was relied on the legal immobility of the serf and went into demise with the growth of the urban population and a system of wage labour.

Fiat Money. Money which the state declares to be legal tender, although its content value may be little or nothing. Most of fiat money has been notes, although token money may also be included in the term.

Fiduciary Issue. Means that portion of the bank-note issue which is not backed by gold.

Filtering. A term which has been used in urban economics to describe a process by which housing changes in quality, generally passing from occupation by higher income groups to occupation by lower income groups. For instance if a house is divided into units for multiple occupancy, or merely loses value by a process of decay, it will become available to lower income groups. In this way, the construction of new housing for high income groups can benefit those on lower incomes as the former residences of the rich 'filter down' to the poor. Filtering also offers an explanation of the process by which slums have been formed; in many cities areas of low-quality housing have been in fact the converted former residences of middle-class households.

FIML. Abbreviation of full Information Maximum Likelihood.

Final Goods. Refers to those goods which are used for the purposes of consumption and not utilized as inputs by firms in the process of production. As such they have to be distinguished from intermediate products. It has been of course possible for a good to be used in both functions.

Final Products. Refer to goods used by consumers in the act of consumption, as distinct from goods used by firms as input into processes which may be considered as intermediate products. Some goods like milk and cocoa may fill a role as final products on the one hand, and as intermediate products on the other.

Finance. Narrowly interpreted it means capital in monetary form, that is in the form of funds lent or borrowed, normally for capital purposes, through financial markets or institutions. But in common parlance the term is applicable to funds from almost any source which are used to undertake any kind of expenditure.

Finance Bill. A bill not involving goods, simply promising to pay a specified sum of money on a specified date.

Finance Commission. Under the Constitution of India, a Finance Commission is to be constituted every fifth year or at such earlier time as the President consider necessary to make recommendations to him as to:

(i) the distribution between the union and the states of the net proceeds of taxes which are to be or may be divided between them under the Constitution and the allocation between the states of the respective shares of such proceeds;

(ii) the principles which should govern the grants-in-aid of the revenues of the states in need of such assistance from the Consolidated Fund of India; and

(iii) any other matter referred to the Commission by the President in the interest of sound finance. The recommendations of the Commission together with an explanatory memorandum as to the action taken thereon are laid before each House of Parliament.

Finance Corporations. Refer to the specialised financial institutions which are established to provide medium and long-term finance where it cannot be provided easily from traditional sources.

Finance House. A financial institution which is engaged in the provision of hire purchase and other forms of instalment credit. Also known as finance companies, hire purchase finance houses, and industrial banks.

Finance Lease. Sometimes termed as a 'full payout lease', a contract between lessor and lessee for the hire of a specific asset selected from a manufacturer or vendor of such assets by the lessee. The lessor retains ownership of the asset. The lessee has possession and use of the asset on payment of specified rentals over a period of time. Though the lessor remains the legal owner, the lessee is given exclusive rights to the use of the asset for the duration of the contract, the contract normally extends for the period of the asset's expected useful life.

Financial Futures Contract. The term used for a futures contract for a financial instruments which commits the seller to deliver and the buyer to take delivery of it at the contracted price.

Financial Institutions. Private or governmental organisations which carry out the vital function of facilitating the flow of savings from those businesses and houselholds with surplus funds to businesses and households with insufficient funds to meet immediate needs, or carry out a central role in the supply of money and credit. Savers are provided with financial assets and borrowers with the type of financing assistance needed to purchase goods and services.

Financial Instrument. Refers to any document which is an evidence of debt, and the sale or transfer of which makes the seller to acquire finance. Examples have been bills, bonds and other securities, certificates of deposit.

Financial Intermediary. Any operator who is engaged in bringing together ultimate providers and ultimate users of finance.

Financial Ratios. Refers to the ratios between particular groups of the assets or liabilities of an enterprise and corresponding totals of assets or liabilities; or between assets or liabilities and flows like turnover or revenue.

Financial Year. Different bodies employ different financial years for financial accounting and this need not be coincident with the standard calender year.

Fine Tuning. The term refers to government policies which aim to make small changes in taxation or expenditures which in turn have been designed to influence employment levels, national income and price levels.

Fine Rate of Discount. Lowest rate of discount.

Firm. Refers to a unit of management which is operating under a trade name organised either to extract minerals, produce or manufacture goods, or to sell goods or services, or to engage in two or three of these activities simultaneously. A firm may be a sole proprietorship, a partnership, a private or public limited company, or a state-owned enterprise. It is important to make a distinction between a firm as a legal entity and as an operating unit. A large conglomerate may be a single firm for the purposes of company law, but will have several operating units managed quite separately.

Firm, Theory of the. Refers to the theory of the ways in which prices have been determined and resources allocated among different used in respect of the products of the individual firm.

First Difference. Refers to the difference between a variable and its own value lagged by one time period. It is also possible to calculate a second difference as the first difference of the first difference. Similarly, the third difference is the first difference of the second difference, etc.

First Mortgage Bond. A fixed interest loan repayable on a given date; similar to debenture. The term 'first mortgage' implies that the bond holders have a claim before other creditors on the assets of the corporation.

First Order Conditions. Refers to the condition which states that the first derivative (s) of the objective function with respect to the choice variable(s) should be equal to zero for the determination of an extreme value (maximum or minimum).

Fiscal Dividend. Refers to the increase in federal or national revenues which results from a rise in the Gross National Product at any given level of tax rates.

Fiscal Drag. Refers to the restraining effects upon growth and demand of increasing effective rates of taxation; this may take place under conditions of inflation when increased wages and salaries have bought people into higher tax brackets.

Fiscal Illusion. Refers to a situation in which the benefits of particular government expenditure have been clearly indentified by recipients but the costs are not, being widely dispersed over time and population.

Fiscalists. Refer to those who believe that fiscal policy has been the most important means available to the government for influencing the level of economic activity.

Fiscal Multiplier. Refers to a coefficient that indicates by how much an increase in fiscal expenditure influences the equilibrium level of income. For example, in the simple Keynesian model.

$$Y=A$$
$$A=C+I+G$$
$$C=\overline{C}+cY$$
$$I=\overline{I}$$
$$G=\overline{G}$$

the reduced form for income, Y, will be as follows:

$$Y=\left(\frac{1}{1-C}\right)(\overline{C}+\overline{I}+\overline{G})$$
$$=\alpha\overline{A}$$

where $\overline{A}$ represents autonomous expenditure and α the fiscal multiplier.

Fiscal Policy. Generally refers to the use of taxation and government expenditure for regulating the aggregate level of economic activity. Thus, if unemployment is considered as excessive, taxes will have to be reduced. Income and expenditure taxes may be varied for this purpose. The overall effect on economic activity will depend on the size of the tax cut and the multiplier.

Fisher's Ideal Index. An index which has been based on a formula devised by the American economist Irving Fisher (1867-1947). It is intended to be a 'true' index, the Laspeyres' index giving an upper limit and the Paasche index a lower limit to this 'true' index, it is in fact an index of the geometric mean of the Laspeyers' and Paasche indices. The formula has been as follows :

$$\left[\frac{\Sigma P_n q_o}{\Sigma P_o q_o} \times \frac{\Sigma P_n q_n}{\Sigma P_o q_n}\right]$$

where P_o=price in the base year ; q_o=quntity in the base -year; P_n=price in the year being considered, and q_n=quantity in the year being considred.

Fixed Asset. Refers to any non-financial capital asset of a company which has been relatively long-live and specific to particular productive processes, and the cost of which has been normally recoverable only over an operating period of some duration, e.g., plant and buildings. Such assets are illiquid compared with current (for short-term) assest like stock of materials or semifinished or finished goods.

Fixed Coefficients Production Function. Refers to a production function in which inputs must be combined in fixed proportions.

Fixed Cost. Refers to the production costs which tend to be unaffected by variations in the volume of output.

Fixed Exchange Rates. Exchange rates among national currencies which have been fixed by governments, and have been not free to vary in response to market forces.

Fixed Factors. Refer to those factors of production which cannot get changed in quanity. Usually it is applicable to some factors, such as capital, in the short run.

Fixed Instalment Method. A method which is used for calculating and allowing for the depreciation of an asset. The fixed instalment, or straight-line, method distributes the cost of an asset uniformly over its depreciable life. The amount to be set a side each year may be calculated from the formula:

$$\frac{P - L}{n}$$

where P represents the initial asset cost, L the expected salvage value at the end of the useful life of the asset and in the plant life expressed in years.

Fixed Interest Securities. Debentures and kindred securities issued by a public company, being known by a variety of names, e.g., mortgage debentures, secured debentures, secured notes.

Fixed Investment. All final goods purchased by firms other than those additions to inventories which have been not intended for eventual reasale. Additions to the capital stock.

Fixed Labour Costs. These include costs of employment that vary less than proportinately with hours worked. There are two main forms of fixed costs. First, there are turnover costs which get associated with the hiring, lay-off or dismissal of employees. These include the costs of recruitment, screening and initial training, in addition to termination costs in the form of servance pay. Second, there have been those costs which, although continuing throughout the period of employment, are not related or fully related to hours of work. Examples include employment taxes that have been based on numbers of employees, and contribution to private pension schemes whose base possesses and annual earnings limit.

Fixed Proportions in Production. Refers to production processes in which the capital/labour ratio has been fixed--i.e., they can only be used in fixed proportions. The resulting iso-product curve has been 'L' shaped.

Fixed Throttle Policy. Refers to a policy which is associated with the name of Professor Milton Friedman (b. 1912) of steadily increasing the money supply by 3-5 per cent per annum so as to support non-inflationary economic growth.

Flexible Exchange Rate. Refer the exchange rates among national currencies which have been free to vary in response to market forces, without government attempts to maintain a fixed exchange rate at which one currency gets exchanged for another. Flexible exchange rates produce greater uncertainty for traders and this can be minimised by an active forward market. Foreign exchange markets depend upon a confidence that obligations will be met.

Flexible-System Production. Refers to a production system in which traditionally separate business functions (design, engineering, purchasing, manufacturing, distribution, marketing and sales) get merged into a highly integrated organisation that can respond quickly to new opportunities.

Flexitime. Refers to the name given to flexible working hours.

Flight from Cash. Refers to moving wealth from cash into interest bearing assets; either because of expectations of price increases or a fall in the interest rate.

Floating Debt. Refers to that part of the National Debt which involves short-terms borrowing; it consists of Ways and Means Advances (q.v.) and Treasury Bills.

Floating Exchange Rate. Refers to a market situation in which the exchange rate between currencies has been free to change from day-to-day in response to supply and demand, the opposite to fixed parity.

Flow. Refers to the quanity of an economic variable measured over a period of time.

Flow of Funds. In the economy, it refers to the transfer of money between the different sectors; the money inflows and out flows by 'transaction group'. Flow of funds accounts have been social accounts giving an overall picture of the financial relationships between the various sectors of the ; they throw light on the processes of economic expansion and contraction.

FOB. (Free on Boad). Terms used of goods shipped where the price is not including shipping or insurance charges; opposite to C.I.F. (q.v). An F.O.B. quotation implies that the exporter will deliver the goods free on board a ship in accordance with the contract at the port named; he pays all expenses up to that point. From then on the buyer must take responsibility, paying for freight, insurance, an all subsequent expenses.

Food and Agricultural Organization. Established in 1945 to FAO is having its headquarters in Rome. With a view to improving the production and distribution of agricultural commodities and food, the organization has been entrusted with the task of collecting and studying relevant data and of promoting international commodity agrrements and technical assistance. As a specialized agency of the UN, the FAO has concentrated its activity upon technical assistance towards less developed countries.

Footloose Industries. Refer to those industries which are not bound to particular locations by specific locational requirements and thus can effectively locate anywhere. They are also known as mobile industries.

F.O.Q. (Free On Quay). Refers to a quotation term where goods have to be delivered to a quay, but the loading expenses have to be forne sepearately by the buyer.

F.O.R. Free On Rail (cf.F.O.B)

Force Majeure. Force beyond the control of a company preventing it from fulfilling a contract; a company unable to deliver in these circumstances may declare force majeure.

Forced Draught Expansion. Refers to the economic expansion which is accelerated by special government measures or strong external influences.

Forced Saving. Refers to a form of saving which takes place because consumers are not able to spend their money on desired consumption goods simply because those goods are not available.

Forecasting, Economic. The use of collected and analysed data derived from the present and the past to predict future economic business or sales developments.

Foreign Aid. Refers to assistance which it given by wealthier countries to aid the less fortunate, often being funnelled through the World Bank and other multilateral development banks.

Foreign Exchange. Currency or interest-bearing bonds of another country.

Foreign Exchange Market. Means the international market in which currencies are transferred between countries.

Foreign Exchange Reserve. See External Reserve.

Foreign Investment. Refers to any investment in another country which is carried out by private companies or individuals as opposed to government aid.

Foreign Payments. Refers to any payment that has to be made to a foreign country whether in return for goods and services or as repayment of debt; these usually have to be made in hard currency.

Foreign Trade Multiplier. Means the net effect on a country's foreign trade following an increase in spending at home after taking into consideration (a) the additonal spending on imports to serve the increase in home demand, and (b) the effect of the increase in imports on the income of the exporting countries and the influence this increase in income may possess on the demand for the exports of the country concerned.

Forestalling Policies. Refer to government measures to correct disturbing trends in the economy which might otherwise cause a disruption of declared objectives, e.g., full employment, steady growth or stable prices.

Forex Markets. Foreign exchange markets including forward foreign exchange markets.

Forward Contract. Refers to a futures contract to buy or sell a specific physical commodity at some time in the future.

Forward Contract (also known as a Future). See Forward Market.

Forward Exchange Contract. A Futures contract which permites a customer to fix the price of a foreign currency for delivery at a future date, irrespective of the market rate at that time.

Forward Exchange Market. The terms used for a market in which currencies are bought and sold at rates of exchange fixed now, for delivery at specified dates in the future.

Forward Linkage. Refers to the relationship between an industry or firm and other industries or firms which employ its output as an input. A change in output or price will get transmitted forwards to users of its product.

Forward Market. Any transaction involving a contract to buy or sell commodities, or securities at a fixed future date at a price agreed in the contract, has been part of a forwardmarket.

Forward Rate. Means the rate of exchange at which a currency may be bought or sold for future delivery, on the forward market.

Forward (or Future) Rate Agreement. Interest rate heding an agreement between a bank and its cutomer on the terms of a national deposit or loan to begin on a futue date.

F.T.O. Free of Tax.

Fractional Reserve Agreement. Refers to the practice by which commercial banks maintain a reserve of highly liquid assets equal to some fraction, normally a small one, of their total assets portfolios. The purpose of the reserve has been to meet unforeseen variations in the outflow of deposits by withdrawals of transfers (by cheque) to other banks, and when calculated as a proportion of total deposits, as it usually is the fraction is known as the 'reserve ratio'.

Franchise

1. Refers to an authorisation or permit to sell products in a particular area;

2. A most important yet least tangible element in the make-up of a successful corporation or bank, the preceived ability in the mind of the client to deliver top-quality services. It distinguishers top firms from the also-rans. Franchise decides the ability to attract and hold important customers and first-class staff.

Free Exchange Rates. Refers to the exchanges rates which depend upon the supply and demand for a currency on the foreign exchange market, without offical intervention.

Freedom of Entry. Means the ability of a new firm to enter a market for a good or service.

Free Good. A good, the supply of which has been at least equal to the demand at zero price. Price in this context refers not simply to money prices but rather to whatever has to be foregone in offering the good--opportunity cost.

Free Market. Refers to a market in which there is an absence of intervention by government and where the force of supply and demand are permitted to operate freely.

Free On Board. FOB.

Free Trade. Refers to the trade which is unimpeded by tariffs, important and export quotas and other devices which obstruct the free movement of goods and service between countries. The formation of a free trade area by two or more countries, however, does not preclude the retention by those participating countries of tariffs against non-member countries.

Free Trade Area. Refers to a loose grouping of countries within which tariffs and other barriers to trade has been removed, while each member country has been its own commercial policy to countries outside the area.

Frictional Unemployment. Traditionally thought of as search unemployment that is the amount of unemployment that corresponds to job vacancies in the same local labour market and occupation.

Fringe Benefits. All those non-wage and salary elements in the total pecuniary rewards an employee receives from his employment.

Front End Loading

1. Refers to a characteristic of loan repayments during period of inflation: high repayments in real terms get incurred in the early years, with lower repayments in real terms towards the end. This front end loading increases as the inflation rate rise. The higher the inflation and interest rates, the more a borrower has to put aside in the early years to service a loan, with less being available for consumption.
2. Often termed as a service fee, cost to an investor of buying into a unit trust or purchasing other securities.

Frustration Hypotheses. A hypothesis which states that the higher the actual rate of growth of real income relative to the long-run expectations of the workforce, the lower will be the sense of frustration and the less likely the workforce will push for higher money-wages.

Full Cost. The sum of average variable cost, average fixed cost and the net profit margin. It is a concept which is used with reference to firm pricing rules.

Full Cost Pricing. Refers to a pricing rule where firms add a net profit margin onto unit costs where the calculation for the latter includes all costs.

Full Employment. Means a situation in which all those persons seeking work in a community are able to find suitable work fairly, with the consequence that a very high proportion of the working population is actually in work at any one time.

Full Employment Budget Surplus. Refers to a measure of the thrust of fiscal policy which is not relying solely on the magnitude of the budget surplus.

Full Employment Surplus (Deficit). Refers to the surplus or deficit which would take place in a federal or national government budget if the economy was functioning with full (or high) employment.

Full-Employment National Income (also known as potential national income and national real output). Refers to a measure of the real value of the goods and services that can be produced when the country's factors of production have been fully employed; when the economy has been at the natural rate of unemployment.

'Full Line Forcing'. Refers to a situation in which a company will not supply certain types of goods or machinery (in which it may have an important monopoly) to dealers who do not order also certain other specified types of good or machinery which the company manufacturers. The company thus enusres the sale of its full line of products.

Funded Debt. Refers to that part of government debt which does not have contracted redemption date.

Funding. The conversion of short-term debts into long-term debts. The sale of long-dated securities by the monetary authorities.

Futures. A term used to designated all standard contracts covering transactions in financial instruments or physical commodities for future delivery on an exchange.

Futures Commission Merchant. The term used for a firm or person engaged in soliciting or accepting and handling orders for the purchase or sale of futures contracts and accepts money or securities as margin on any resulting trades or contracts.

Future Options. An Option is a contract that gives a buyer the right, but not the obligation, to buy something at a stated price within a certain time; an option on a future gives an investor the right to buy or sell a futures contract covering a commodity.

Future Price. The price of a given commodity unit which is determined by open outcry on a futures exchange.

G

GAB. Refers to abbreviation of General Arrangements to Borrow.

Grains from Trade. Means the increase in welfare to the world economy as a whole or to an individual country, depending on the viewpoint, because of engaging in international trade. The gains may take the form of a greater real income for the world or country for the same input of factors or the same real income for a lesser input of factors or some combination of the two. The gains get originated in two sources, which have been the possibility of exchange and the possibility of increased specialization.

Galloping Inflation. It is the name given to rapid growing inflation, such as that which characterized by Germany and several other European countries just after the First World War, when prices rose so rapidly that money quickly lost its value, people lost broke down and people resorted to the system of barter. In recent years, the increase in the price of petroleum and allied products by oil producing countries has caused a galloping inflation round the world.

Game Theory. Means a theory of individual rational decisions which are taken under conditions of less than full information cencerning the outcomes of those decisions. Modern game theory starts with the theory of games and economic behaviour (1944) by Von Neumann and Morgenstern. The theory examines the interaction of individual decisions given certain assumptions concerning decisions made under risk the general environment, and the co-operative or non-co-operative behaviour of other individuals, while conventional micro-economic theory offers a theory of decisions under conditions of certainty it is by no means obvious what decisions a rational individual should make under conditions of uncertainty and interaction. Games have been often described as 'zero sum' where one person's gain has been another's loss, 'non-zero sum' where all players may gain from an individual decision, 'co-operative' where antipathy has been the rule.

GAIT. Abbreviation of General Agreement on Tariffs and Trade.

G.A.T.T. Anti-Dumping Code. A code which was introduced by the General Agreement on Tariffs and Trade setting out the criteria for the investigation of complaints of alleged dumping and the imposition of appropriate remedies.

Gazumping. Means the practice of raising the price of a home after accepting a deposit from a prospective buyer, the buyer is told by the real estate agent to pay the increase or miss out on the sale. Between placing a deposit and discovering that a house has been sold to someone else, a person may get engaged a solicitor, arranged finance and incurred expenses such as a value's fee. The practice becomes more common place when the housing market has been buoyant and buyers possess little resistance against smart operators.

Gearing. Refers to the relationship between ownership and borrowing. The higher the use of borrowing, the higher the gearing. The higher the gearing, the greater the risk of loss or potential for profit.

G.E.M.M. Abbreviation of a Gilt-edged Market Maker. It is a company functioning as a primary dealer in the gilt-edged market.

General Agreement on Tariffs and Trade (G.A.T.T.). An international commercial treaty which came into force on 1 January 1948. Some 88 governments, accounting for over 80 percent of world trade, had by 1982 become contracting members of the Agreement. Two-thirds of the membership is made up of developing countries. The basic principle of G.A.T.T. enshrined in Article 1 of the Agreement is that trade should not be discriminatory; what applies to one partner should apply to all. Exemptions from the rules granted to some branches of agricultural trade have been gradually extended so that G.A.T.T. rules apply largely to industrial products. Furthermore, the trading system embodied in Gait has been progressively undermined by nontariff protectionist measures, like national subsidies, import restraint agreements, and free trade agreements restricted to two or a few countries.

General Equilibrium. The term used for a theoretical situation when supply equals demand in all market—in an economy. An economic system is said to be in equilibrium when producers' plans and consumers' plans have been consistent, and the forces which bring about changes in prices have been in balance.

General Equilibrium Analysis. Distinguished from partial equilibrium analysis by the assumption that the price of every good has been free to vary and that all markets must come into balance, i.e. that all markets must clear. Such analysis usually assumes perfect competition and private ownership of the means of production.

Generalized System of Preferences

(a) E.E.C.A system of tariff reductions which had been granted by the European Economic Community to developing countries. The E.E.C. was the first major trading power to introduce generalized preferences in 1971;

(b) U.S.A. system of tariff reductions which were offered by the United States of America to poorer countries allowing more favoured treatment in trade.

General Linear Model (GLM). It is the most commonly used functional form in econometrics analysis, which is able to specify the dependent variable as a linear function of a set of independent variables.

General Mortgage Bond. Refers to a bond which has been secured by a blank mortgage on a company's property.

General Unions. Refers to trade Unions which organize workers in a range of different skills. Refers to unions which do not confine themselves to organizing a particular industry or group of skills.

Geneva Round. Refers to the popular name for both the first (1947) and fourth (1955-56) rounds of trade negotiations under the General Agreement on Tariffs and Trade.

Genoa Conference. An international monetary conference which was convened in Genoa in 1922. This conference considered and eventually rejected a British proposal for a strict gold exchange standard whereby central banks would regulate their credit policies so as to maintain fixed currency parities and control excessive fluctuations in the purchasing power of gold. The plan did not get succeeded due to the joint efforts of the US, which expressed concern regarding the rapidly accelerating German inflation, and France, which refused to engage in international monetary management while the question of post World War I reparations payments remained unsolved.

Geographic Frontier. Refers to a term which is used in the theory of economic development to describe an area in which with the existing population, level of technical ability and tastes and preferences, there will occur increasing returns to labour and capital. This constitutes a step forward from an economic frontier where a change in population, technical knowledge or preferences would be necessary for increasing returns. The word frontier has been used in the context of a barrier to development which has to be crossed. The geographic frontier gets crossed when production reaches levels of maximum efficiency for the techniques in use.

German Historical School. A school of economists associated with the names Roscher, List, Schmoller, Hildebrand, Butcher, and to some extent Sombart. The school argued that economics was by its very nature incapable of allowing the formulation of abstract and general hypotheses, and that the correct procedure for the study of economic problems was by means of historical investigation. Through such study and the process of induction some 'general laws' might be identified, but they would be specific to certain stages of history.

Ghosting. Means the practice by workers of collecting pay packets for non-existent colleagues; claims by employers with regard to business expenses involving the wages of non-existent employees.

Gibrat's Law of Proportionate Growth. Due to R. Gibrat this is a formulation which is describing how a process of random growth can produce a *lognormal distribution* of firm sizes. Specifically, the law assumes that the number of firms has been fixed, the distribution of growth rates confronting each firm has been identical, and has been therefore independent of both firms' absolute size and past growth history. Thus whether the firm has been large, medium or small it is having the same average proportionate growth rate, and the dispersion around this common average will also be invariant across all firms. Such a law of growth can be shown to produce a size distribution of firms whose relative dispersion increases overtime.

Giffen Good. Means a good whose demand tends to fall as its price falls, thus apparently contradicting the law of *demand*. This situation occurs when the absolute size of the *income* effect (with respect to price) has been greater than the negative size of the *substitution effect*. The income elasticity of *demand* for an inferior good has been negative.

Gilt-Edged. Refers to a high-grade bond issued by a company which has demonstrated its ability to earn a comfortable profit over a period of years and pay its bondholers their interest without interruption.

Ginne Mase (U.S.). Mortgage-backed certificates which were issued by the Government National Mortgage Association.

Giro System. Refers to a mechanism for the transfer of payments operated by the post-office in many European countries and in Japan. Any concern or person may open an account with the 'giro' by paying cash or a cheque into the post office. Transfers from one account to another take place by a written instruction to the post office to debit the 'giro' account of the payer and credit that of the payee. Several payments could be made on a single instruction.

Giving and Taking Cable. In London means selling and buying U.S. dollars.

Global Marketing. Refers to marketing in which all markets have been served which provide scope for sales, there being no rigid distinction in thought between home and export markets. Global marketing provides an opportunity for a larger volume of production in which lower costs of production per unit of output may be achieved. The prospects while there are greater opportunities to counter falling demand in one area by increasing demand in others.

Gold-bricking. Refers to the restriction of output by workers under *incentive payment system* so as to avoid the introduction of higher effort standards per unit of payment.

'Golden Age' Growth. In growth theory it refers to a situation of balanced growth in which the warranted rate of growth will be equal to the naural rate of growth at full employment. The term was introduced by Joan Robinson indicating in her opinion the low probability of such a state of affairs arising in a capitalist economy without intervention by government.

Golden Avalanche. Descriptive of the flow of gold into the United States of America during the 1930s because of an export surplus, high domestic gold prices, and fear of war in other countries. The golden avalanche continued until checked by restrictions imposed during the Second World War.

Golden Handshake. Refers to a non-negotiable award given to a top executive whose services are being dispensed with; the discretional golden handshake has tended to be displaced by the contractual golden parachute.

Golden Parachute. Means a financial compensation package which is designed and negotiated by top executives prior to any threat of displacement or takeover. If, in adverse circumstances, the top executive gets displaced ('let go' is the usual euphemism) or he or she finds it necessary to 'bale-out', the individual descends to earth with the dignity of his golden parachute. Such contracts have been usually restricted to the chief executive and the top three to six executives. Ordinary employees have been simply dispensed with, subject to any terms negotiated by the relevant trade unions or imposed by national or state legislation.

Golden Rule. Refers to the optimal growth path which provides the maximum sustainable level of consumption per person in an economy.

Golden Rule of Accumulation. Refers to that path of balanced growth where each generation saves for future generations that fraction of income which past generations saved for it. The biological interest rate has been an aspect of the same idea. It has been sometimes called the biological interest rate rule.

Gold Exchange Standard. Means a variant form of the gold standard under which a country pegged the value of its currency to the value of the currency of a centre country, e.g., sterling, which was itself on gold. The pegging got effected by the monetary authorities holding all or part of the country's external reserves in reserve assets, and by exchanging the domestic currency for the reserve currency at determined and stable rates.

Gold Market. Refers to the market in which metallic gold, coin or bullion, is being traded. There are gold markets in all the main financial centres.

Gold Points. Refers to those exchange rate levels at which, when a currency is on a gold standard, it becomes profitable to buy gold from the central bank and export it (the 'gold export point') or import gold and sell it to central bank (the 'gold import point'). These points are lying on either side of the central gold parity, the export point below, the import point above, the range being determined by the difference between the central banks' determined by the difference between the central banks' buying and selling prices for gold and in the earlier phases of the gold standard, the costs of shipping gold to other centres.

Gold Standard. Refers to a monetary system in which each unit of currency is worth a fixed amount of gold. The rules of a gold standard have been:

(a) all paper currency must be convertible at its face value into gold;

(b) there must be no restrictions on the import or export of gold;

(c) a gold reserve must be maintained, fully sufficient to meet all demands made upon it.

One of the advantages of a Gold Standard has that it maintains stable exchange rates 'automatically' between countries operating the system. This depends one the 'mintpar of exchange' balance of payments crises do not arise. However a marked disadvantage has been that changes in the stocks of gold cause fluctuations in production and employment. If imports exceed exports, the deficit is met by the export of gold. This reduces the amount of money in the country leading to restriction of credit and falling prices and incomes. As wages generally resist reduction, the effect of deflation is to cause unemployment.

Goodhart's Law. A law which states that any measure of the money supply that is officially controlled promptly loses its meaning.

Goods. Tangible commodities which contribute positively to economic welfare. To be distinguished from bads.

Gosplan. Refers to a Russian term for the State Planning Commission in the USSR. It has been responsible for working out production plans and passing them on to the relevant organizations for execution.

Gossen's Laws. These were developed by Hermann Heinrich Gossen (1810-1858). The first law states that the pleasure obtained from each additional amount consumed of the same commodity diminishes until satiety is reached. The second law states that once a person has spent his entire income, he will have maximised his total pleasure from it only if the pleasure or satisfaction gained from the last item of each commodity bought is the same for each commodity. The third law states that a commodity has a subjective value, and the subjective value of each additional unit owned diminishes and eventually reaches zero.

Government Securities. A general term which is used for marketable debt of the Central Government, from the shortest term, i.e. Treasury bills, to very long term and undated debt.

Gradualism. Means an approach to economic development policy which indicates that the development process is a slow, steady, gradually increasing phenomenon and that the necessary policy measures should also be of this nature.

Grand Factor Price Frontier. A concept which was used by P. Samuelson in his attempt to rehabilitate the use of aggregate capital in neoclassical economic models. He took into consideration the assumption (equivalent to Marx's assumption of a 'uniform organic composition of capital') that the capital to output ratios and labour to output ratios for different production sectors were equal. This made the Factor Prices Frontier for each technique of production to be drawn as a straight line, ensuring that such lines with different slopes would only intersect once. A large number of these lines were able to produce an envelope made up of linear segments.

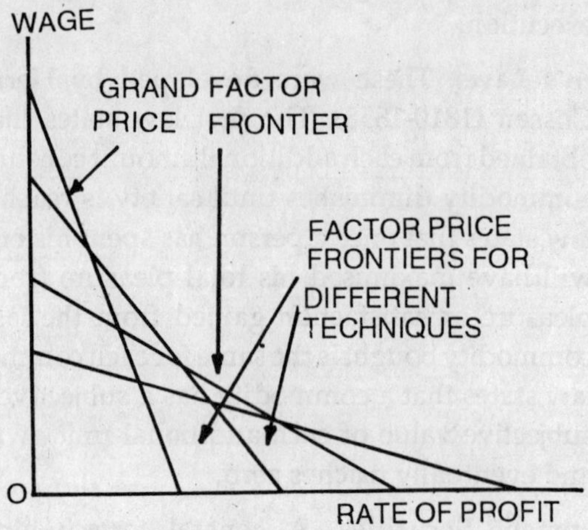

Grand Factor Price Frontier.

When the underlying factor price frontiers were not linear then the same underlying factor price frontier could form part of the grand factor price frontier for different ranges of wage and rate of profit combinations resulting in the problem of Reswitching or Double-switching.

Grant. Refers to the funds which are provided by some agency or individual to other agencies or individuals which do not form part of some exchange but represent a one-way transfer payment. Grants could be paid by one level of government to another (inter-governmental grant), from government bodies to private groups or individuals or from private groups or individuals to other private groups or individuals. A grant could be a 'general grant' which has been available for any type of expenditure or a 'selective grant' tied to specific uses. Grants may also be matching grants which have been calculated as some proportion of the recipient's total expenditure or may be non-matching grants which are not determined by the recipient's expenditures.

Gravity Model. This is commonly used approach to certain problems in Regional Economics and transport studies. It represents the amount of interaction between two places as being determined by the size or importance of the places and the distance between them. One such from of interaction has been population movement. Others would be car travel or air travel. A general from to the gravity model would be.

$$I_{ij} = \frac{A. P_j^{x} . P_i^{y}}{D^{z}_{ij}}$$

where I_{ij} denotes the amount of interaction between places *i* and *j*. A is a constant, P some measure of significance such as population or income level, D the distance and x, y and z parameters. Thus migration between J and I could be represented as a function of the population of each center and the distance between them. Despite its common use, the approach is criticized as lacking firm foundation in economic theory.

Greenback. The United States Dollar.

Green Currency. The term used for agricultural unit of account for the European Economic Community. An accounting device only, the exchange rates between the national currency and the unit of account have been called 'green monies'.

Green Money. Refers to a set of special exchange rates which are used to convert common farm prices into national currencies, in the European Economic Community.

Green Pound. Means the exchange rate for the pound sterling which is used for converting agricultural prices agreed under the Common Agricultural Policy in terms of the European unit of Account into domestic UK prices.

Green Revolution. A term applicable to an increase to the major increase in agricultural productivity obtained in developing countries by the introduction of high-yielding, disease resistant seeds. It is applicable to rice and wheat in particular. Adequate water supplies and the use of artificial fertilizers have been necessary requirements for the success of this policy. In some developing countries double and even triple-cropping have become possible because of the new seeds. Yields have increased dramatically in some areas.

Green Stamp Plan. Refers to a proposal given by Professor Kenneth E. Building to offer a market mechanism for population control. According to the plan each human being would receive in adolescence, saw, 110 green stamps, 100 of which would enable the owner to have one legal child. A market would then be set up in these instruments so that those who had a strong desire for children could buy stamps from those who did not want to have children. Individual preferences in this matter could thus be expressed while at the same time society could maintain overall social control of the rate of growth of population. There would presumably have to be mild sanctions, argues Professor Bounding, for having illegal children which might entail temporary sterilisation until the illegal children are paid for in green stamps. Professor Bounding has remarked that (not surprisingly) his scheme has met with a good deal of disapproval.

Gresham's Law. A 'law' which was formulated by Sir Thomas Gresham (1519-79), an English businessman and public servant. Although usually expressed in the phrase 'bad money drives out good' and applied to episodes of currency debasement or depreciation, the 'law' actually embodies a morose general principle. This theory is able to predict that where two monetary media circulate together, then if their intrinsic relative values as determined by market forces diverge from their legally determined values, the money of higher intrinsic value will be withdrawn from circulation and hoarded. Such a situation will arise with arise without any currency debasement; for example, historically, where gold and silver coin are circulated together at legally established values which have come to differ from the relative commodity values which have come to differ from the relative commodity values of the two metals.

Gross and Net Output. The gross output of a firm or industry has been the total selling value of production of that firm or industry within a given time-period. Gross output has been including value of materials, fuel and other supplies bought from firms outside the industry. To establish the 'net output', or the value of the contribution made by the industry itself, it has been necessary to deduct from the gross output what has been spent on incoming supplies. Net output has been therefore the value added by a firm or industry in the productive process in a given time-period. Net output has been a useful indicator of an industry's importance in the economy.

Gross Cash Flow. Equal to company profit plus depreciation. It does not measure the actual flow of funds in an organisation as it does not take into consideration the movements in assets and liabilities or capital raisings. It is important, however, as an indicator of potential cash that may be raised through normal operations.

Gross Domestic Fixed Capital Formation. Investment in fixed assets, e.g., expenditure on buildings, vehicles, plant and machinery for replacing or adding to the stock of existing fixed assets, expenditure on maintenance and repairs being excluded.

Gross Domestic Product at Constant Prices. Refers to the Gross Domestic Product at Factors Cost or the Gross Domestic Product at Market Prices (taken over a series of years and adjusted to discount changes in the value of money).

Gross Domestic Product at Factor Cost. Means the value of goods and services produced within the nation, representing only the sum of the incomes of the factors of production. It is equal to the Gross Domestic Product at Market Prices minus indirect taxes plus subsidies. Valuation at factor cost is able to display product in terms of the factors of production employed, the contributions of the factors being measured by the incomes they receive.

Gross Domestic Product at Market Prices. Refer to the value of goods and services which are produced within the nation, charged at ruling prices. Prices include all taxes on expenditure, subsidies being regarded as negative taxes. In the estimate of gross domestic product only goods for final consumption and investment goods (capital) have been included, the values of intermediate goods have been implicitly included in the prices of the final goods.

Gross Income. As distinguished from Net Income gross income of a firm implies the total income earned by it before taxes and overheads.

Gross Interest. Distinguished from Net Interest, gross interest is one which is calculated with due consideration to extra income earned from the use of money so borrowed.

Gross Investment. Refers to the total investment that takes place in the economy within any specific time period. It comprises replacement investment and net investment.

Gross Margin. Refers to the difference between the price paid to the wholesale supplier and the price received by the retailer.

Gross National Product (G.N.P.). Refers to a comprehensive measure of a nation's output. It may be measured in two ways; from the demand side as the sum of consumer expenditures, private investment, government purchases, and net exports; and from the supply side as the sum of employee earnings, proprietors' earnings, corporate profit, net interest, rental income, capital consumption allowances and indirect business taxes.

Gross National Product Deflator. Refers to a prices index which is used to correct the money value to all the goods and services entering Gross National Product for price changes. This makes the changes in the real output of the goods and services in the economy to be isolated.

Gross Trading Profit. Profit which are earned on operations before allowing for depreciation and interest on debt finance and stock appreciation.

Group of Eleven. Initially, a group of ten countries such as the United States, United Kingdom, Canada, France, West Germany, Sweden, Netherlands, Belgium, Italy and Japan, which agreed to lend if requested to the International Monetary Fund for the purpose of increasing the lending resources of that body. Under the General Arrangements to Borro, adopted in 1962, the Group of ten offered the Fund with an additional $6 billion of their currencies. These resources were used to help in a massive rescue operation of the pound in 1964. The Group of Ten agreed on 19 December 1971, on a realignment of currency exchange rates which devalued the U.S. dollar by 7.89 per cent. In January, 1983, Switzerland was admitted to full membership. In the same month, the eleven nations expanded their General Arrangements to Borrow in the International Monetary Fund from $7.1 billion to $19 billion, further the International Monetary Fund could lend this money to developing countries, instead of only to members of the Group of Ten as in the past.

Group of Five. A group of leading industrial countries such as the United States of America, Britain, West Germany, France and Japan; representatives meet from time to time to discuss issues of mutual concern, e.g., interest rates, problems of large debtor countries, and other financial matters.

Group of Seventy-Seven. Means a group of less-developed countries (actually over 100) who banded together in 1964 to press for better terms of trade with the richer countries. The group has played an important role in international trade and tariff negotiations.

Growth-Gap Unemployment. Refers to long-run demand deficient unemployment. The growth in the productive capacity of the economy through time has been insufficient to offer jobs for all those who wish to work. The production techniques adopted have been 'too capital intensive' and this is therefore one form of technological unemployment.

Growth Pole. Refers to a group or cluster of industries which are centered on an linked with one of more propulsive industries and form a centre of growth and dynamism in an economy. The concept was introduced by the French economist Perroux.

Growth Recession. A period of slow expansion.

Growth-Profitability Function. Refers to the maximum profit rate which a firm can sustain at different rates of growth.

Growth Theories of the Firm. Due to the pioneering work of E.T. Penrose and R.L. Marris growth theories are a branch of the managerial theories of the firm, regarded appropriate to a corporate economy within which corporations' managers passed an element of discretion over the objectives they choose to pursue. In contrast to the other managerial models growth theories are, as the label implies, concerned with the time path of expansion of the firm. In this dynamic context managers have been presumed to satisfy instinct of power, dominance and prestige by pursuing growth as an objective, while motives such as security and professional excellence induce them to accept the firm's valuation ration as an objective. The capital market will impose a constraint on the value of the valuation ratio through the merger and takeover mechanism. Representative of growth theories of the firm has been the following formal presentation of the constrained optimization problem facing the firm.

$$\text{maximize } U_M = U_M(g, v)$$

$$\text{subject to } v \geq \bar{v}$$

where U_M denotes the managerial utility function, g is firm's growth rate, v the firm's valuation ratio and $\bar{v}$ the capital market constraint. Given a growth-valuation function whithin which v becomes negatively related to g beyond some level of g, managers will face a trade-off as illustrated in the diagram. An unconstrained optimum will be achieved at the tangency point g* v* between the highest possible managerial indifference curve I_m^3 and growth-valuation function. If this were however to yield a valuation ratio which does not satisfy the capital market constraint $v \geq \bar{v}$ then the optimal growth rate would be given by the constrained maximization solution of $\bar{v} \cdot \bar{g}$.

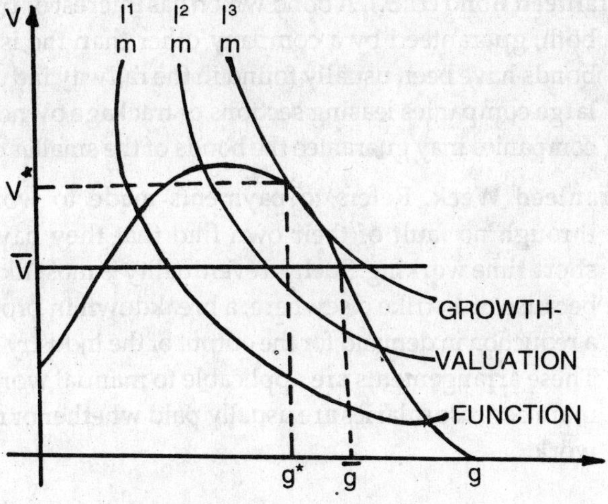

Growth Teories of the Firm.

Growth Theory. Refers to a part economics which deals with the analysis of the determinants of the rate at which economies grow over time, that is with changes in the major economic aggregates such as national income, capital consumption and employment.

Growth-Valuation Function. This function provides the maximum valuation ratio a firm can sustain at different rates of growth and is a common features of growth theories of the firm. Reflecting the growth theories of the firm. Reflecting the growth-profitability relationship this function has been likely to be bell-shaped. Assuming steady-state growth conditions, initial positive increments in the growth rate stimulate growth economies yielding a higher profit rate thus leading, for a given dividend-payout ratio, to a larger initial dividend payment and faster expected growth of that payment. This possesses a positive effect on the valuation ratio. Beyond that rate of growth at which growth diseconomies have set in and have been 'dominant', the consequent fall in the profit rate depresses the initial dividend payment and prevents the continuance of a positive relationship between growth and the valution ratio.

Guaranteed Bond (U.S.). A bond which has interest or principal, or both, guaranteed by a company other than the issuer. Such bonds have been usually found in the railway industry when large companies leasing sections of trackage owned by small companies may guarantee the bonds of the smaller companies.

Guaranteed Week. Refers to payments made to workers who through no fault of their own find that they have been on short-time working. Such an eventuality is most likely to arise because of a strike elsewhere, a breakdown in production or a reduction in demand for the output of the industry concerned. These arrangements are applicable to manual workers in the main because salaries are usually paid whether or not there is work.

H

Haberler Gottfried (1900—). Australian born American economist who is best known for his work in international trade. In his Theory of International Trade (1936) he gave an alternative demonstration of the gains from trade in terms of the opportunity cost of producing goods as seen in the goods foregone. This has freed the case for trade from the real costs of the approach of Ricardo.

Habit-Creation Demand Function. Refers to a demand function for non-durable goods which is reflecting the fact that demand in any one period may get influenced by the cumulated purchases of the goods in the past. The higher this past 'stock' (it is not a stock in the strict sence since past goods will not be extant) the greater would be the influence of past consumption on demand in the current period.

Hammer Price. Means a price which is calculated according to the rules of the Stock Exchange of Great Britain and many other countries. It represents the market value of a security at the time of the default of a member firm.

Hard-Core Unemployed. Refer to those whose average term of unemployment has been significantly longer than the average, extending to many months and perhaps years with an increasing proportion regarded as unemployable.

Hard Currency. Means a currency which is having a continuing high level of demand, relative to supply in the market for foreign exchange. Currencies of stable industrialized nations are generally included while those of underdeveloped countries and the Eastern Bloc are not.

Harrod-Domar Model. Refers to one of the earliest analyses of the process of the growth of an economy. It is being a synthesis of the independent work of two economists, Sir Roy Harrod (b.1900) and Evsey D. Domar (1914). The model comprises (a) firms which produce and sell goods, spend on new investment, and pay incomes to households for productive services; and (b) household which spend part of the income they receive on consumption goods and save the rest. The model is able to demonstrate that if the amount saved has been equal to the amount invested in every period, then the economy will tend to grow at a rate which has been determined by the marginal propensity to save and the incremental capital-output ratio (q.v.).

Harrod Neutral Technical Progress. Refers to a classification of a disembodied technical progress which is comparing points in the growth process at which the capital to output ratio is constant. Harrod Neutral Technical progress is then equivalent in effect to an increase in the supply and/or efficiency of labour. It means a change in the labour coefficient in the production function.

Heckscher-Ohlin Law. A principle which was first put forward by Eli F. Heckscher (1879-1952) in 1919, and subsequently refined by Bertil Ohlin (b. 1899). This principle states that advantages in international trade arise from the different relative factor endowments of the countries trading. A country will tend to export those commodities which intensively embody the factor with which it has been most well-endowed. From this basis theme, Professor Paul A. Samuelson (b.1915) developed his factor price equalisation theorem. He demonstrated how an increase in the price of a commodity can increase the income of the factor of production which has been used most intensively in producing it. The theorem also states the conditions under which, as free trade in commodities narrows differences in commodity prices between countries, the prices (or incomes) of the factors of production also become closer; to some marked degree, therefore, free trade becomes a substitute for the free mobility of the factors of production.

Hedge. Refers to an action taken by a buyer or seller to protect his business or assets against a change in prices.

Hedger. Refers to one who deals in a physical commodity and who uses futures contracts to manage his price risk.

Hedging. Refers to a technique of insurance against fluctuations in the prices of raw materials or goods scheduled for future delivery by dealing in 'futures'. The two basic types of hedge operation have been the 'buying hedge' and the 'selling hedge'.

Hedonic Price. Refers to the implicit or shadow price of a characteristic of a commodity. The quantity of a particular commodity could be resolved into a number of constituent characteristics which determine its quality. A part of the price of that commodity may get associated with each characteristic and variations in quality may thus be valued. The application of hedonic price theory to quality changes was done by Zvi Griliches and has found valid applications in the analysis of housing demand and environmental economics.

Hedonism. Means the philosophy according to which human behaviour is to be guided by the search for pleasure. As a philosophy, however, Hedonism is typically modified by concepts of duty, obligation, etc. As a school of positive thought it simply states that people do behave as pleasure seekers, not that they ought to.

Heterogeneity. Means the quality of goods, services or factors which permits their distinction in the minds of consumers and producers.

Heterogeneous Capital. Refers to physical capital of different types which are highly specific to certain production processes and not transferable to alternative processes. This concept is at variance with the idea of a single malleable capital good which can be used for the production of many different goods by different processes. If capital is regarded to be heterogeneous than, as noted by the Cambridge School, it raises serious problems for the use of an aggregate production function such as is commonly the case in neoclassical growth models.

Heterogeneous Product. If commodities or services supplied by economic agents in a given market possess attribute combinations which have been not identical in the eyes of buyers, the product is regarded to be heterogeneous.

Heteroscedasticity. Refers to an econometric problem in which the variance of the error term in a regression equation does not remain constant between observations. The problem is arising most often in cross section data, and results in the ordinary least squares procedure not producing best linear unbiased estimates.

Hicks Neutral Technical Progress. Means a classification of disembodied technical progress which compares points in the growth process at which the capital to labour ratio has been constant. The innovative process is regarded Hicks Neutral when the ratio of the marginal product of capitals to that of labour has been left unchanged such that the share of output going to Labour (and Capital) is unchanged.

Hidden Unemployment (also known as disguised unemployment). As the labour force varies procyclically, it has been argued that the unemployment by excluding discouraged workers, who are considered to form the hidden or disguised unemployed. On this view, such workers would otherwise be available for work if they did not regard the search as hopeless. Accordingly, an estimate of the hidden unemployed should be added to the official unemployment figures to get a true reading of labour market slack.

High-Powered Money. Money consisting of currency (notes and coin) and bank's deposits at the central bank of a country. Part of the currency is held by the public, the remaining currency being held by banks as vault cash. Also called the monetary base; the terms have been interchangeable. The manner in which 'the Fed' most often after the stock of high powered money is through open-market operations.

High Technology. Refers to more complex and advanced technology which is relative to the general level in society at any time; thus in its time the steam locomotive would have been high technology. At the present time, the term includes computer software and hardware: scientific, mechanical and professional instruments various kinds of electronic equipment: lasers; robotics; solar energy systems; and biotechnology.

Hire Purchase. Means a procedure which is used for purchasing goods under which the purchaser pays a deposit on receipt of the goods followed by a number of instalments until the debt gets cleared. The goods do not become the property of the purchaser until the last instalment has been paid. In the event of the default of the purchaser in respect of the instalments, the firm can resume possession of the goods in question.

Hire Purchase Finance Houses. Finance houses which deal with the granting of credit for the purchase of certain classes of goods on the condition that their advances will be repaid by regular instalments over a fairly short period of time, together with interest charged on the amount borrowed. Credit will be extended to private persons for the purchase of consumer durables, and to industry and agriculture for the purchase of motor vehicles and machinery.

Histogram. Refers to a graphical representation of a frequency distribution (or probability distribution) in which the frequency (or probability) with which a variable takes on values between certain limits has been given by the height of a block covering the horizontal axis between those limits.

Historical Costs. Means the charge incurred at the time a factor input or resource was originally purchased and which will be not thus equal to the cost of replacing the input (replacement cost) if prices rise in the meantime.

Historical Models. Economic models which have been capable of analysing charges and situations in the real world as opposed to equilibrium models which have been largely theoretical.

Historic Costs. Refers to the actual monetary cost of raw materials, machinery, products, etc., at the time they were bought or made. Depreciation based upon historic costs will be not sufficient to cover replacement costs, particularly during inflationary periods.

Hoarding. Refers to the act of holding money. If the desire to hoard increases the result will be (assuming that no new money is created) that money incomes will fall. Conversely, if there is occurs a fall in the desire to hold money, incomes will rise. If an increase in the quantity of money circulating causes a fall in the velocity of circulation or an increase in the volume of trade, then the increased quantity of money need not be accompanied by any rise in the price level. The holding or accompained by any rise in the price level. The holding or hoarding of money should be carefully distinguished from money used for investment in capital assets; in the latter case, the money returns to the economic system as income. The term 'hoarding' was first of all coined by John Maynard Keynes (1884—1946) to denote liquidity preference (q.v.) as distinct from saving proper.

Holding a Call. Buying a call option.

Holding a Put. Buying a put option.

Holding an Option. Buying an option.

Holding Company. A company which is having control over a number of other companies, through ownership of a sufficient proportion of the latters' common stock.

A holding company is concerned itself with control over the financial, managerial or marketing functions of its subsidiaries, and thus performs more of a monitoring role. The subsidiaries are then given an element of independence, which facilitates the retention of the individual subsidiary's image and control over its production and investment plans.

Homogeneity. Refers to the quality of goods, services or factors which ensures that they cannot be differentiated in the minds of suppliers and consumers. A range of commodities have been said to be homogeneous if all commodities in that range are perfect substitutes for each other. The commodities may be physically distinct but economically homogeneous. Individual workers have been physically distinct, but may be almost identical in their ability to work and may therefore be treated as a homogeneous group by firms.

Homogeneous Product. If the commodities or services supplied by economic agents in a given market are having attribute combinations which are identical in the eyes of buyers, the product is considered to be homogeneous.

Horizontal Equity. Refers to fairness of justice in the treatement of individuals in similar circumstances. In general, the principle that like-individuals is to be treated in a like manner where economic arrangements have been most frequently used with regard to tax and income, thus horizontal equity has been held to be attained if individual with the same income face the same tax burden.

Horizontal Integration. Horizontal Integration is said to take place if two firms at the same stage of the production process merge to form a single business organization.

Hot Money. Refers to money which gets transferred rapidly from one financial centre to another to take advantage of differences in short-term interest rates or to escape the financial penalties of devaluation.

Human Capital. Refers to those investments which are made in human resources so as to improve their productivity. Costs are incurred in the expectation of future benefits; hence, the terms 'investment in human resources'.

Human capital theory underpins many of the important developments in modern economics and provides one of the main explanations for wage and salary differentials by age and occupation, the uneven incidence of unemployment by skill, the job regulatory practices of trade unions and so on, as well as contributing to policy decisions on, say, the allocation of resources to schooling and training vis-a-vis other claims on resources.

Hyperinflation. Inflation which has got out of control; runway inflation. A particularly outstanding example of this occurred in Germany in the 1920s when savings were destroyed in value by an astronomical rise in prices. To the middle classes the effect was disastrous.

Hypothecation. Refers to the pledging of securities as collateral, for example to secure the debit balance in a margin account.

I

IBRD. Abbreviation of International Bank for Reconstruction and Development.

IDA. Abbreviation of International Development Association.

Identification Problem. Means an econometrics problem which arises in the estimation of the parameters of simultaneous equations. The difficulty arises when it is impossible to distinguish from the data which equation is being estimated.

Idle Balances. Refers to money that has been withdrawn from circulation and held as a store of wealth. Keynes identified a speculative demand for money. He argued that money would be held in idle balances because of uncertainty as to the future price of financial assets which represented the principal alternative form of holding wealth.

Idle Money. As inactive money that does not contribute to productive effort in an economy. It results from what Keynes called Liquidity Preference i.e., the desire to hold money rather than risk it on interest-earning assets, or goods which may have little utility.

Illiquidity. Refers to lack of liquidity in a specific asset, or in a portfolio of assets held by a transactor. Being the observe of liquidity the condition has been always a relative one because almost all assets vary in degree of liquidity.

ILO. Abbreviation of International Labour Office.

IMF. An abbreviation of International Monetary Fund.

Imitative Growth. Refers to an aspect of firm growth by diversification. Referring to that growth stimulated by the introduction of products whose attributes have been such that consumers don't perceive the product to be new, that is they don't arouse and satisfy some latent need. The impact of imitative growth will be realized on a small number of producers, (Growth).

Immiserizing Growth. Refers to the possible but improbable case where an increase in economic output within a country results via repercussions through trade to a situation where its economic welfare gets diminished. The circumstances which could commodity, for which foreign demand has been price inelastic, and a high marginal propensity to import. The growth in real output is able to induce a demand for more imports. To earn the extra foreign exchange to pay for them the export commodity in the face of a price inelastic demand is to be sold at so low a price that the terms of trade deteriorate to such an extent that this wipes out the gain from the extra output.

Impact Analysis. Refers to a technique which attempts to measure the effect on a regional or local economy of a given change in economic activity.

Impact of Taxation. Means the person, company or transaction on which a tax is levied. Someone has been responsible for handing the levy over to the tax authorities. This is thus referring essentially to the legal situation.

Impact Multiplier. Refers to the immediate effect on an endogenous variable of a change in an exogenous variable, as opposed to the total or long-run effect of such a change. In macroeconomics it has been the multiplier effect of a change in one of the components of aggregate demand in the period immediately following the change. In econometrics models impact multipliers have been the estimated parameters on exogenous variables in the reduced form.

Imperfect Competition

1. Refers to any form of market structure other than perfect competition and would thus include monopolistic competition, oligopoly and monopoly.
2. Refer to any market structure other than perfect competition and monopoly.

Imperfect Market. Means a market in which the following conditions, necessary for a perfect market, do not hold good:

1. A homogeneous product;
2. A large number of buyers and sellers;
3. There exists freedom of entry and exit for buyers and sellers;
4. All buyers and sellers possess perfect information and foresight with respect to the current and future array of prices;
5. In relation to the aggregate volume of transactions the sales or purchases of each market agent have been insignificant;
6. There exists no collusion amongst buyers and sellers;
7. Consumers maximize total utility and sellers maximize total profits;
8. The commodity is transferable.

Imperialism. According to Marxist or socialist thought, it refers to a foreign policy which seeks political and economic control over backward areas to guarantee the home country an outlet for idle savings and surplus manufactured goods in exchange for strategic raw materials. Most Marxist or socialist thought believes that a closed capitalist economy must suffer from a chronic deficiency of 'effective demand' which can only get corrected by the opening of foreign markets.

Implicit Costs. Mean the costs in the form of lost opportunities to use resources, including time, in another way, e.g., a major implicit cost of a university education has been the foregone opportunity to work and receive an income.

Implicit Price Deflator. A price index which is used to deflate the various spending series that comprise the gross national product.

Implicit Rental Value. Refers to the price the owner of a physical factor of production like capital should charge the firm for the use of that factor.

Implementation Lag. Refers to the time taken to implement monetary policy. It is also known as the inside lag. It is subdivided into a recognition lag, and an administrative lag.

Import. Refers to a good or service which has been consumed in one country but bought from another country. A visible import has been good, while an invisible import has been a service.

Import Duties. The taxes which are levied by the state on imported goods. Besides being a source of revenue these are used for giving protection to domestic industries and for conserving foreign exchange. The latter two functions are carried out by import control. In countries where imports are severely restricted, import duties are regulated under certain import licensing policy in force. From the purely revenue angle, imported products must be subjected to at least the same rate of taxation as products of domestic origin. A somewhat higher levy could also be justified on the ground that those who consume imported products may be made to pay higher price as they consume a service resource, namely foreign exchange.

Imported Inflation. Refers to price rises due to the increased cost of imported raw materials and goods.

Import Licence. A Government licence required for goods imported into a country. A licence may be an 'open general licence' permitting the unrestricted importation of certain goods in accordance with schedules which are published from time to time. Sometimes an "individual open licence" may be issued, granting to a particular importer the unrestricted right to import a certain commodity as long as the licence is valid. Frequently a 'specific import licence' is issued to cover shipments up to a certain value only.

Import Restrictions. Refers to the restrictions on the quantity or types of goods imported into a country, through the use of tariffs or quotas.

Imputed Rent. Refers to the rent notionally paid by the firm tc itself for the use of the land it occupies.

Inactive Money. Refers to that portion of total stock of money or money supply in existence at any one time which is not utilised to finance current transactions or being lent out on the money market.

Incidence of Taxation. Refers to the eventual distribution of the burden of a tax.

Income. Refers to the wealth, measured in money, which has been at the disposal of an individual or a community, per yer or other unit of time, it may be considered to be a flow of purchasing power which may be expended at once on goods or services or retained for the purposes of capital accumulation.

Income Bonds and Debentures. Bonds and debentures or debenture stock, the interest on which is only payable out of profits.

Income Consumption Curve. The tangency of the consumer's indifference curve and his budget line are able to define the consumer's equilibrium. If income gets varied such that the budgen line moves outwards in a parallel fashion, new equilibria will be established. The locus of all such equilibria has been the income consumption curve. If the curve slopes upwards in commodity space it reveals that both goods (measured on the axes) are normal goods. If it slopes backwards or downwards one of the goods is an inferior good. (See diagram.) The income consumption curve has been widely referred to as an Engle curve although some writers distinguish the two.

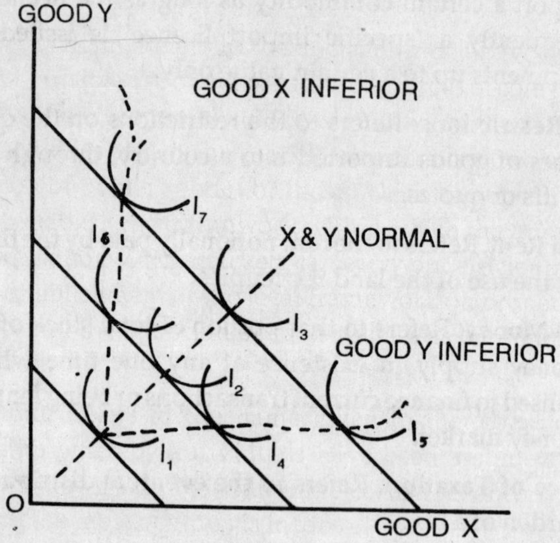

Income Consumption Curve

Income Differentials. Refers to the difference in income levels between different people. These can occur due to types of job, i.e. skill differentials or geographical location in that some areas have higher wage levels. This has been a particularly marked phenomenon in less developed countries.

Income Effect. Refers to the effect which a change in price of a good or service has on a consumer's demand for the good or service, taking into account the change it induces in his real income. An increase in real income due to a fall in the price of a good may cause a standard demand analysis.

Income Elasticity of Demand. Refers to a measure of the responsiveness of the quantity demanded of any good. In order to avoid the measure being sensitive to the units used, the measure were be put as follows:

Income Elasticity of Demand

$$= \left(\frac{\Delta Q_i}{Q_i}\right) \div \left(\frac{\Delta Y}{Y}\right)$$

$$= \frac{\Delta Q_i \cdot Y}{\Delta Y \cdot Q_i}$$

where Q_i represents the quantity demanded of good i, Y income and the symbol Δ refers to a change in the variable in question.

Income Expenditure Model. It is a simple Keynesian one sector model. It shows the determination of the equilibrium level of national income. Under the assumptions of a fixed capital stock, labour force and technology and rigid wages and prices and, therefore, expectations, it describes the static equilibrium in which the supply of real national output is equal to the quantity of national output people wish to buy. In the model the volume of aggregate expenditure finds out the volume of output and the associated level of employment the model concentrates exclusively on the demand side of the macro-economy. Graphically equilibrium is shown as the point at which the aggregate expenditure function cuts the 45° line as below. This diagram is also called the Samuelson Cross after Samuelson who first suggested the diagrammatic approach.

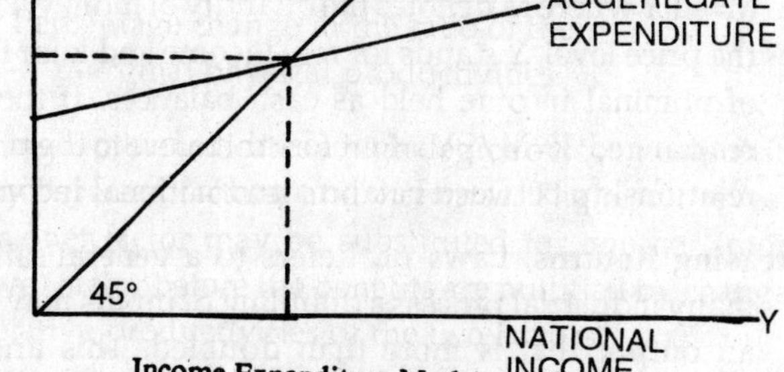

Income Expenditure Model

Income Maintenance. Refers to policies which are designed to raise the income levels of specific groups or individuals. Policies or this type are including social security benefits such as those paid to the sick or unemployed but also programmes designed to support the incomes of particular producers such as farmers.

Income-Sales Ratio. Refers to the ratio of a firm's or industry's value added to total sales revenue. This ratio can be regarded to be a measure of the extent of vertical integration, the greater the integration the higher the index.

Income Tax. It is the most important single tax and plays an important role in the fiscal regimes of all countries. In India it is levied on taxable income of individuals at progressive rates. Income has been widely recognized as being a suitable base for taxation on equity grounds though there are many problems with the definition of taxable income and some economists suggest that an expenditure tax is superior.

Income Tax, Progressive. Refers to a system of graded tax payment, individuals with small incomes paying a smaller proportion of their incomes than individuals with large incomes. The system has been based on the theory of diminishing marginal utility.

Income Velocity of Circulation. Refers to the measure of the velocity of circulation of money which arises from the Cambridge analysis in which average cash balances get related to the level of income in a given period. The equation is $M=kPY$ where M denotes the quantity of money, P represents the price level, Y stands for real income and k for the fraction of nominal income held as cash balances. If the terms get rearranged: $k=M/PY$ and refers therefore to the proportional relationship between balances and national income.

Increasing Returns, Laws of. Refers to a generalisation that in many industrial process a doubling of inputs may give rise to an output that is more than doubled. This arises due to economies that may arise in mechanisation and specialisation in energy utilisation and avoidance of waste.

Incremental Capital-Output Ratio (ICOR). Refers to the number of additional units of capital that are needed to produce an additional unit of output: $\frac{\Delta K}{\Delta Y}$ where ΔK denotes the change in the capital stock and ΔY the change in output. Since in the naive accelerator $\Delta K = \alpha \Delta Y$, it is evident that α the accelerator coefficient is also the incremental capital-output ratio.

Indexation. Means a mechanism for periodic adjustments in the nominal value of contracts in line with movements in a specified price index. Escalator clauses in wage contracts offer one example of these. The complete indexation of all contracts has been frequently advocated as a policy to prevent the arbitrary redistribution of income caused by inflation. If all contracts, both explicit and implicit, have been escalated by the known rate of inflation, inflation would possess small effects and costs.

Index Number. A single number which gives the average value of a set of related items, and stated as a percentage of their average value at some base period.

A price index number finds the price of a given physical quantity of each item in the current period, express this as a percentage of the price of the same quantity in the base period and then takes a weighted average of these percentages for 'price relatives' to give the overall price index.

Index numbers are a very concise and efficient way of providing information. They have the usual property of averages in summarising the values of a large number of items. Also, by the device of ralating all values to a single base period, they make comparison of values at different periods easy.

The index number for a particular year can be determined by using the following formula:

$$\frac{\text{Price of selected commodities in the particular Year X 100}}{\text{Prices of selected commodities in the base year}}$$

The average of the index number of both years i.e., the base year and the particular year:

$$\frac{\text{Total Index Number of the Year}}{\text{Total number of selected commodities}}$$

Index Number — Uses of

(i) Knowledge of the Economy.

(ii) Knowledge regarding standard of living.

(iii) Comparison between countries.

(iv) Guide to government.

(v) Measure for the value of money.

Indifference Analysis. Refers to an analysis of consumer demand which is based on the notion of ordinal utility. The consumer has been assumed to possess a given amount of money while being faced with the prices of all the goods that might be consumed, the consumer will then decide on a set or bundle of goods to buy influenced by the money available, the prices, and the tastes of the buyer. The consumers may have regarded several alternative sets of goods which could be purchased; they are then ranked in order of preference, i.e., given any two bundles, the consumer can judge whether one is preferred to the other, or whether there is an indifference between them both being regarded as equally desirable.

Indifference Curve. A curve which shows the locus of combinations of the amounts of two goods, say X and Y, such that the individual has been indifferent between any combination on that curve. An indifference curve is usually considered to be convex (see diagram).

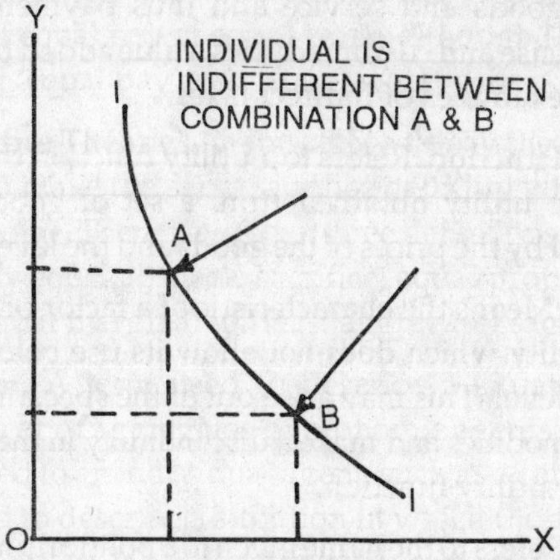

An Indifference Curve

Indifference Map. Means a set of indifference curves in which each successive curve is lying outside the previous one and in a north east direction. 'Higher' indifference curves reveal higher levels of utility. Indifference curves cannot cross, if they do they are violating the axiom of transitivity of preferences. They can touch the axes (see diagram) but are usually drawn such that this does not happen. Note that the distance between indifference curves does not reveal absolute differences in utility because indifference curve theory has been based on ordinal utility.

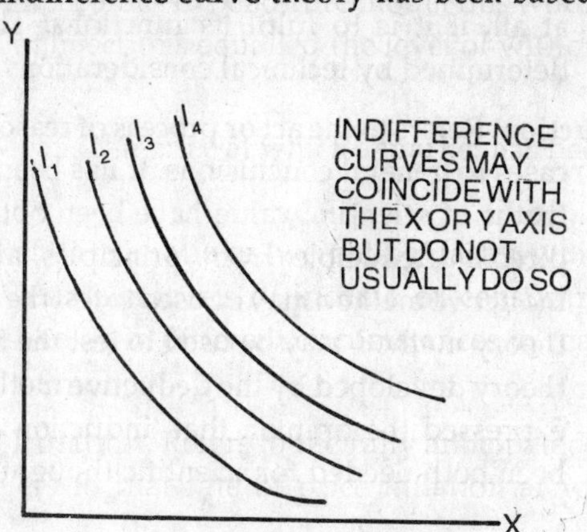

An Indifference Map

Indirect Taxes. Traditionally these are defined as taxes which are levied on goods and service and thus payment was only indirect. Excise and customs duties, value added tax and rates have been examples of indirect taxes.

Indirect Utility Function. Refers to a utility function that is able to express the utility obtained fron a set of goods as being determined by the prices of the goods and the level of income.

Indivisibilities. Means the characteristic of a factor of production or commodity which does not allow its use below a certain minimum level. This may arise out of the specialist nature of many commodities and make a discontinuity in the production function or utility function.

Individualism. Refers to the name given to a political and economic system that favours the development of the individual rather than that of the state or other association. It has been the antithesis of collectivism and socialism. Individualism has found strong advocacy among the English speaking peoples. As a philosophy it rested on the teachings of Adam Smith (1723—1790) and Jeremy Bentham (1748—1832) and was accepted with some modification by John Stuart Mill (1806—1873). Its most extreme exponent was Herbert Spencer (1820-1903).

Indivisible Plant. Plant which must be used on a large-scale, or not at all, if it is to fulfil its functions. The minimum size is determined by technical considerations.

Induction. Refers to the act or process of reasoning from particular cases to general conclusions. It has been a method by which truths of scientific value have been obtained which are not directly deducible from principles already known. The inductive method may be used to test the findings of economic theory method may be used to test the findings of economic theory developed by the deductive method. Alfred Marshall expressed the opinion that 'induction and deduction have been both needed for scientific thought as the right and left foot have been both needed for walking'. There is no one method, therefore, which can be properly called the method of economics.

Industrial Action. Refers to the sanctions which are employed by individuals or groups of individuals in an attempt to resolve an industrial dispute in their firm. The sanctions may take the form of either a complete or partial withdrawal of labour, that is strikes or at the other extreme complete adherence to the rules governing work, which is work to rule.

Industrial Bank. An alternative name for a finance house. An organization which provides hire purchase credit.

Industrial Complex Analysis. Refers to a technique for use in regional planning which is able to emphasize interrelationships between various industrial activities located in the same geographical area. An industrial complex may be defined as a group of economic activities which when located together benefit from mutually advantageous external economies, also termed as agglomeration economies. The analysis involves estimating the flows of inputs and outputs which occur between the component industrial sectors and estimating costs of production for the complex as a whole (rather than the individual industries) at various locations. The techniques means that policies to stimulate a regional economy should concentrate on complexes rather than individual industries.

Industrial Democracy. Refers to an extension of the decision-making process within an enterprise away from a single body and towards the whole work force.

Industrial Dispute. Refers to a dispute or difference either between employers and employees or amongst employees dealing with the terms and conditions of employment of any person or group of people or indeed the non-employment of any person. An industrial dispute may give rise to industrial action.

Industrial Inertia. A term which is used to describe the observed phenomenon whereby firms fails to alter location when the existing location ceases to be the most profitable location.

Industrialization (in developing countries). Refers to the development of industries as a general development strategy.

Industrial Relations. Refers to the study and practice of the rules that govern employment. These rules have been of three main kinds. Substantive rules that are to regulate pay and employment, procedural rules that govern the making and challenging of substantive rules and finally disciplinary rules that deal with a breach of both the above sets of rules.

Industrial Unions. Means trade unions which are able to organize all workers within a given industry regardless of the jobs they perform.

Industrial Wage Differentials. Refers to differences in the average levels of pay groups of workers which are classified according to the industry in which they are employed.

Industrial Wage Structure. Refers to the ranking of the average pay levels of different groups of workers which are classified according to the industry in which they are employed.

Industry. In its widest sense it refers to all the manifold activities of a country which offer employment, but more narrowly those activities concerned with the production of goods rather than services. Specifically, an industry comprises all those activities which get directed to the production of a given class of goods, e.g., aircraft, ships, machine tools, foodstuffs, etc.

Inelastic Demand. A change demand is not always proportionate to the change in price. A small change in price may lead to a greater change in demand. In such cases, the demand is called elastic or sensitive. On the other hand, even a big change in price may not cause any change in demand such demand is said to be inelastic. For example, even if the price of salt varies widely, people continue to buy almost the same quantity. Hence, the demand is inelastic.

Inequality. Refers to a relationship whereby a function of a variable (or set of variables) has been represented as being greater than, or less than, some quantity, and denoted by the symbols:

$>$ greater than,

$<$ less than,

$\geq$ greater than or equal to,

$\leq$ less than or equal to.

Than normal application of inequalities in economics has been in the formulation of constraints. For instance

$$rK + wL \leq TR$$

where r denotes the per unit cost of capital,

w denotes the per unit cost of labour,

K denotes the amount of capital,

L denotes the amount of labour, and

TR denotes total revenue.

would be interpreted to mean that factor payments must be less than or equal to total revenue.

Inertia Selling. Refers to a practice in which goods have been sent to householders without having been ordered. The recipient suffers inconvenience in having to return unwanted goods, tending to retain them, later he receives a bill for the merchandise.

Infant Industry. Means a young and growing industry. It is often considered not quite able to stand on its own feet in the face of foreign competition.

Inferior Goods. Goods of which less have been bought by people in higher-income groups because they all able to afford to consume more expensive commodities. Inferior goods possess negative income elasticities.

Inflation. Refers to a sustained rise in the general price level. Also, refers to the proportionate rate of increase in the general price level per unit of time.

Inflationary Spiral. Refers to an upward trend of prices, which has been partly the result and partly the cause of increases in wages and salaries and other incomes such as profits, dividends, interest and rent.

Inflation, Cost-Push. Inflationary trends which are initiated by pressure for higher incomes, greater spending not being accompanied by a corresponding increase in goods and services. Cost-push inflation may also arise from increases in the prices of imported raw materials.

Inflation, Creeping. Inflation which is characterised by a slowly rising price level.

Inflation Demand-Pull. Refers to excessive demand for goods and services, the symptoms of which have been rising prices and scarcities of labour and materials; bidding trends to raise the price of these resources which leads to further increases in the prices of goods and services.

Inflation, Suppressed. This takes place if price controls are holding down prices when general inflationary tendencies have been present in the economy.

Inflation Accounting. Refers to techniques for dealing with the impact of inflation on accounts and accounting procedures.

Inflationary Gap. Aggregate expenditure exceeds the maximum attainable level of output with the result that there occurs upward pressure on prices. In the simple income-expenditure model this is shown by an aggregate expenditure function which cuts the 45°, where E=Y, beyond the full employment level, Yf. At Yf the resources of capital and labour have been fully employed with the result that this represents the maximum attainable level of output. Because of this, there exists an inflationary gap of magnitude AB with the associated upward pressure on prices.

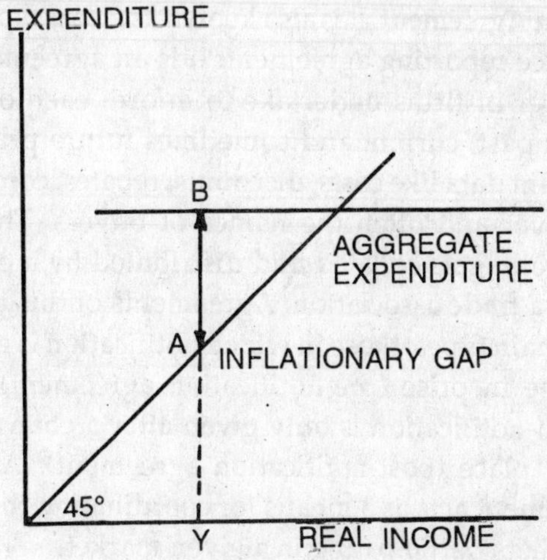

Inflationary Gap

Inflation Subsidy. Due to institutional inflexibilities interest rates and debt repayments are unable to rise in line with inflation and as a result real interest rates and the real value of debt will fall indeed real interest rates may even become zero. In this case there exists an inflation subsidy to those borrowing although of course there exists a corresponding tax on those who made the loans.

Inflation Tax. Refers to the situation where a government adopts a policy of promoting inflation in place of an increase in taxation to pay for its expenditures. If the government finances its purchases by using as increase in the money supply when the aggregate supply curve in the economy is inelastic, prices will rise so that all holders of money balances will rise so that all holders of money balances will get their real purchasing power diminished in a manner analogous to an increase in e.g., income taxes.

Informal Sector. Refers to self-employed in a developing country who are engaged in small-scale labour-intensive work like tialoring, food preparation, trading, shoe-repairing, etc.

Information Agreement. It is also known as an open price agreement or price reporting agreement. It is an agreement whereby a number of firms undertake to inform each other regularly about past, current and sometimes future prices, and other relevant data like costs, discounts, rebates, conditions of sale, turnover and often the names of buyers. The information generally gets collated and distributed by a central agency, often a trade association. Agreements of this nature fall into two main types; those in which notification is given prior to a change in price (pre-notification agreement) and those in which notification is only given after a change in price has taken place (post-notification agreement). An information agreement acts as a means for coordinating the behaviour of suppliers participating in a given market.

Infrastructure. Services which are regarded as essential for the creation of a modern economy, e.g., power, transport, housing, education and health services.

Infrastructure of an Economy. Refers to the underlying capital of a society involving basis amenities for economic development in the country like roads and rail transportation, communication systems, water supplies, electric power, and other public utilities. Often called 'social overhead capital', the term is also at times widened to include education, health, skills and other amenities available to people for self-development and professional proficiency.

Initial Margin. Refers to the deposit which a user of futures markets must make on purchasing or selling a contract; the amount of the deposit is representing only a small proportion of the full value of the contract.

Injections. Refers to an exogenous addition to the income of firms or households. An addition to the income of domestic households or firms that does not result from the immediate expenditure of the private sector. In the simple income expenditure model injections get magnified via the actions of the multiplier and as a result give rise to some multiple rise in national income. The three broad categories of injections usually considered have been investment, government expenditure and exports.

Inland Bill. A bill which is drawn for the finance of domestic production or trade. Although such bills have been still significant (and have increased in volume in recent years) the term has been now little used.

Innovations. Often used to cover both technological advances in production processes as well as the introduction of different attributes and attribute combinations in marketable products. In the latter context innovation has been a source of product differentiation and has been used by producers to create demand and enhance market share.

Input Orientation. Refers to the tendency for some forms of production or manufacturing to locate near raw materials or input sources. It is generally explained in Location Theory on the grounds that the production has been 'weight-losing' that is large amounts of raw material are required per unit of output, which do not transfer their full weight to the output.

Input-Output Analysis. Means the quantitative analysis of inter-industry relations. All transactions that involve the sale of products or services within an economy during a given period have been arranged in a square indicating simultaneously the sectors making, and the sectors receiving, delivery. The preparation of input-output tables processes significantly added to our knowledge of the industrial economy in past periods. Input-output analysis is closely associated with the name of Wassily Leontief.

Input-Output Coefficient. Refers to a coefficient of proportionality which is used in input-output analysis. Industry *j*'s demand for the output of industry *i* has been proportionate to the total output of industry *j*. Thus:

$$X_{ij} = a_{ij} X_j$$

where

X_{ij} = output of industry *i* which is sold to industry *j*;

a_{ij} = coefficient of proportionality, or input-output coefficient;

X_j = output of industry *j*.

The value of the coefficient may be zero if industry *j* does not buy any input from industry *i*; otherwise it will be positive and is generally assumed to be less than utility.

Inputs. The materials and factor services fed in at one end of the production process and its implementation. The inside lag may be subdivided into three components, recognition, decision and action lags.

Inside Money. Forms of money which have been based on private sector debt, the prime modern example being commercial bank deposits to the extent that they have been matched by bank lending to private sector borrowers. By contrast, 'outside money' has been money which has been a direct debt of the public sector, e.g., circulating currency; or has been based on such debt, e.g. commercial bank deposits matched by bank holdings of public sector debt.

Inside Information. Information of commercial value which is obtained from someone within an organisation, being information not available to the public, such information, if reliable, may ensure an avoidance of loss or the making of a profit.

Insolvency. Means the state of being unable to pay one's debts. An insolvent person or company may, after various legal processes, be declared bankrupt, or they are able to agree an arrangement with the creditors to discharge the debts.

Instalment Credit. The term used for finance lent on conditions which offer repayment of the principal, together with the interest by regular instalments. The greater part of instalment credit will be advanced to finance the purchase of consumer goods under hire purchase contracts, where the finance has been linked to a particular transaction with the lender and purchaser having certain legal rights in the object purchased. Such credit may get financed by the retailer concerned, although in the case of hire purchase the contract may be between the buyer and a finance company. Other forms of instalment credit have been personal loans by banks, and credit extended through credit card and budget account facilities.

Institutional Economics. Refers to a type of economic analysis which emphasizes the role of social, political and economic organizations in determining economic events. This movement got flourished in the early twentieth century particularly in the US under the influence of T.B. Veblen and W. C. Mitchell (1874-1948).

Institutional Training. Usually used to describe job training which is provided directly by the government. Its rationale, at a micro-level, has been that the private market does not offer a socially optimal amount of training.

Instrumental Variables (I.V.). Variables which have been used to replace actual explanationary variables as weights in regression analysis. The I.V. technique has been often used where one or more of the explanatory variables get correlated with the error term of the equation.

Insurance. Refers to the elimination of risk of loss by the payment of premiums to an insurance company which undertakes to pay for specified losses. The losses of the few have been thus met from the premiums of the many. Insurance services are divided into the following classes:

(a) fire, and other hazards such as riots, explosion, earthquake and hurricane;

(b) accident, including motor, third party liability and personal;

(c) marine, both hull and cargo;

(d) aviation, both hull and cargo;

(e) life and endowment; and

(f) cover against default by a borrower. This category includes credit insurance, mortgage insurance, and financial guarantees.

Insurance Broker. Broker acting on behalf of the insured.

Intangibles. Costs or benefits which either cannot be quantified, or at least cannot be priced.

Integrated Economy. A term which refers to a situation when different sectors of an economy, usually the agricultural and industrial sectors, work together efficiently, and have been mutually interdependent. As part of the development process, this situation has been usually coincident with the achievement of sustained growth.

Intended Inventory Investment. Refers to the deliberate build-up of stocks. The deliberate run-down of stocks has been intended inventory disinvestment.

Intensive Margin. Refers to the case of decreasing physical returns to capital or labour applied to a fixed quantity of land. Often accredited to David Ricardo, this theory states that if to a given piece of land equal increments of labour (or capital) have been applied the increment in the output of the crop produced will at some point reach a maximum and thereafter continuously decline.

Interest. The reward for the use of capital in the processes of production. The term 'interest' generally means gross interest. Net profit refers to the payment for the use of capital when there is no risk of non-payment or trouble to management. Gross interest is composed of a number of elements and net interest is only a part of the gross interest. Gross interest includes:

(i) payment against risk

(ii) payment against inconvenience

(iii) payment against keeping accounts, and

(iv) payment for the use of capital, i.e., pure interest or net interest.

Interest Arbitrate. Refers to the drawing on overdraft facilities, not for the purposes for which the facilities had been sought but to invest in higher, yielding certificates of deposit or other money market instruments.

Interest, Classical Theory of Rate of. Refers to a theory that the rate of interest, under the play of market forces, comes to rest at the point where the amount of investment at that rate of interest has been equal to the amount of saving at that rate. John Maynard Keynes (1883-1946) argued that the total amount of saving got influenced by many factors, and that the rate of interest merely influenced individual decisions as to what proportion of savings would be invested in industry and how much held as cash.

Interest Cover. The number of times the fixed interest payments made by a company to service its loan capital get exceeded by earnings. The cover serves as a guide to the ability of a company to meet interest payments out of current income.

Interest, Monetary and Real Theories of. Theories which are seeking to discriminate between and relate monetary theories of interest and real theories of interest. A contemporary view argues that the market (monetary or nominal) rate of interest has been equal to the real rate plus the expected inflation rate. Essentially, monetary theories of interest have been short-run theories in which the monetary or nominal rate of interest has been the cost of borrowing money and selling securities, and the yield on lending money and purchasing securities. The real rate of interest, on the other land, has been determined by the demand for and supply of real savings. If the monetary rate of interest on investment in securities has been 15 per cent per annum, and the rate of inflation has been 10 per cent per annum, then the real rate of interest will approximate to 5 per cent per annum.

Interest, Productivity Theory of. Refers to a theory which emphasises the yield from investment as the explanation for the existence of a rate of interest. Eugen Von Bohm-Bawerk (1851-1914) adopted this theory as one of his reasons for the existence of a positive interest rate. It got related to his theory of 'round-about' production methods.

Interest Rates, Real. Actual interest rates, discounted against inflation to give a real rate; for an actual interest rate of 15 per cent and a rate of inflation of 10 per cent, the real rate of interest may be regarded to be about 5 per cent.

Interest Rates, Social Effects of. Refers to the effects of interest rates at various levels on different segments of the population. If interest rates have been high those with loanable funds and cash self-evidently benefit, and have an interest in the continuation of such rates. Other may be in a socially natural position: affluent citizens who do not need to borrow money, or self-financing companies, or those who borrow but are able to as the full cost along to the public. Those who must borrow money to obtain housing, provide a car, or finance a business, pay the full penalty. High interest rates, even if introduced to ensure the economic health of the country, are able to operate by rewarding the rich and penalising the poor.

Interest, Time Preference Theory of. Refers to a theory of the existence of interest rates. It is based on the assumption that an individual prefers consumption now to consumption in the future. It is argued that the individual prefers present consumption due to the following reasons: (a) the slaking of thirst now takes a natural preference over the contemplation of slaking thirst at some future time; (b) the benefits of deffering consumption may never be enjoyed due to death or incapacity; and (c) the tendency of people to undervalue future benefits.

Intergovernmental Grants. Refers to the funds which are provided by one level of government in a country to another level of government.

Interim Dividend. A dividend paid out of profits not yet audited.

Interlocking Directorates. The term used for a situation in which one or more person(s) sit on the board of directors of two or more companies. Where these firms are having similar product lines, such conditions may be conductive to collusive activities.

Intermediate Good. A good which finds use at some point in the production process of other goods, rather than final consumption. Common examples include steel and wood. It has been quite possible for some goods to be both instance which is used both the purposes of producing electricity and steel, as well as directly for domestic heating purposes.

Intermediate Lag. Refers to a part of the operational lag which is associated with monetary policy. It represents the time which is taken for the action of the authorities to have an effect on the intermediate target varibles; money supply interest rates and credit availability.

Intermediate Technology. The term used for a set of techniques and technological processes which has been halfway between the highly capital-intensive technologies of the Western world and the primitive, indigenous techniques of underdeveloped countries. The name was invented by Dr. E. F. Schumacher.

Internal Balance. Means a situation in which full employment and price stability are simultaneously achieved.

Internal Drain. Means a movement of cash, i.e., circulating media, from the banks into domestic circulation.

Internal Effects. Benefits (or costs) which are received (or paid) by persons within a particular grouping, generally a decision-making unit, like a governmental unit or business firm.

Internal Finance. Means those fund which are retained from net profits for use in financing a firm's activities.

Internal Growth. Refers to that part of a firm's expansion which has been produced by investment within the firm rather than investment in acquisition of other firms and merger activity, i.e., external growth.

Internal Inflexibilities. Inflexibilities in organisations which arise from ingrained patterns of thought and behaviour, long established procedures and policies, and the typing up of available funds in specific projects; all these factors are able to impede progressive pianning.

'Internal' Labour Market. Means an arrangement whereby labour has been supplied and demanded within the firm without direct access to the external labour market.

Internally Generated Fund. Trading profits before depreciation and after interest, tax and dividends.

International Bank for Reconstruction and Development (I.B.R.D.). Bank set up under the Bretton-Woods Agreement in December, 1945, for two purposes; to help finance the rebuilding of wardevasted areas and to aid in the advancement of less developed countries. Nearly one-third of all funds have gone for power projects. Besides lendings funds, the Bank provides technical advice to governments or other borrowers on a wide range of development problems. It undertakes general economic surveys for governments wishing to study resources and to plan long-range programmes of development. The Bank has also lent its 'good offices' to help governments solve economic or financial disputes. The Bank's loan funds come in part from member's subscriptions to capital shares. The powers of the Bank are vested in a Board of Governors. It is often referred to as the World Bank.

International Cartel. The term used for an agreement among producers, when their number has been small, to apportion the world market in a particuiar good among themselves to get profits above the competitive level and in times of depression to avoid cutthroat competition.

International Commodity Agreements. Agreement which are made between producer and consumer countries, but occasionally only on the part of producers, in an attempt to attain price stability for primary commodities.

International Development Association (I.D.A.) An affiliate of the International Bank for Reconstruction and Development (q.v.). It was formed in 1960 to help developing nations by extending financial aid on easy terms. I.D.A. finances carefully studied and well prepared projects. It will help countries whose credit standing has not enabled them to borrow from the Bank, and it is prepared to finance a wide variety of projects e.g. by extending credits for municipal water supply, industrial estates and special training programmes.

International Economics. Deals with that part of economics which is concerned with transactions between countries in the fields of goods and services, financial flows and factor movements. It is mainly divided into two subject areas, pure theory and monetary theory. In the former, attention has been focused on real magnitudes like gains from trade, terms of trade, patterns of trade, etc. where as the latter has been preoccupied with the determination of the exchange rate between currencies and with adjustment mechanisms for attaining equilibrium in the balance of payments.

International Finance Corporation (I.F.C.). A United Nations agency established in 1956 as an affiliate of the International Bank for Reconstruction and Development to help finance productive private undertakings by investing in them, without government intervention or guarantee. It invests only in the less-developed areas, and in enterprises which are primarily industrial. I.F.C. will not however, finance more than half of the total cost of an enterprise.

International Firm. A firm which is undertaking operations on an international basis, without the ownership being on an international basis.

International Gold Pool. An organisation established in 1961 by a number of central banks to operate in the London market for the purpose of stabilising the price of gold. The participating countries had been the United States of America. Belgium, Italy, Netherlands, Switzerland. Western Germany and the United Kingdom. France was also a member but ceased to take an active part in the pool from July, 1967, onwards.

International Investment Bank. A regional development bank which was established in 1970. It grants long and medium term credits for industrial development projects in the COMECON countries of Bulgaria, Cuba Czechoslovakia, East Germany, Hungary, Mongolia, Poland, Romania, USSR and Vietnam. The Bank also accepts deposits and executes foreign exchange transactions for member countries. A special fund for financing economic and technical assistance to developing countries get established in 1974.

International Labour Office. An intergovernment organization which was established in 1919 by the Treaty of Versailles and finally become a specialised agency of the United Nations in 1946. The aim of Organization is to promote international co-operation regarding policies designed to achieve full employment, improve working conditions, exited social security and raise general living standards.

International Liquidity. The term used for the ability of countries to meet their international transactions. Countries keep reserves of gold and foreign currencies and settle their indebtedness to other countries by using either a transfer of gold or payments in their own or foreign currencies. A country in temporary balance-of-payments difficulties may get the assistance of the Interntional Monetary Fund.

International Monetarism. Refers to a school of thought which holds that changes in the world money supply have been the principal source of inflationary and deflationary pressure in the International economy.

International Monetary Fund. It is an international financial institution which was set up in December 1945, because of the Bretton-Woods Agreement of the previous year. It is an association of governments designed to:

(a) Promote international monetary cooperation through a permanent institution;

(b) Facilitate the expansion and balanced growth of international trade;

(c) Promote exchange stability maintain orderly exchange arrangements among members, and avoid competitive exchange depreciation;

(d) Assist in the establishment of a multilateral system of payments in respect of current transactions between members; and

(e) Provide members with an opportunity to correct maladjustments in their balance of payments without resorting to measures destructive of national and international prosperity. Each member government has been set a quota to be paid into the Fund, payable partly in gold and partly in the member's own currency; the quota decides the member's voting power and the amount of foreign exchange that it may draw from the Fund. A member may purchase foreign exchange, paying its own currency, but the member must 'repurchase' its own currency within 3 or, at the outside, 5 years to maintain the balance in the Fund pool. Currencies drawn from the Fund may be used for relieving a member's balance of payments difficulties; the funds may not be used for military purposes or for programmes of economic development.

International Payments System. A general term referring to the way in which international financial transactions have been carried out i.e. payments between residents of different countries who hold different domestic currencies. The term covers the various systems of exchange rates, exchange control and questions concerned with international liquidity.

International Price Arbitrate. Means the mechanism by which domestic prices get influenced by world prices.

International Standard Industrial Classification. The term used for an industrial classification of economic activity which has been designed to promote international comparability in statistics compiled and published by the United Nations. The classification has been essentially a compromise between the systems of industrial classification employed by countries throughout the world.

International Sugar Agreement. An agreement between world sugar exporters. It has been aimed at stabilising world sugar prices.

International Trade. The term used for the trade which is carried out between nations in goods and services.

International Trade Theory. A body of economic theory which is relating to international trade, including the following:

(a) the theory of comparative advantage which states that mutually advantageous trade will always be possible with trade patterns based on relative prices, rather than absolute prices; no one country can have a comparative advantage in all commodities;

(b) the Heckscher-Ohlin theory which states that a country will tend to export the commodity that used relatively more of the factor of production that is relatively abundant in that country. The theory assumed that countries possess different quantities of the various factors of production such different quantities of the various factors of production such as land, labour, and capital, but identical production functions; and

(c) the factor-price equalisation theory which states that under free international trade, not only the prices of the traded products but also the prices of the factors of production (inputs) such as land, labour, and capital will be equalised among countries.

Intra-Firm and Inter-Firm Comparisons. Refers to the comparisons of business efficiency which are made between firms within the same industry, so as to stimulate improved performance. The members of an industry often collaborate in the regular publication of statistics and organisations have been set up to define, collect and compare financial and operating ratios on a confidential basis. The more common ratios used in interfirm comparisons have been as follows.

$$\frac{\text{Net profit}}{\text{Capital employed}}$$

$$\frac{\text{Fixed assets}}{\text{Stocks}}$$

$$\frac{\text{Total capital employed}}{\text{Liquid assets}}$$

$$\frac{\text{Fixed assets}}{\text{Depreciation provision}}$$

$$\frac{\text{Current assets}}{\text{Current liabilities}}$$

$$\frac{\text{Fixed interest capital}}{\text{Equity capital}}$$

Inventory-Led Recovery. Descriptive of a recovery from an economic recession which starts with the rebuilding of depleted business stocks or inventories; this will take place if firms anticipate a recovery of demand for goods.

Investment Bank. A bank which advises corporations and governments on how to raise capital; guarantees the sale of new bonds and shares, and distributes them to investing institutions and individuals.

Investment Grants. Funds which have been made available by government or other agencies for the purpose of encouraging firms to make expenditures on the acquisition of physical capital.

Investment Trust. A company whose main function has been to invest in other organizations.

Involuntary Unemployment. Refers to that unemployment which would get eliminated by a rise in a aggregate demand which resulted in higher prices and a lower real wage.

Iron Law of Wages. The hypothesis which states regardless of the possibility of upward movements in wages in the short run, wages would inevitably return to the subsistence level in the long run. This 'law' has been a combination of the wages fund doctrine and Malthus law of population.

Islamic Development Bank. A regional development bank which was formed in 1974 by the Organization of the Islamic Conference to encourage economic growth in Muslim countries and communities.

ISLM Diagram. The diagram which details the simultaneous determination of equilibrium values of the interest rate and the level of national icome because of conditions in the goods and money markets; the integration of the real and monetary sectors of the economy by Hicks and Hansen to reveal the determination of macroeconomic equilibrium.

The IS curve has been the schedule detailing the combination of interest rates (r) and levels of national income (Y) which ensure equilibrium in the goods market. At all points along this schedule total with drawls, savings and taxation in the closed economy case, equal total injections, investment and government expenditure. The title IS curve reflects the simple case dealt with in Hicks' initial exposition when only savings and investment had been considered. The LM curve has been the schedule which details the combination of interest rates and levels of national income and ensure equilibrium in the money market. At all points along this schedule the demand for money market. At all points along this schedule the demand for money transactions (and precautionary motives if we subsume this into transactions demand) and speculative purposes has been equal to the exogenously determined supply of money. Initially this schedule called the L curve by Hicks, but Hansen christend it the LM curve, emphasizing that it represented a curve along which L, the demand for money =M, the supply of money.

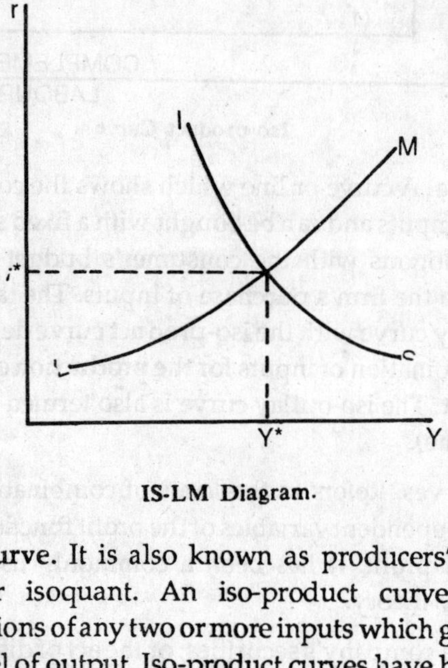

IS-LM Diagram.

Iso-product Curve. It is also known as producers' indifference curve, or isoquant. An iso-product curve details the combinations of any two or more inputs which give rise to the same level of output. Iso-product curves have been typically drawn as being convex to the origin because of the assumed substitutability of inputs (Curve 2 in the diagram), where inputs have been complementary, the iso-product curve will be a perfect 'L' shape (Curve 1), where they are perfect substitutes the iso-product curves, are straight lines.

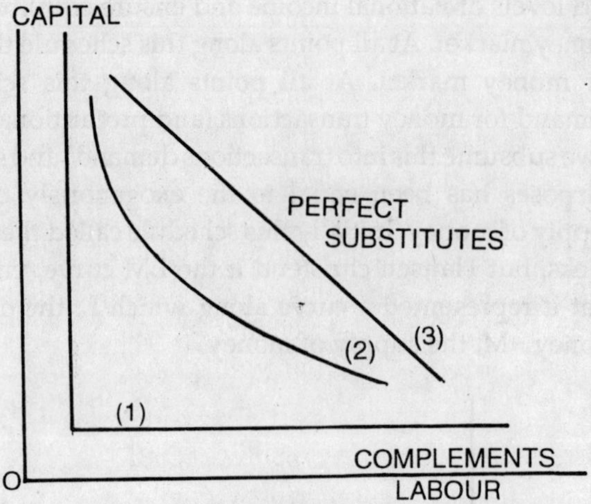

Iso-product Curve

Iso-Cost Curve. A curve or line which shows the combinations of any two inputs and can be bought with a fixed sum of money. It is analogous with the consumer's budget line, but gets related to the firm's purchase of inputs. The tangency of the iso-outlay curve with the iso-product curve defines the least-cost combination of inputs for the production of a given level of output. The iso-outlay curve is also termed as the iso-cost curve (line).

Iso-Profit Curves. Refers to the locus of combinations of two or more independent variables of the profit function which yield an equal profit. It has been a commonly used concept in oligopoly theory.

Issue. Any of a company's securities; or the act of distributing such securities.

Issued Capital. Refers to that part of the authorised capital of a company which has been subscribed. Such capital will be fully-paid-up, or partly-paid up.

J

Jawbone (U.S.). Descriptive of verbal appeals as an aspect of the voluntary approach to the implementation of monetary policy. During periods when restraint in bank lending has been desirable, the Federal Reserve Board and Reserve Banks may appeal to the commercial banks to secrutinise loan applications particularly carefully giving priority to loans which will add to productive capacity.

J. Curve. In the period immediately following a depreciation or devaluation of its currency a country may experience a balance of payments deficit. In the subsequent period however this will get eliminated and the current account slowly get moved into surplus. The J curve is so called because it describes the shape of the time path the current account figures may follow if time has been plotted on the horizontal axis and the balance of trade on the vertical.

Jelly Capital. The term used to refers to that capital when it is theoretically assumed that the capital-labour ratio can get altered immediately.

Jobcentres. Refers to a concept in employment office which offer self-service facilities; freed from the task of distributing unemployment benefit.

Job Cluster. The term used for a stale group of occupations or work assignments within an internal labour market which have been so linked that they have common wage settling characteristics. The jobs get linked together (a) because for the technology of the work place, (b) because of the administrative organization of production, or (c) because of social custom. Each job cluster will have one or several 'key rates' of pay and associated with each of these will be further jobs which enjoy an established differential between their rate of pay and that of the key rate.

Job Competition Theory. A theory which replaces the orthodox wage competition model in which workers tend to compete with each other for jobs by altering the wags rates for which they will work. The main elements of the theory have been that the number and type of jobs available have been technologically determined; that workers skills and their wage offers have been irrelevant in determining the number and type of jobs actually filled; that wages have been rigid and as such determined by custom and institutional factors; that queues of workers at fixed wages constitute the supply of labour-workers thus compete for places in a labour queue; that employers have been employing screening devices to hire workers based upon their presumed adaptability and trainability; and that all training has been acquired on the job, so that the labour market is a market for training slots.

Job Duplication. This takes place when an individual is having more than one form of employment at the same time and therefore is not dependent only one source of income. It has been particularly prevalent in underdeveloped countries especially in the informal sector.

Job Evaluation. The term used for a process whereby the various elements of a job — such as different skills, acquired knowledge, responsibility, and physical working conditions—have been each rated and an overall rating for the job obtained. Points have been accorded to the various job obtained. Points have been accorded to the various job factors and these points are aggregated following the weighting of each component. The differences in the weighted totals for different jobs are then employed for determining relative wages. The processes have been however, related to the market rates ruling for certain key jobs. From these key rates a curve, or regression line, is obtained which is relating pay to the job evaluation. The wage rates for the remaining non-market jobs can then get slotted into the structure and differences between current pay levels and evaluated pay levels met by upgrading or downgrading (which maintaining 'personal' wage rates at the old level) as appropriate. It is to be noted that job evaluation has been a subjective process, the success of which has been depend on its concordance with what the market would dictate.

Jobless Growth. Refers to increases in production which is made possible by more and better use of machinery and innovations; without an increase in employment.

Job Search Channels. Refers to the methods through which jobs have been identified and or obtained. They have been classified as either 'formal' or 'informal'. Formal methods are the public employment service, private employment agencies and trade union networks. Informal methods are employee referrals and gate applications.

Job Shopping. Means a tendency among younger workers, and in particular teenagers, to search for suitable employment on a trial and job to another, finding out in a rather expensive way what kind of work they are liking.

Job Splitting. Refer to a practice where two people share the same job for one wage.

Joint Costs. Means costs which have been incurred in the production of two or more products and which cannot get attributed to any one of them; an allocation of costs may prove a wholly arbitrary business.

Joint Demand. The term used for describing a situation which exists when the satisfaction of a want involves two or more separate commodities being used in conjunction with each other, e.g., knives and forks, petrol and motor-cars, pens and ink, records and record players.

Joint Products. Commodities having such a property that in production a change in the rate of output of one makes a similar change in the others(s). Any change in supply and demand conditions will therefore get transmitted between the markets of joint products. Examples of joint products have been wool and mutton, gas and coke, petrol and heavier oils.

Joint Profit Maximization. Means the maximization of the combined profits of an existing group of firms. It is a feature which is able to characterize oligopolistic market structures, where firms mutually are able to recognize their interdependence and thus get motivated to overcome rivalry and adopt goals such as joint profit maximization.

Joint profit maximization needs the group of firms to find that industry output level at which industry marginal cost and marginal revenue have been equal.

Joint Profits. Means the profits which are earned by a small group of rival firms. Firms in a small group may get motivated towards a set of policies which will maximise the combined profits of the group, i.e. the group will behave as a single firm acting as a monopolist, or conversely each firm may act in a way which seeks a larger share of smaller joint profits. The actions of rival firms thus influence the size of the joint profits, as well as the division among them.

Joint Products. Two or more products ordinarily produced under a given process.

Joint Sector. That sector in an economy in which public and private sectors collaborate.

Joint Stock Banks. The banks whose stocks are jointly held by the public and private investors. These banks are of two categories: (i) scheduled, and (ii) non-scheduled.

Joint Supply. Refers to a situation in which the supply of one commodity inevitably involves the supply of another, e.g. meat and hides. An increase in the supply of meat involves an increase in the supply of hides; and increased demand for one may be accompanied by reduced prices for the other.

Joint Ventures. Mean a situation where both public and private sectors have been working together in an economic activity. It is particularly prevalent in underdeveloped countries where capital has been very scarce in the private sector and government funds have been often needed so as to develop industry, or banking services etc.

Juglar Cycle. Business cycles of between 9 and 11 years' duration which were identified by Clement Juglar of France. He has been credited with being the first to speak of business cycles. Juglar divided business cycles into three phases: prosperity, crisis and liquidation. He argued that the sole cause of the crisis had been the prosperity phase that preceded it, and that depression always followed the crisis; the excesses and maladjustments of the prosperity phase made the crisis and depression inevitable. Standard business cycle theory deals mainly with explanation of the Juglar cycle. These theories have been classified by Gottfried Haberler as: purely monetary theories, monetary over investment theories, nonmonetary over investment theories, underconsumption theories, and psychological theories. Most modern theories have been based on time lags occurring in necessary adjustments between production and demand, investment and interest rates, and so on.

K

Kabutocho. Tokyo's equivalent of Wall Street.

Kaffirs. South African mining shares.

Kaldor-Hicks Test. This test was posulated by N. Kaldor and J. R. Hicks in articles published in the Economic Journal in 1939. State A has to be preferred to state B if those who gain from the move to A can compensate those who lose and still be better off. Compensation here has been hypothetical and the Kaldor Hicks criterion suggests that A has been preferable to B even if compensation does not actually take place.

Kennedy Round. The sixth of multilateral trade negotiations which was conducted under the auspices of the General Agreement on Tariffs and Trade, and occurred in Geneva between 1964 and 1967. The Kennedy Round resulted in across-the-board tariff negotiations on specific groups of goods as opposed to negotiations conducted on a single good basis. This general approach to tariff reductions was made possible by the US Trade Expansion Act of 1962 which allowed the administration of President J. F. Kennedy to negotiate up to a 50 percent reduction in tariffs on a reciprocal basis. By 1973 the Kennedy Round agreements got reduced the average level of world industrial tariffs by approximately one-third.

Kerb Market, South Korean. An unofficial money-lending market in the Republic of Korea, where interest rates charged have been sometimes more than twice the official lending rates. The market attracts borrowers because the official lending rates. The market attracts borrowers because the official banking system has been not able to meet demand.

Key Bargain. Refers to a specific from of wage leadership in which a single pay settlement acts as a point of reference for all subsequent wage claims. The key bargain has been often thought to establish the 'going rate' for ensuring wage rounds.

Keynes Effect. Refers to a change in the demand for commodities because of a change in the general price level. For example, a fall in the general price level will increase the quantity of real money balances and therefore more money will become available for speculative purposes. Because of this the price of bonds will rise and the interest rate fall which in turn will stimulate a rise in investment and an increase in the demand for commodities. Clearly a rise in the general prices level will set in motion an opposite sequence of events. This indirect change in the demand for commodities for investment should be distinguished from the direct effect of a change in the general price level on the demand for commodities for consumption as described by the direct real balance effect. The Keynes effect is depicted by a shift in the LM curve in the ISLM diagram while the direct real balance effect manifests itself via a shift in the IS curve.

Keynesian Economics. A term which is used to describe macroeconomic theories of the level of economic activity using the techniques developed by J. M. Keynes. The methodology of Keynesian economics could be distinguished from neoclassical economics by its concern with aggregate behaviour, especially the income generating effect of total expenditure and the emphasis placed on the investment component in determining the level of activity. The development of Keynesian theory is centered around three related topics:

(1) the stability of a market system and particularly its ability to maintain full employment,

(2) the role of money in such a system and

(3) the long term dynamics of the market economy.

Keynesian Revolution. Appellation for the profound changes in fundamental economic thinking brought about by the challenging contributions of John Maynard Keynes (1883-1946). In 1936 appeared Keynes' most famous work The General Theory is basically an analysis in terms of fundamental economic principles of the cause of unemployment, that is, unemployment over and above 'frictional' unemployment arising from people changing jobs.

Keynesian School. A school of economists which in whole or substantial part supports the following tenets:

(a) Fiscal policy has a greater influence in the economy than monetary policy, i.e., money supply is regarded to have a negligible effect on output and prices —'money does not matter';

(b) an incomes policy is important in helping to achieve an inflation rate limitation;

(c) it is possible to obtain a more stable macroeconomic environment if policy instruments are used in a discretionary manner by the authorities rather than being set according to some simple rules;

(d) exchange rates have been an important policy instrument in achieving a balance-of-payments target;

(e) tax rates (and to a lesser extent government expenditure) may get adjusted so as to keep unemployment at a reasonable level, ensure low inflation, and achieve a balance-of-payments equilibrium.

Key Rates. The term used for the wage rates of those occupations in the internal labour market which act as points of contact with the external market. Associated with each key rate is a job cluster; a set of associated rates for occupations of varying job content and description which are specific to the firm. The wage rates of these occupations have been generally tied to the key rate and move in association with these.

Kinked Demand Curve. It is a demand curve which may be characteristic of firms in certain oligopolistic industries; it occurs when a firm judges that if it cuts its prices, other firms will cut theirs too; but that if it raises its prices, other firms may be content to leave theirs unchanged (in this event a potential loss of market is involved). Thus the demand curve has been relatively inelastic below the going price, and relatively elastic above the going price.

Kitchin Cycle. A notion which was developed by the Joseph Kitchin. According to him the business fluctuations could be divided into two categories; major cycles and minor cycles, the major cycles being aggregates of two or perhaps three minor cycles each minor cycle averaging some 40 months in length. Kitching based his findings on commodity prices, bank clearings, and interest rates in the United States and Great Britain for the period 1890 to 1922. Kitchin did not try a serious theoretical explanation of the observed phenomenon suggesting only rthythmical movements due to psychological causes and variations crops.

Kite. A bill, often called 'accommodation bill' drawn on a person who has received nothing in return. It is an expedient for getting credit for a short period.

Knife Edge. In growth theory refers to an obstacle to steady growth where the warranted rate of growth has been unstable, apart from the further problem of whether or not the warranted rate is equal to the natural rate of growth. The role of expectations about the future level of output has been central to the knife edge problem: if the expected rate of growth of income has been below the warranted rate then entrepreneurs will invest too little, making a fall in aggregate demand and an increase in excess capacity making a further fall in the expected rate of growth of income.

Kondratieff Cycle. Identified by the Russian economists Nikolai D. Kondratieff, the longest cycles or waves found in economic history. An analysis of economic time series for England, France, Germany and the United States, by Kondratieff suggested that there existed a cycle of an average duration of some 54 years. The hypothesis has been subjected to a great deal of criticism; some students have found different patterns when using different techniques, other that Kondratieff's position had been supported by price level series and interest rates but not by production and consumption data.

Krugerrand. A legal coin which was struck by the South African mint in 1967, and minted each year since as part of a public policy to encourage private gold-holding. The coin has been made of 22-carat gold and weighs 33.93 grams.

L

Labour. All human resources which are available to society for use in the process of production.

Labour-Costs Per Unit of Output. Refers to the cost of the labour in real terms which is involved in making each unit output from a factory. High wages associated with high productivity may imply a lower labour cost per unit than low wages associated with low productivity.

Labour Economics. Deals with the study of the nature and determinants of pay and employment. The study emphasizes the role of institutions which are playing a significant role in determining the pattern and speed of adjustment in the labour market. While the traditional tools of micro and macro economics find use in this analysis their limitations give rise to a more discussive treatment of certain topics.

Labour Force. Refers to the proportion of a population that is entering the labour market i.e., employed plus unemployed.

Labour Intensive. A process or technique of production A is considered to be more labour intensive than an equivalent process of technique B if the ratio of labour to capital used has been greater in A than in B.

Labour Intensive Industry. Refers to an industry in which the ratio of labour input to capital input has been higher than the average ratio for industry as a whole. The capital input may be calculated by the depreciation costs of plant and equipment. Examples of labour-intensive industries have been the textile, leather products, furniture industries and service industries.

Labour Market. Concerns the activities of hiring and supplying certain labour to undertake certain jobs, and the process of determining how much shall be paid to whom in performing what tasks.

Labour Power. A term which is used by Karl Marx to describe the commodity which workers sell to capitalists.

Labour-Saving Techniques. Refers to a technological process or production method which has been biased towards mechanization and sparing use of manpower. If manpower has been scarce then these have been ideal processes to implement, and have been more common in industrialized nations than less developed countries.

Labour's Share. The share of wages in the national income. There are two competing theories of labour's share: the marginal productivity theory and the neo-Keynesian theory.

Labour Standard. A term coined by J.R. Hicks to express his particular interpretation of the manner in which wages (and hence prices) were determined.

Labour Supply. Or supply of effort, the total number of hours of work that a population has been willing to supply. It has been a function of:

(a) Size of population;

(b) Proportion of population able and willing to work; and

(c) Number of hours worked by each individual.

Labour Theory of Value. A theory which is employed by the classical economists, e.g., Ricardo and especially Marx, to explain the determination of relative prices on the basis of quantities of labour, immediate and accumulated, embodied in goods.

Labour Turnover. Means the number of workers who leave, or are replaced, in a given period. It is expressed as a percentage of the average number of workers employed during the period.

Laffer Curve. Refers to an illustration of the thesis that there exists some optimal tax rate, shown as t* in the diagram below, which maximizes government tax revenues. The thesis could be expressed in terms of either personal or corporate taxes and it proposes that taxes above the optimal rate discourage production and hence results in lower revenues. These arguments represent an aspect of supply-side economics and the curve has taken its name from its originator, the American economist Arthur Laffer.

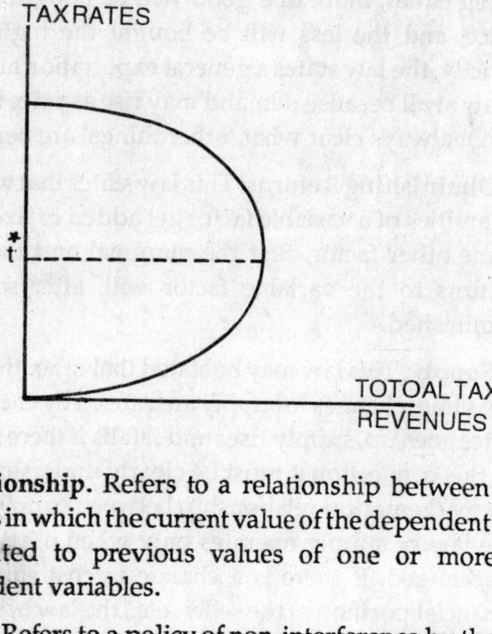

Lagged Relationship. Refers to a relationship between a set of variables in which the current value of the dependent variable gets related to previous values of one or more of the independent variables.

Laissez-Faire. Refers to a policy of non-interference by the State in economic affairs. The underlying philosophy is that man is moved predominantly by self-interest and that there exist certain immutable laws which produce a natural harmony.

Land. In economics this term is used to cover not only that part of the earth's surface not covered by sea, but also all those natural resources like forests, minerals, resources of the sea, soil fertility, etc., which can be used in the process of production.

Land Tax. A tax which is based on the land values or size of land holdings. Its is proposed by some economists as a device for mobilizing any surplus from agriculture and for encouraging productivity growth.

Lausanne School. It is a school of economic thought which is based at the University of Lausanne in Switzerland. It has placed great emphasis on the use of mathematical techniques to show the interdependencies in a market economy.

Law of Demand. The widely accepted view that, other, things being equal, more of a good will be bought the lower is its price, and the less will be bought the higher is its price. Strictly, the law states a general expectation and has been not a law at all because demand may rise as price increases and it is not always clear what 'other things' are being held equal.

Law of Diminishing Returns. This law states that when increasing quantities of a variable factor get added to fixed quantities of some other factor, first the marginal and then the average returns to the variable factor will, after some point, get diminished.

Law of Supply. This law may be stated that other things remaining the same, changes in supply are caused by changes in price. If price goes up, supply rises and it falls if there is a fall in price. In this connection it must be clearly understood that there is no mathematical relationship between supply and price and the law of supply operates only when other things remain unchanged. If there is a change in cost structure, fashion, financial position of the seller, etc., the law of supply may not hold good.

Law of Variable Proportion. The law of variable proportions states that "If one factor of production is fixed while another factor of production (variable) is increased, average and marginal products will rise, reach a maximum and then decline". We can state the law in another way also thus: "As the proportion of one factor (variable) and in a combination of factors (fixed) is increased, the total output will increase at an increasing rate, and after a stage, will increase at a diminishing rate".

Leap-Grogging. A process which is also known as the wage/ wage spiral. It is held to be an independent cause of wage and price inflation by those who espouse cost-push inflation theories.

Learning Curve. A relationship which shows an increase in cumulative average output per man and the cumulative number of units of output produced, usually in some manufacturing industry. For a typical learning curve, see diagram given below:

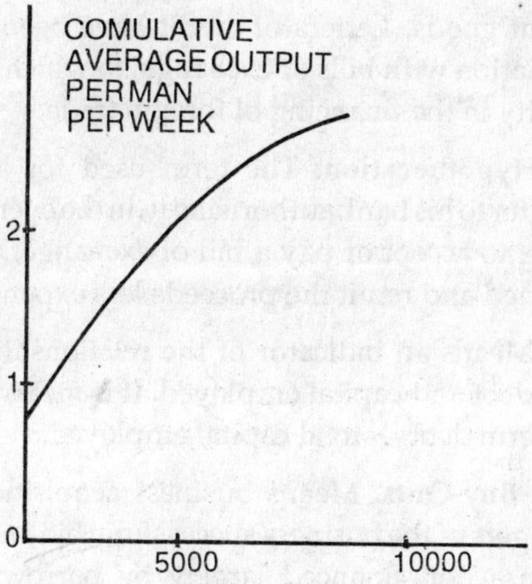

Learning Curve

Lease. The term used for an agreement in which one agent obtains the use of some property owned by another agent for a given period of time in return for an agreed fixed charge which is generally paid in periodic instalments.

Lerner Index. Refers to an indicator of monopoly power which is defined as

$$\frac{\text{Price} - \text{Marginal Cost}}{\text{Price}}$$

If perfect competition exists, price equals marginal cost; therefore the index assumes a value of zero. If price exceeds marginal cost, the Lerner index becomes positive and varies between zero and unity. The closer the index to unity the greater the degree of monopoly power has been said to be possessed by the firm.

Letter of Credit. A document which is issued by a bank on behalf of a customer which guarantees payment by the bank of cheques drawn by the customer, or more commonly today of bills drawn on that customer by parties from whom he has bought goods. Letters of credit have been used largely in association with bills of exchange, to which they give added security in the financing of foreign trade.

Letter of Hypothecation. The term used for a letter from an exporter to his bank authorising it, in the event of the importer failing to accept or pay a bill of exchange, to sell the goods exported and remit the proceeds less expenses.

Leverage. Means an indicator of the relationship between long-term debt and capital employed. It is measured by the ratio, longterm debt ÷ total capital employed.

Leveraged Buy-Outs. Means business acquisition in which the managers of the business successfully bid and take control, in a transaction financed largely by borrowing; the debt is ultimately paid either out of the earnings of the business, or from the sale of its assets.

Liabilities. Refers to any claims, actual or potential, on an individual or institution. The term usually refers to financial liabilities of which the commonest form has been a debt of any kind. Thus, bank deposits, which are bankers' debts, are commonly termed as 'deposit liabilities'.

Lien. Means a claim against property; a bond has been usually secured by a lien against specified property of the company.

Limited Information (L.I.). A term descriptive of a family of econometric estimation techniques which are used in estimating the parameters of simultaneous equations. The distinctive feature of this type of estimator has been that they do not take the entire structure of a simultaneous equation model into account, but merely the form and variables of a subset of those equations.

Limited Liability. It is the restriction of an owner's loss in a business to the extent of the capital that he has invested in it.

Limit Pricing. Means the way in which established firm within an industry is able to set price with the objective of preventing new entry. In the presence of barriers to entry, this can be realised by setting a price just below the minimum long-run average cost of the best placed potential entrant. Such a price level is termed as the maximum entry forestalling price.

Linear Expenditure Systems. In linear expenditure systems the demand functions have been expressed for groups of goods rather than for individual goods. Substitutability within the group has been significant but has been zero between the groups. The demand functions for the groups may then be added to secure a total expenditure function. The implied utility function is additive and has the form:

$$U=U_i+U_j+U_k$$

where i, j and k refer to groups of commodities.

Liquid Assets. Means assets either in the form of money, or which can be quickly converted into money. The liquid assets of a commercial bank have been coin, notes, and balances at the Central Bank of a country; money at call or short notice; and discounted bills.

Liquidation (also known as winding-up). Refers to the process where-by the existence of a company gets terminated, its property having been realized and distributed among its creditors and in the event of a surplus, among its members.

Where the company has been insolvent, the process resembles bankruptcy, but it may also be used in the case of solvent companies as, for instance, in certain types of merger or reconstruction.

Liquidity. The term used the availability of cash, and of assets readily convertible into cash (called liquid assets), to meet immediate obligations; a volume of reserves plus credit facilities, reflected in an ability to meet current financial liabilities in cash.

Liquidity, Preference Theory of Interest. It is a Keynesian theory which attributes the rate of interest to the demand for and supply of money and money substitutes, with demand being determined by liquidity preference and the supply by banking policy. Liquidity preference will be held to vary inversely with the rate of interest, and vice versa.

Liquidity Ratio. Refers to the ratio of the total assets of a bank which are held in the form of cash and liquid assets. The latter may consist in general of money lent out to the discounting banks at call and short notice, and short-term bonds issued by the government and other borrowers.

Liquidity Trap. Refers to a situation in which an increase in the money supply does not cause a fall in the interest elasticity of demand for money becomes infinite.

Liquid Market. Means a market where the selling and buying can be accomplished with ease, due to the presence of a large number of interested buyers and sellers.

Liquid, to be. To hold cash.

Loan. Means an advance of finance by a lender to a borrower. Interest will be normally payable on a loan, and the term to maturity (repayment) can vary from the very short to the very long.

Loanable Funds Theory of Interest. A theory which states that interest rates are determined by the supply of, and the demand for, funds available for lending. The supply of such funds has been determined mainly by: (a) the extent of savings, and (b) the net increase in deposit currency. The demand for such funds is determined mainly by:

(a) the opportunities for new capital formation, and

(b) the desire to increase cash balances. The theory is more in common with the liquidity preference theory of interest.

Locational Interdependence. Means an interrelationship between firms where one firm's decision concerning a choice of location for its plant gets affected by the locational choices of its competitors.

Location Quotient. Refers to a statistical measure of the extent to which a particular economic activity is comparatively over or under-represented in the economy of a region, compared to its representation in the economy as a whole. The location quotient will be calculated as follows:

$$\frac{E_{ir}}{E_{in}}$$

where E_{ir} denotes the percentage of economic activity (usually measured by employment) in region *r* accounted for by activity *i*, and E_{in} denotes the percentage of national economic activity accounted for by activity *i*. This ratio may then be multiplied by 100 and expressed as a percentage.

Location Theory. Refers to that body of economic theory which analyses the forces which determine the location of economic activity, and seeks to explain and predict the spatial pattern of the location of economic agents.

Lockin-ing Effect. Refers to the effect by which a holder of an asset is deterred from selling it due to a fall in its market value and the consequent loss that would be incurred. Typically, it may be affecting holders of gilt-edged or other fixed-interest securities when a marked rise in interest rates causes a fall in the market prices of these stocks.

Lockout. Means the closure of the workplace by the employer in an attempt to compel the employees to accede to the terms of employment which are desired by management.

Long Cycle Theory. A prolonged period of relatively prosperous times followed by a period of hard times of similar duration, often called the Kondratieff cycle. It extends much beyond the periodicity of the trade cycle. A full cycle being considered of about 50 years in length. Some economists regarded that price and interest rate movements alone were involved, with the Kondratieff a price and not an output phenomenon. Long cycles may be regarded as long-run cumulative movements, one view is that they are caused by wars, related to high government expenditures on armaments during prosperous times. Evidence on long cycles has cycles has been inconclusive.

Long-Haul Economies. Refers to the tendency for transport costs to rise less than in proportion to distance travelled. Thus where long-haul economies have been present the average cost per unit distance travelled has been a decreasing function of distance. These economies arise principally because any mode of transport will involve certain costs which are fixed and uninfluenced by the distance of the journey.

Long Rate. The rate of interest, or rather set of interest rates, obtainable on long-dated securities, and therefore payable on new long-term borrowings.

Long-Run. A time period which relates to the process production during which there is time to vary all factors of production, but not sufficient time to change the basic technological processes big used. The term was introduced originally by Alfred Marshall. In the very long run it has been possible totally to change the type of technology being used.

Long-Run Average Cost. In the long-run all cost tend to be variable costs. The long-run average cost curve will therefore relate to the minimum cost sections of a series of overlapping short-run cost curves, as shown in the diagram. Thus it has been possible to use either plant 1 or plant 2 to produce an output between X1 and X2. Clearly, for X1, it would be more sensible to use plant 1 than plant 2 because the average cost of producing X1 is lower. At X2, however, it is better to use plant 2. Each of the overlapping sections of the short-run average cost curves may therefore be 'deleted', leaving a cost curve which has been seen to be an 'envelope' of the points on the short-run average cost curves which correspond to the lowest possible short-run costs for a given level of output. The 'bumpy' shape of the curve shown has been due to indivisibilities—i.e., it is not possible to change the size of the factory or plant by very small discrete amounts. If, however, such small changes could be made, the SRAC curves would overlap more closely until, in the case of perfect divisibility a perfectly 'smooth' long-run average cost curve would result. Note that the 'loci of the short-run cost' points may get lower and lower because of economies of scale. In the diagram shown, the curve is seen to rise eventually due to the presence of diseconomies of scale. Note that there exists no 'law' which dictates the shape of the long-run average cost curve and it has been entirely a matter of empirical observation as to whether the final curve is one reflecting decreasing costs (increasing returns), constant costs (constant returns) or increasing costs (decreasing returns).

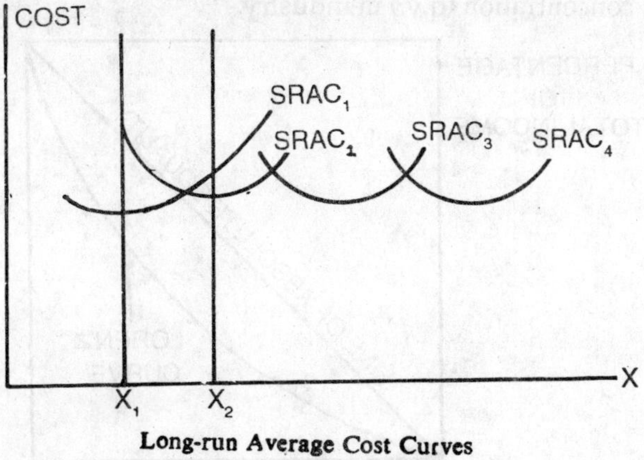

Long-run Average Cost Curves

Long-Run Consumption Function. Refers to the functional relationship between consumption and income over periods of over 50 years. In these studies 10-year averages of income and consumption are regarded to remove the effects of the business cycle. These studies found:

1. Marginal propensity to consume < 1;
2. Average propensity to consume < 1;
3. Marginal propensity to consume = average propensity to consume.

These findings are able to contradict Keynes' absolute income hypothesis on the shape of the consumption function and suggest a straight line function from the origin, i.e., C=bY, where C denotes consumption, Y denotes income and b denotes a constant.

Long-Run Marginal Cost. Means the extra cost of producing an extra unit of output in the long run.

Lorenz Curve. In measuring the income distribution of a community, a curve showing what percentage of families receive what percentage of the community's family income; the curve indicates the degree of inequality in income distribution. The Lorenz curve has other uses e.g., the measurement of concentration (q.v.) in industry.

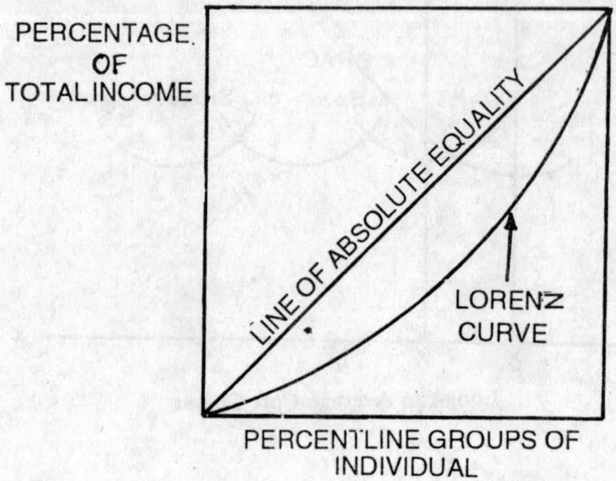

Loss Leader. A good sold by a retailer below normal price, not for the purpose of making a profit on the sale of the good, but for the purpose of attracting customers likely to purchase other goods at his shop.

Loss Leader Pricing. Refers to the practice of diversified firms who offer some portion of their product range at prices below cost, in the belief that this will encourage sales of other higher profit margin products. It is common amongst retailers, who use 'loss leaders' to attract customers, who then may buy high profit margin goods as a matter of convenience or impulse.

Loss-Offsetting Provisions. Means the arrangement whereby losses from a reject can be offset against income from other sources.

Luxury. Not a widely used in modern economics. However, if it is used, it is taken to refer to a good with an income elasticity of demand greater than unity such that, as income rises, the good accounts for an increasing proportion or the consumer's income. It is also known as an 'elitist' good.

Luxury Taxes. Raising taxes for government funds can be very problematic in less developed countries; many people are self-employed or paid in kind and cannot be made liable for income tax.

M

MI-B. A United States money supply concept which consists of currency plus demand deposits; currency consists of notes and coin in circulation, while demand deposits are deposits against which cheques can be writtenin commercial banks and thrift institutions.

Macro-Dynamics. Refers to an area of economic study which examines the determinants of the rate of increase (or decrease) of the main categories of demand for capital goods, consumer goods, exports, and so on.

Macro-Distribution. Means distribution of national income into such broad aggregates as wages, rent, interest and profits.

Macro-Economic Policy. Public policy which is concerned with the ways in which certain policy instruments such as government expenditure, the money supply, and rates of interest, may be used for achieving certain desirable targets like full employment, balance-of-payments equilibrium, and a low rate of inflation.

Macro-Economics. A branch of economics which is concerned with the analysis of the economy in the large, i.e. with such large aggregates as the volume of employment, saving and investment, the national income.

Malleable Capital. It is an assumption about the nature of physical capital which is much used in neoclassical economics. It implies that the materials incorporated into a particular machine may be instantly and costlessly changed into a different machine.

Malthusian Theory of Population. A theory of population which was developed by Thomas Malthus (1766-1834) and published in An Essay on the Principle of Population 1978. The essence of the theory may be given as follws:

(a) that population would soon out-strip the means of feeding it, if it were not kept down by vice, misery or self-restraint;

(b) that in a state of society where self-restraint does not act at all, or only acts so little that we need not think of it, population will augment until the poorest class of the community have only just enough to support life;

(c) that in a community where self-restraint acts effectually, each class of the community will augment until it reaches the point at which it begins to exercise that restraint.

Population according to Malthus tended to increase in a geometrical progression, whereas the means of subsistence increased in only arithmetical progression.

Management. Refers to those staff within the firm who are able to exert control over its activities on behalf of owners. Of interest to economists has been the influence which the pursuit by management of their objectives can have on firm behaviour.

Management Science. In the context of the study of firms, this discipline refers to scientific principles to aid pursuit of operational efficiency with regard to business objectives.

Manager-Controlled Firm. A company which is having no individual shareholder or group of shareholders owning a sufficiently high proportion of the voting stock to exert control over company policy. The execution and design of policy have been thereby placed in the hands of the company's managers.

Managerial Capitalism. Refers to the organization of the economy into large corporations having the power over resources located within a definable managerial class separated from property owning calss and largely independent of their control. It is different from corporate capitalism in that the managerial class pursues goals which may be independent of those of workers, the state and society.

Managerial Discretion. The ability of a corporation's managers to pursue objectives which they themselves deem beneficial. The extent to which this discretionary behaviour can get sustained will be determined by how competitive product and capital markets are.

Managerial Revolution. A label which is associated with the Galbraithian idea that economic power has passed from capital to the owners of technical expertise, i.e., the marginal class. It is due to the alleged inelastic supply of managers relative to that of capital.

Managing Director. A person who is appointed as a director of a limited company. He takes chief responsibility for the day to-day running of the company's activities. In general managing directors are having a shareholding within the company.

Manoilescu Argument. A version which was developed by the economist of that name, of the infant industry argument and is based on the empirical observation that the average wage in the manufacturing sector in an underdeveloped country sexceeds that in the agricultural sector though labour productivity may be similar. The manufacturing industry has been at a disadvantage vis-a-vis imports and the argument has been that it should be compensated by a tariff on manufactured goods.

Manpower. In ordinary language, manpower means the working population of a country. In economics, manpower means the organisation of work force for its utilization in different sectors of the economy.

Manpower Policy. There are two main forms of manpower policy. The first accepts the existing characteristics of supply and demand and aims for better 'matches' between workers and jobs by improving placement efforts and by counselling workers looking for jobs and employers looking for workers. Programmes of this kind may also be able to include schemes for increasing the mobility of workers. The second form tries to influence the pattern of the supply of labour by upgrading skills and abilities. There also exists a third form, which tries to influence the composition of demand by establishing measures to increase the number of employment opportunities, especially by opening up good jobs for disadvantaged workers.

Manual Workers. Employees engaged in physical work and who are paid a wage. They are frequently used interchangeably with blue-collar workers. The opposite of non-manual workers.

Margin. In economics, 'at the margin' implies at the point where the last unit has been produced or consumed.

Marginal Analysis. A tool of analysis which is found in all branches of economic theory. It is concerned with the relationships between marginal changes in related economic variables; marginal changes being very small increments or decrements in the total quantity of a variable. The search for optimum values, maximand and minimands, are involving the definition and analysis of marginal concepts.

Marginal Cost. Means the extra cost of producting an extra unit of output. Algebraically it may be written as follows:

$$MC = \frac{\Delta C}{\Delta X}$$

where Δ implies 'a small change in', C is total cost and X is output. In the short run the marginal cost curve slopes upwards due to the operation of the law of diminishing returns. In the long run marginal costs may rise, fall or stay constant depending on the presence of economies or diseconomies of scale.

Marginal Cost Pricing. Refers to a concept in which selling prices have been brought into equality with the marginal costs of production, through variations in output. It is a situation which arises automatically under equilibrium conditions with perfect competition and which some economists have thought could well be introduced as a general pricing policy, to achieve optimum public benefits.

Marginal Costs, Long-Run. Refer to the costs of supplying on a continuous basis those services and products which can be costed separately; they are including provision for replacement of fixed assets needed for the continued provision of services, together with a satisfactory rate return on capital employed.

Marginal Costs, Short-Run. Refer to the increase in total costs which results from an increase in production when not all the inputs used by the form can be varied; the additional costs of increasing output within existing capacity. In electricity generation, the main element of cost in short-run marginal costs has been fuel.

Marginal Damage Cost. Means the extra cost of damage done, generally by pollution, from an extra unit of the nuisance-creating activity.

Marginal Disutility. Means the extra disutility which is resulting from a small change in some variable.

Marginal Efficiency Capital. Means the earning power of the last increment of capital invested. It is also as defined by Keynes in his General Theory of Employment, Interest and Money (1936), 'the relation between the prospective yield of one more unit of a type of capital and the cost of producting the unit.

Marginal Efficiency of Capital. Means that unique rate of discount which would be able to make the present value of the expected net returns from a capital asset just equal to its supply price when there is no rise in the supply price of the asset.

Marginal Efficiency of Capital Schedule. Refers to the schedule which details the long-run equilibrium relationship between the desired capital stock and the interest rate. At all points along this schedule the marginal efficiency of capital will be just equal to the interest rate.

Marginal Efficiency of Investment. It is also known as the internal rate of return. It refers to that rate of discount which would make the present value of the expected net returns from the capital asset just equal to its supply price wheter it is recgnized that this price will be rising in the short-run.

Marginal Efficiency of Investment Schedule. Refers to the demand curve for investment. Also, refers to the schedule detailing the relationship between the marginal efficiency of investment and the interest rate.

Marginal Firm. A firm which has been the last to enter, or the first to leave, a particular line of production. It is not necessarily the least efficient firm and may, indeed, be the most efficient.

Marginal Land. Means the land which is the last to be brought into, or the first to be taken out of, a particular line of production. This will not necessarily be land which is just worth cultivating.

Marginal Producer. Means a prducer who would be just induced to produce a certain commodity at the prevailing level of profits being obtained from it, but if profits fell slightly would withdraw from production.

Marginal Product. Refers to the amount added to the total product by the addition of one more unit of capital-and-labour.

Marginal Productivity Doctrine. A hypothesis which states that an employer who seeks to maximize his profits will get guided by the law of diminishing marginal productivity while successive units of labour hired yield successively diminishing returns to output.

Marginal Propensity to Consume. Means the change in consumption because of an additional unit of income. It can be put as follows.

$$MPC = \frac{\Delta C}{\Delta Y}$$

where C denotes consumption, Y income and Δ 'small change in'. It may be stated as a propensity to consume out of either national income or disposable income.

Marginal Propensity to Import. Refers to the change in imports because of a unit change in income.

Marginal Propensity to Save. Refers to the change in savings because of an additional unit of income.

Marginal Propensity to Tax. Refers to the change in tax revenues because of a unit change in income. Tax considers to be one of the major withdrawals from the circular flow of income, and thus the marginal propensity to tax has been one of the major constituents of the marginal propensity to withdraw.

Marginal Propensity to Withdraw. Refers to the change in withdrawals (W) because of one additional unit of income (Y) which may be written as follows:

$$MPW = \frac{\Delta W}{\Delta Y}$$

Marginal Rate of Substitution. In consumer demand theory it refers to the amount of one good, say Y, which is needed to compensate the consumer for giving up an amount of another good, say X, such that the consumer possesses the same level of welfare (utility) as before. In indifference curve analysis it is in fact the slope of the indifference curve which, in turn, is equal to the ratio of the marginal utilities (MU) of the two goods in question, i.e.

$$MRS_{x.y} = \frac{\Delta MUx}{\Delta\, MUy}$$

Marginal Rate of Tax. Refers to the rate of tax on an incremental unit of income but is also applicable to increments of expenditure, wealth or gifts. The higher the marginal rate of tax the greater would be the substitution effect likely to be.

Marginal Revenue. Means the change in total revenue which is resulting from varying the output sold by one unit, it equals the total revenue from N units minus the total revenue from N-1 units.

Marginal Revenue Product. The marginal physical product multiplied by the marginal revenue from the sale of the extra unit of output from the employment of the extra unit of input.

'Marginal' Revolution. A description which is accorded to the contributions of William Stanley Jevons (1835-1842), Cart Menger (1840-1821) and Leon Walras (1834-1910), who solved the apparent conflict between value and utility by considering that it was the specific utility depending on the last available or marginal unit of a commodity and not the genetic utility which determined its value. Jevons did not use the adjective 'margin', using the term 'final utility' instead. He published his Theory of Political Economy, embodying this new theory, in 1871.

Marginal Utility. Refers to the increase or decrease in the total utility of consumption of a good which is resulted from increasing or decreasing the quantity of the good consumed by one unit. A good may be having a very low marginal utility, but a very high total utility e.g., water.

Marginal Utility, Law of Diminishing. A proposition which states that the marginal utility of a commodity to anyone, other things being equal, diminishes after some point with every increase in his supply of it. Alfred Marshall stressed an implicit condition in this law -- that we do not consider time to be allowed for any alteration in the character or tastes of the person concerned.

Marginal Utility of Money. Refers to the rate at which an individual's utility gets increased as his personal budget (income) gets expanded by one unit.

Market. Refer to an area, however large or small, where buyers and sellers come in sufficiently close contact with each other to ensure that the price of a commodity tends to be the same in all parts of the market, allowance being made for transportation costs, tariff barriers, and other obstacles.

Market Clearing. Refers to a situation in which the forces of supply and demand have been so in balance that all the goods have been sold, i.e., the market has cleared.

Market Demand Curve. Means the aggregation of a set of individual demand curves for a good.

Market Economy. Means as economy in which the crucial economic decisions and choices have been made in a decentralised manner by numerous private individuals and firms operating through a free price-and-market machanism. Equilibrium prices and quantities have been determined in a market economy through the laws of supply and demand.

Market Failure. Means the inability of a system of private markets to offer certain goods either at all or at the most desirable or 'optimal' level.

Market Forces. Refer to pressures which are produced by the free play of market supply and demand and induce adjustment in prices and or quantities traded.

Market of Touched Order. A market order executed when a transaction takes place at, or better than a specified price after the order has been transmitted. Unlike a stop order used to limit losses the market if touched order is kept above the existing market if a sell, and below the market if a buy.

Marketing. A term used to cover those activities of firms which are associated with the sales and distribution of products.

Market Orientation. Refers to a tendency for producers to locate their factories near the markets in which the products will be sold rather than (say) near a raw material source.

Market Performance. Refers to the performance of a firm or industry in a market measured against specified criteria. These criteria or goals may be including: (a) the efficient employment of scarce factors of production to yield the greatest possible real income; (b) the full employment of the factors of production; (c) growth and progressiveness in enlarging and improving the flow of gooods and services; and (d) equity in the distribution of income.

Market Power. Refers to the ability of a single or group of buyer (s) or seller (s) to influence the price of the product or service in which it is trading. A perfectly competitive market in equilibrium, will ensure the complete absence of market power.

Market Price. Means the price what is determined by the equilibrium between demand and supply in a market period or very short run. The market period refers to a period in which the maximum that can be supplied is limited by the existing stock. In case of perishable commodities like vegetables, fish, eggs, etc., this market period may be a day or two, because in their case, the supply gets limited by the quantity available at a point of time. Since it must be sold away on the same day, price equilibrium has been flexible in such cases.

Market Research. Refers to a management aid which is involving the systematic collecting, recording and analysing of data about problems relating to the marketing of goods and services.

Market Share. Refers to the proportion of total market sales accounted for by one firm.

Market Structure. Refers to the economically significant features of a market which affect the behaviour of firms in the industry supplying that market. The main elements of market structure have been : (a) concentration and concentration ratio; (b) product differentiation; (c) barriers to the entry of new firms; (d) growth rate of market demand; (e) price elasticity of market demand; (f) ratio of fixed to variable costs in the short run.

Mark-Up. Refers to that portion of price which the seller adds onto average variable costs so as to cover overheads and yield a net profit margin.

Marshallian Demand Curve. The term refers to the most widely used demand curve in which the responsiveness of quantity demanded to price incorporates both the income effect and the subsitution effect. It is in contrast to the compensated demand curve where income effects have been netted out.

Marshallism Economics. The neo-classical economics which is associated with Alfred Marshall (1842-1924) and his followers.

The more striking contributions to economic science made in his Principles of Economics were:

(a) The clarification of the respective roles played by demand and by costs of production in the determination of value.

(b) The general theory of economic equilibrium in which all the elements of the economic world are kept in their places by mutual counterpoise and interaction, a theory, strengthened by two subsidiary concepts--the 'margin and 'substitution';

(c) The explicit introduction of the element of time as a factor in ecnomic analysis, with the concepts of the 'short' and 'long' period;

(d) The distinction between, 'external' and 'internal' economies;

(e) The doctrine of 'normal profit' assisted by the concepts of 'quasi-rent' and the representative firm'.

(f) The concept of consumer's surplus;

(g) The introduction of the idea of elasticity;

(h) Proof that laissez-faire regarded as a principle of maximum social advantage breaks down in certain conditions theoretically and not merely practically; and

(i) An examination of the effects of monopoly.

Marshall's successor was A. C. Pigou (1877-1959).

Marshall Lerner Condition. A devaluation of the currency may under certain conditions improve the balance of payments. The Marshall-Lerner conditioons has been one such condition.

Marshall-Lerner Criterion. In its simplest form it refers to a rule which states that the price elasticities of demand for imports and exports must sum to greater than unity for an improvement to be effected in the balance of trade through a change in country's exchange rate.

Marxist Economics. Means a school of economic thought which seeks to analyse the social and economic development of the capitalist economic system. Modern Marxist economists have been a diverse group ranging from the more dogmatic followers of the works of Karl Marx to those sympathetic but critical, economists, who are prepared to modify the tenets of orthodox Marxism.

Marxist Socialism. A creed developed by Karl Marx (1818-1883) which had its origin in the conditions created by the Industrial Revolution.

Marx tried to show that the capitalist system could not by its very nature survive that it would in the course of time get replaced by socialism, and that the class which would effect the revolution would be the new industrial working-class or 'proletariat'.

Materials Balance Principle. In environmental economics, it refers to the principle whereby the amount of waste products discarded to the environment is held to be approximately equal to the withdrawal of resources to generate production of goods.

Material Forces of Production. The term which is used by Marx to define the real economic foundation of any society. The forces of production have been the factories equipment, tools, production skills, scientific knowledge, techniques of production, education of the labour force etc., and they differ according to the state of development attained in any society.

These forces of production have been the major determinants of the social relations of production.

Mathematical Economics. Means the application of the techniques of mathematical analysis to economic variables, with the object of discovering relationships between those variables.

Maturity. Means the date on which a loan or bond or debenture becomes due and is to be paid off i.e., the capital refunded.

Means-Tested Benefits. Benefits that may only be paid if the claimant's income has been less than a certain value.

Mercantilism. Refers to the economic philosophy of merchants and statesmen during the sixteenth and seventeenth centuries. It relied upon a strong state and the extensive regulation of economic activitiy. Bullion or treasure was seen as the key to the wealth of the state, so that foreign trade was regulated to obtain a surplus of eports over imports and an inflow of specie by such means as Navigation Acts (concerning the carriage of goods at sea), confining the trade of colonies to the mother country, subsidizing exports and taxing imported manufactured goods.

Merchant Banks. Denote one of a group of institutions that carry on a very varied range of financial or finance-related activities.

Merchanting. A type of trade which involves the buying of goods in one overseas country and selling them in another.

Merger. Means a union of two or more firms in a transaction by which one absorbs the other (s), or a new firm gets created utilising the assets of the absorbed firms.

Methodology. A term which is often very loosely used in economics to describe the way in which economists take place in their analysis of a problem. It is often also used to describe the set of problems which a group of economists are prepared to analyse.

Metzler Case. Refers to the situation in tariff theory which is analysed by the economist of the name, where the imposition of a tariff on an import improves the terms of trade to such an extent that not only the external terms of trade improve but even the domestic terms of trade inclusive of tariff.

Micro-Dynamics. An area of economic study which examines the forces governing the rates of increase (or of decrease) of demand for particular commodities, or those governing the rates of increase or decrease in the prospects of particular firms or industries.

Micro-Economics. Or economics 'in the small'; a branch of economics which deals with the analysis of the behaviour of individual consumers and producers, particularly with the optimising behaviour of individual units such as households and firms.

Minimum Wage Legislation. Protective legislation which is to establish minimum wages for workers in certain industries. The need for such legislation has usually arisen because the trade unions in the industries concerned have been either non-existent or too weak to negotiate wage rates for their members.

Mixed Market Economy. Refers to a system which combines competitive private enterprise with some degree of central control.

Modern Sectors. It is another name for the industrial sector, or sometimes the government sector, which has been often used with reference to less developed countries where the legacy from the colonial era was the sector comprising plantations, mines, oil fields and refineries and now includes other capital-intensive industry sponsored by governments as well as multinational corporations. Wage levels have been often high although there occurs widespread unemployment.

Monetarism. Refers to a school of economic thought which argues that distrubances within the monetary sector are the principal cause of instability in the economy. The term 'monetarism' was introduced by Karl Brunner in 1968.

Monetary Control. Refers to the systematic action adopted by governments to regulate the volume and terms of monetary intermediation.

Monetary Policy. Refers to that part of economic policy that regulates the level of money or liquidity in an economy with a view to achieve some desired policy objective, such as the control of inflation, improvement in the balance of payments, a certain level of employment or growth in the Gross National Product. It contrasts with more direct measures of control like taxation, etc.

Monetary Theory. This terms is used to refer to the branch of macro economics which studies money in all its aspects.

Money. The term used for anything which is widely accepted in exchange for goods, or in settling debts, not for itself but because it can be similarly passed on, has the character of money because it serve the primary function of money, i.e., means of payment.

Money Market. Money market can be defined as comprising the financial institutions that deal in short-term securities and loans, gold and foreign exchange. Money has a 'time' value and so the use of it is bought and sold against payment of interest. Short-term money is bought and sold in the money market, and long-term money on the capital market.

The Reserve Bank occupies a central strategic position in the money market. It is the key constituent of the money market as the residual source of supply of funds and it is this virtue which invests the Bank's operations with significance.

Money Supply. A supply of purchasing power comprising several streams.

Money, The Demand for. The demand for a commodity which performs the role of both a medium of exchange and a store of value.

Money Transmission. All the ways by which the ownership of money may be transferred from one person to another in the course of making payments.

Monoculture. Refers to the practice of cultivating only one type of crop in any area which occurred before the agrarian revolution and is still prevalent in tropical areas.

Monopolistic Competition. Refers to a market situation in which competition exists between each of two or more (perhaps numerous) sellers whose products are close, but not perfect substitutes for one another. Products have to be differentiated by means of distinctive brand names, variations in preparation and presentation, and by skilful advertising. Monopolistic competition is descriptive of imperfect competition in general, and includes oligopoly.

Monopoly. A market structure having a single seller of a commodity or service dealing with a large number of buyers; the seller has complete control over the quantities of goods offered for sale and the price at which the goods are sold; further, the goods have no close substitutes and entry to the industry may present for midable obstacles. The monopolist tries to maximise profits, which may involve higher prices and more limited supplies than a competitive or oligopolistic situation would permit.

Monopoly Power. It is the ability of a firm or group of firms to influence the market price of the commodity or service it sells.

Monopsony. A single buyer in the market; a buyer's monopoly.

Monte Carlo Methods. Refers to a technique for discovering the small sample properties of econometric estimators. A hypothetical economic model with known parameters has been used to generate artificial data having known characteristics, and the estimator has been used to estimate the parameter of the model. By comparing these estimates with the actual parameter values information about the performance of an estimator under specific conditions can get gained.

Moonlighting. Refers to the practice of having a second full or partime job.

Mortgage. Refers to the conveyance of property by a debtor (mortgagor) to a creditor mortgagee) as security for a debt, with a condition that the property will have to be reconveyed on payment of the debt.

Mortgage Loans. Refer to loans for which specific assets in land and buildings are used as security.

Most Favoured Nation Clause. Refers to a clause in an international trade agreement which states that contracting parties to the agreement are bound to grant to each other treatment as favourable as they extend to any other country regarding the application of import and export duties and other trade regulations.

Multicollinearity. Refers to an econometric problem in which two or more of the explanatory variables in a regression analysis have been highly correlated with each other.

Multilateral Aid. Aid in money or kind given by one group of countries collectively or through an international agency to another group of countries.

Multilateralism. International trade and exchange between more than two countries without discrimination between those involved, in contrast to bilateralism.

Multilateral Trade. Refers to trade among several countries, whose exports and imports have been not in balance between pairs of countries, though countries will tend to be in balance with regard to their total foreign payments and total foreign receipts. Such trade usually conforms to comparative advantage, with countries which are buying in the cheapest market and selling in the dearest.

Multinational Corporation. Means a corporation or company which is operating in a number of countries with production or service facilities outside the country of its origin; the principal decisions of the company are taken in a global context. Also known as international companies.

Multiplier. A ratio which indicates the effect on total employment or on total income of a specified amount of a real capital investment.

Multiplier-Accelerator Interaction. An approach to the explanation of fluctuations in the level of economic activity--the trade cycle--which rests on interactions between the multiplier and the accelerator. The basic analysis combining the Keynesian consumption function and the accelerator principle to produce a self-generating cyclical mechanism had been provided by Samuelson.

Multiproduct Firm. Refers to an enterprise which combines factors of production to produce a range of products. With such firms the concepts of a physical volume of total output and unique price have been less applicable.

Multisector Growth Model. A model which is used in growth theory. It allows for many types of good. It is an extension of the problems considered in general equilibrium continued into growth theory. Considerable mathematical competence is needed to understand such models fully. A two sector growth model may be regarded as the first step from the one sector growth model to the multisector case.

Mulivariate Analysis. An analysis (normally of a statistical nature) which involves more than two variables.

Mutually Exclusive Projects. A situation where two or more projects cannot all be executed because they all need an input which can only be utilized on one project.

MV = PT. The equation of exchange of the quantity theory of money.

N

National Accounts. Means the compilation of accounts to derive estimates of the national income.

National Bargaining. Refers to the collective bargaining between employees and employers representatives to establish pay and conditions of work in a single industry or industry group throughout the country. Most frequently such negotiations involve a number of different employers and trade unions but occasionally only a single employer or employer's representative is involved. If a single employer is involved, this form of bargaining can be equivalent to company bargaining.

National Capital. Comprises of fixed and circulating capital used in the process of production plus the consummer's durables and other goods lying for the use of consumers or households.

National Debt. Refers to the total of outstanding debt obligations of central government and, among other distinctions. It is divided into marketable debt, i.e., securities traded on markets like the stock exchange or the discount market; and non-marketable debt, e.g., national savings certificates. The term may be used to mean 'public sector debt" that is to include the obligations of other public bodies that borrow, e.g., local authorities and nationalized industries.

National Economic Goals. Generally refer to a high and stable level of employment, a satisfactory growth rate, reasonable price stability, and equilibrium in the international balance of payments.

National Income. Refers to a measure of the money value of the goods and services becoming available to the nation from economic activity. There are three approaches to measuring this; first, as a sum of the incomes derived from economic activity, these broadly divide into incomes from profits and incomes from employment; second, as the sum of expenditures with the main distinction being between expenditures on consumption and expenditure which add to the capital stock (investment); finally, as the sum of the products of the various industries of the nation.

Nationalisation. State ownership and control of any of the means of production, distribution or exchange.

Nationalized Industry. Refers to a industry which produces output for sale to consumers and other producers by way of markets but which has been solely owned by and under the control of the government.

National Wealth. Comprises of national capital and land with all the productive resources given by nature and existing in their natural state. In short, wealth includes all reproducible and irreproducible resources. Part of national wealth has been the gift of nature which is non-renewable or irreproducible and the other part is man-made which is renewable or reproducible. In brief, national wealth comprises of all those things which belong to the society as a whole such as machines, rivers, land mines, minerals, metals, oils and gas, forests etc.

Natural Economy. Natural economy of a country comprises of its natural resources like land, climate, forests, mountains, rivers, mines etc. These include the basic facilities which help the manpower to develop the economy for its utlization with the use of science, technology and management techniques.

Natural Increase. Refers to that part of increase in the economic resources of a country which are caused by improvement in its natural resources. For example, more rainfall may cause better agricultural crops.

Natural Law. The term used for a set of rules which have been imposed by nature on man are consequently immutable. The doctrine of natural law associated with Scholars like St. Thomas Aquinas and the Physiocrats who equated natural laws to that set of rules which conform to social necessity.

Natural Monopoly. Refers to that monopoly which a country or a part of it has specially as a gift of nature. For example, gold mines at Kolar fields in Karnataka, tea gardens in Assam, etc.

Natural Price. Refers to a term which is used by Adam Smith to describe the value of a commodity around which market prices fluctuate. In essence the natural price has been the long-run equilibrium price of a commodity and is dependent upon the costs of production.

Natural Rate of Growth. Refers to the rate of growth of the effective labour force in the Harrod-Domar growth model. With a fixed coefficients production function the natural rate has been the maximum sustainable rate of growth of real income. The natural rate (GN) has been composed of the rate of growth of population (n) plus labour-augmenting technical progress (λ) (also known as Harrod-neutral technical progress). Thus

$$G_N = n + \lambda$$

Natural Rate of Unemployment. Refers to a level of unemployment in a country regarded 'normal' as it embraces those changing jobs including seasonal workers and permits a certain amount of restructuring of industries.

Natural Selection Hypothesis. Refers to the argument that competitive product or capital markets ensure profit maximizing behaviour on behalf of firms. Under such conditions, those firms who fail to maximize profits will not be able to survive.

Nearby Month. Refers to the nearest active trading month of a financial or commodity futures market.

Near Money. Assets which are readily convertible into money e.g., deposit accounts, deposits with savings banks and building societies, and certain short-term government securities.

Necessity. Refers to a good with an income elasticity of demand of less than unity. That is, a smaller and smaller proportion of income will be spent on the good as income rise.

Negative Gearing Refers to a situation which arises when, for example, the interest payments due on the borrowing for an investment exceed the net revenue from the investment.

Negative Income Tax. Means a government payment to individuals whose income falls below prescribed levels; the opposite of an income tax.

Negative Real Growth. Refers to a contraction in the value of economic activity, taking inflation into account.

Negative Real Interest Rate. Refers to an interest rate which is less than the rate of inflation e.g., when money is lent at a return of say 7 per cent annum while money is losing value at the rate of 15 per cent per annum. Despite the interest earned the lender is worse off in real terms at the end of each year than at the beginning.

Negotiable Instrument. A claim, the title to which passes by delivery. Examples of such claims include bills of exchange, cheques promissory notes, share warrants dividend warrants, and debentures payable to bearer. Transfer has been by delivery only. A bill of exchange payable to a certain person 'only' has been not a negotiable instrument. Neither is a cheque with 'not negotiable' written on it. Bills of lading, dock warrants, share certificates and postal orders have been not negotiable. A creditor is not bound to take a negotiable instrument in payment of a debt; he may insist on payment in legal tender.

Neo-Classical Economics. Refers to a body of economic theory which uses the general approach methods and techniques of of the original nineteenth century marginalist economists. The term neo-classical derives from the view that the originator of the so-colled 'marginalist revolution' had been extending and improving on the basic foundations of the classical economists such as D. Ricardo and J.S.Mill. The founders of the neo-classical system. J.M. Clark, F.Y. Edgeworth, I, Fisher, A. Marshall, V. Pareto, L. Walras and K. Wicksell used marginal analysis (the concept of marginal utility and marginal productivity) to analyse the pricing of goods, services and factors of production in competitive markets. They emphasized that the market prices of goods and factors had been related to their scarcity. In particular they studied the possibility of a set of market prices which ensured the equality of supply and demand in all markets. The idea of a perfectly competitive economy in equilibrium, which might be attributed especially to Walras, has been central to the neo-classical scheme.

Neo-Classical Equilibrium. A concept of neo-classical economics in which the equilibrium between production and purchasing power got established at a level where all willing and useful workers had been employed.

Neo-Classical Growth Theory. A general term which refers to the models of economic growth developed in a neo-classical frame-work, where the emphasis has been placed on the case of substitution between capital and labour in the production function to ensure steady-state growth, so that the problem of instability found in the Harrod-Domar Growth Model because of the assumed fixed capital to labour coefficients is avoided.

This approach is also to be distinguished from Vintage Growth Models, which regard that new technology can only be incorporated in new machines neo-classical models typically assume that technical progress is exogenous ("manna from heaven") and that technical advances can be incorporated in exiting, as well as new, machines. Neo-classical growth models are able to identify the sources of growth as being population growth and technical progress with capital accumulation simply determining the capital to labour ratio in the steady state.

Neo-Classical Model. Refers to a view of the economy held in whole or substantial part by the neo-classical economists; the essentials of the system appeared to be as follows. Individuals are using income in the main derived from their own productive activities in the purchase of various goods and services available in the market their tendency has been to so distribute their income that the satisfaction derived from the last unit of expenditure for any particular purposes has been equal to that derived from expenditure for any other purpose.

At this point satisfaction (and occasionally, happiness) gets maximised. The patterns of expenditure convey important messages to producers.

Neo-Classical Synthesis. Refers to the argument that the existence of an unemployment equilibrium had to be attributed to the Keynesian assumption of rigid money wages. It is a synthesis of the Keynesian integration of the real and monetary sectors of the economy, to show the simultaneous determination of money income and the interest rate, and the classical views that the tendency to full-employment equilibrium might only be thwarted by rigidities in the system.

Neo-Imperialism. According to socialist and Marxist writings it refers to the control of the economies of less developed countries by giant corporation with headquarters in developed capitalist countries.

Imperialism in its orginal form usually means the political control of the satellite economy by the government of the metropolitan country as well as the commercial and industrial penetration of the satellite economy by metropolitan economic interests.

Neo-Orthodoxy. The name assigned to the opponents of the new-orthodoxy in the debate over the control of the money supply. According to the neo-orthodoxy view led by Newlyn in the 1960s, the control of the cash base was both necessary and sufficient for the control of the level of bank deposits. This contrasts with the new-orthodoxy view that the liquid assets ratio had been the variable to be controlled, and bankcash ratio control would not be sufficient to control bank deposits.

Net Book Value. A statement of the value of fixed assets which is used in accounting. The appropriate amount of depreciation has been deducted from the original cost of purchase of the asset to give its net book value. It may often differ from market value through inflation or other changes in value affecting the purchase price of the asset.

Net Investment. Means the addition to the economy's total capital stock, i.e., the amount of investment net of depreciation. It is also known as net capital formation.

Net Profits. Means that portion of total profits which is left after the deduction of taxation payments and depreciation provisions.

Neutrality of Money. It is a theorem which states that via the operation of the real balance effect in the money market, there will exist an equal proportionate increase in equilibrium money prices for a given increase in the money supply.

New Cambridge School. The term used for a school of economists which have been associated with certain members of the Cambridge Economic Policy Group at the Department of Applied Economics. University of Cambridge Since the 1970s, the school has made a number of distinct analytical contributions concerned with the long-run behaviour of the economy.

New Classical School. A school of economies which has been associated with the names of Lucas, Sargent and Minford. The school believes that (1) expectation are rational, and (2) markets clear very quickly when wages and prices and flexible, up and down. Thus, willing buyers and willing sellers try to strike bargains which satisfy reasonably all parties. Involuntary unemployment can happen only when wages get inflexible or get fixed at infrequent intervals with workers being temporarily priced out of employment. In a flexible system, unemployment tends to be at its 'natural rate'; it exists because some people choose to be unemployed. If the system has been flexible, it is argued, governments cannot use a fiscal and or monetary boost to increase output and employment.

'New Classical Macroeconomics'. It is a restatement in a more rigorous form of orthodox classical economics. This restatement is based on the notion of rational expections combined with a natural rate of unemployment which emerges because of efficient market clearing.

New Economic Policy. A term which was used to describe the workings of the economic system in the USSR in the 1920s.

'New Economics'. Descriptive of the analytical and philiosophical approach to economic policy-making used by the Kennedy and Johnson administration in the 1960s. The New Economics emphasised the goal of reatraining full employment and to move towards a full utilisation of resources. It emphasized economic growth in order to achieve full employment and potential output.

New Inflation. Means the notion that the current inflation that western economics have experienced since World War II has been of a different nature or origin to previous inflations in history. The basic argument here has been that trade union pushfulness constitutes the 'vital parameter' or 'motive force' of the current inflation.

New Keynesian School. A school of ecnomics which is associated with the names of Klein, Tobin, Hicks and Meade. In common with monetarists, its adherents believed that economies tend towards a full-employment equilibrium, however, they also believed that this may require many years to reach unless governments take steps to boost demand during a recession.

'New Microeconomics'. The name assigned to a body of economic literature which has sought to identify the microeconomics of macroeconomics; specifically, to offer a firm microeconomic rationale of the mechanisms underlying the aggregate relationships between price changes and unemployment. The new microeconomics is based upon the natural rate (of unemployment) hypothesis, and abandons the notion of fully and costlessly informed market participants.

'New-new' Microeconomics. The name assigned to model building exercises which try to explain wage and price contracts in terms of microeconomic optimizing behaviour. The existence of wage and price contracts implies that prices will react sluggishly to underlying changes in aggregate demand and that the latter will predominantly induce quantity changes in the short run.

New Socialism. A concept given by Professor John Kenneth Galbraith in his Economics and the Public Purpose (1974) as a remedy for unequal development, unequal income, unequal and bizarre distributions of public expenditures, environmental damage discriminatory and ineffective stabilisation policies.

Noble. A coin made from platinum (for white gold as it is known because of its colour). It is legal tender in the Isle of Man, an offshore tax haven.

Nominal Gross National Product. Refers to the measure of the value of output in the national economy in a given period at the market prices of that period.

Nominal Income. Means the monetary value of income; changes in nominal income may be ascribed to either changes in real income of changes in the level of prices.

Non-Bank Financial Intermediaries. The term used for those financial intermediaries whose liabilities have been not included in the money supply on the more usual definitions.

Non-Excludability. A good is considered to be non-excludable of its provision to any one person automatically makes it available to others. The term is also applied from the producer's point of view where the supplier cannot prevent individuals from getting the good from the consumer's point of view where the consumer has been a characteristic of public goods.

Non-Labour Income. Means the income that accrues outside the labour market either from investments or, more importantly, from transfer payments.

Non-Manual Workers. The term used for employees and employers who are engaged in mental rather than physical labour who are paid a salary. The opposite of manual workers.

Non-Pecuniary Goals. Refer to those objectives which are pursued by individuals or organization and are not directly measurable in monetary units. Objectives such as prestige, power, professional excellence and status have this property and have been commonly referred to within managerial theories of the firm.

Non-Price Competition. Refers to the adoption of any policy other than price reduction, which has been designed to attract new customers from rivals. Commonly referred to forms of non-price competition have been advertising marketing and product innovation.

Non-Profit Institutions. Those institutions who either explicitly or implicitly do not exist to make a profit, for example, many educational institutions.

Non-Recourse Finance

(a) Finance offered by a specialist finance company which, for a commission, assumes financial responsibilities on behalf of an exporter. The company passes on to the exporter any down-payments credited from the overseas buyer and most of the amount remaining due within 15 days of shipment, this being without recourse once the goods have been accepted by the buyer.

(b) A loan, the repayment of which has been conditional upon the project making a profit, no repayment. Such a high-risk loan means a high potential return to the lender.

Non-Renewable Resource. The term used for any resource which exists in a limited stock and cannot be replenished other than by recycling. The most obvious finite resources have been oil, coal, gass and metals such as tin, mercury, aluminium etc.

Non-Rival Consumptions. When one individual's consumption of a good in no way diminishes the supply of that good to other individuals, the good is considered to be non-rival in consumption. There have been no opportunity cost of consumption of such a good. Non-rivalness has been a characteristic of public goods. An example of a good which is non-rival in consumption has been a broadcast television singal; one person's use of that signal does not dimnish its availability to other individuals.

Non-Uniqueness. In partial and general equilibrium theory it refers to a situation in which more than one equilibrium price exists.

Non-Wage Labour Cost. Costs of employment to the firm over and above earnings per hour paid for.

Normal Cost Pricing. A hypothesis which states that the process of price fixing has been based on the cost of some national output level rather than upon actual current costs or excess demand.

Thus, when output and costs fluctuate in response to cyclical or other factors, price will not get adjusted.

Normal Good. A good whose demand gets reduced as income falls. For normal goods a price fall would give rise to an increase in real income such that the income effect always has the same sign (with respect to the price change) as the substitution effect; both are negative.

Normal Price. Means the long-run price of a commodity. It is defined by Alfred Marshall as the 'value which economic forces would bring about if the general conditions of life were stationary for a run of time long enough to enable them all to work out their full effect.'

Normal Profit. Refer to that minimum amount of profit which a firm must acquire so as to induce the firm to remain in operation. This is where all opportunity costs have been just covered by total revenue and therefore corresponds to a zero level of profits.

Normative Economics. Economic studies consisting of statements on what individual business or public policy ought to be, the statements being based upon the value-judgments of the economist concerned.

North-South Dialogue. The term used for the discussions between the developed and developing countries, *e.g.*, as took place at the Conference on International Economic Co-operation in 1976 at which a prospective New World Economic Order was debated. The essence of the dialogue has been whether and to what extent there should be a permanent transfer of resources from developed to developing countries.

Numeraire. Refers to a unit of account, or an expression of a standard of value. Money has been a numerate, by which different commodities can have values compared.

O

OAPEC. Abbreviation of Organization of Arab Petroleum Exporting Countries.

Occupational Mobility. The mobility which is prevalent in an economy and provides for inter-change of work force from one occupation to another. Occupational mobility has been very much less in an under-developed country compared to a fully developed country, where occupations of different sort have a tendency to merge into each other at the higher management levels.

Occupational Wage Differentials. Refers to the differences in the average level of pay of groups of workers that classified according to the occupation in which they are employed.

Occupational Wage Structure. Refer to the ranking of the average pay level of different groups of workers that are classified according to the occupation in which they are employed.

Offer. Means the price at which a person is ready to sell as opposed to bid, the price at which one is ready to buy.

Offsetting Contract. A future contract which offsets or closes out an earlier obligation to deliver or take delivery of the commodity in question.

Offshore. A marketing area beyond the regulation of the home country.

Offshore Investment Centres. Refer to the place where because taxes on income and wealth have been low or non-existent, and where there are developed laws relating to trusts, it is particularly advantageous to hold assets; or from which business, especially financial business, can be conducted again with tax advantages. Prominent among such places are the Channel Isles, some Caribbean states and Luxembourg.

Ohlin's Theory of Relative Price Difference. According to this theory, relative price differences result in the absolute price difference where a rate of exchange has been settled. These differences indicate in what commodities each region should specialize. The rate of exchange and the value of interregional and international trade has been determined by reciprocal demand. Ohlin extended his analysis to any number of regions or nations without in any way alternating its basic methods or conclusions. However, the application of the theory was impractical. Also Ohin's theory has been objected on the ground that even if two regions may have identical factor units it would be possible to specialise because of the existence of a large market which would permit large scale economies of production to come into existence.

The existence of qualitative difference in the different factors of production could be easily solved by classifying these factors under different groups for purposes of inter-regional comparison.

Ohlin takes into account transport costs also and thus points out how these will reduce trade and weaken its effects on prices. He tries to explain the barriers to inter-regional mobility of factors and says how factor movements act as substitute for movements of commodities under certain circumstance.

Okun's Law. Refers to a relationship between real economic growth and changes in the rate of unemployment. Accounting to this law for every 2.5 percentage points growth in real gross national product, above the trend rate that is sustained for a year, the unemployment rate declines by 1 percentage point. The law has been simply a rule of thumb for assessing the implications of real growth for unemployment.

Obligopolistic Behaviour. Means conduct by firms which is characterized by perceived interdependence in decision-making with regard to major policy areas like pricing, advertising and investment.

Obligopoly. The term refers to a market structure within which firms have been aware of the mutual interdependence of sales, production, investment and advertising plans. Hence manipulation by any firm of variable under its control has been likely to evoke retaliation from competing firms. These features have been commonly ascribed to markets in which the number of sellers has been few.

Oligopsony. Means a market in which a few buyers have to face a very large number of sellers. This type of market is comparable to that of oligopoly.

One Sector Growth Model. A model which is used in growth theory where a single homogeneous product is produced which is equally useful as a consumption or as an investment goods. An example of this model has been the Harrod-Domar model.

One-Stop Banking. Universal banking in which customers can obtain every financial service in one branch. One stop banking encourages cross-subsidisation, that is the offering of loss leaders in the hope of more than making up for them once a customer is booked into range of services.

On-The-Job-Training. Refers to either formal or informal training which is undertaken at the place of work. On-the-job training offered by employers varies from formal programmes of apprenticeship to the most basic forms learning by doing and observing. On-the-job training may be either specific or general, although much training is an admixture of both.

OPEC. Abbreviation of Organization of Petroleum Exporting Countries.

Open Contracts. In a commodity market contracts which have been brought or sold without the transaction having been completed by subsequent sale or purchase, or by making or taking actual delivery of the financial instrument of physical commodity.

Open Economy. An economy which has been engaging in international trade. The degree of openness of an economy may be approximated by the size of its foreign trade sector relative to its gross domestic product.

Open Interest. The total number of futures contracts, whether purchased or sold, recorded on the books of a commodity exchange which are not offset by the opposite transactions or by physical delivery of the commodity.

Open Market. Open market in the context of world economy implies that a country permits international exchange of goods and services and currencies without much restriction. Within a country, open market is considered to prevail when movement of goods from one unit to another is allowed unrestricted.

Open Market Operations. In many countries Central Banks undertake open market operations to control the credit creating capacity of commercial banks. This is carried out by selling government securities to the public or to the banks themselves. This reduces the amount of cash with the banks and forces them to reduce the supply of risky credit.

Open Unemployment. Refers to the situation where an individual accepts that he has no employment and he may then subsequently register with a labour exchange if that facility is available.

Operating Cost Ratio. Operating costs which are expressed as a proportion of the value of net sales.

Operating Gearing. Refers to a measure of the percentage of a firm's operations that are constituting fixed costs. Break-even analysis can be used to measure this.

Operating Income. The income which arises of the normal business of a firm. It will exclude any extraordinary items such as sales of land, buildings or other capital assets, unless the firm is engaged normally in buying and selling of such assets.

Operating Lease. Refers to a lease under which goods are leased for only part of their estimated life, and so the rental covers only part of their capital costs.

Operating Profit. Refers to that profit which would be earned if no resources get diverted to the future expansion of the firm.

Operating Ratios. Ratios which indicate the operating efficiency of a business. Examples of operating ratios are:

$$\frac{\text{Cost of Sales}}{\text{Stock (including stores and work in progress)}}$$

$$\frac{\text{Stock of Furnished goods}}{\text{Production costs for period}}$$

$$\frac{\text{Trade Creditors}}{\text{Purchasers}}$$

Opportunity Cost. Means the real cost of satisfying a want. It is expressed in terms of the cost of the sacrifice of alternative activities. For example, if capital funds could earn 15 per cent elsewhere, then that is their cost in present use.

Opportunity Cost Approach to International Trade. This approach considers the cost of producing a particular goods not as a certain amount of real costs but as the goods which have to be foregone to obtain this good. Provided opportunity cost ratios differ between countries, it has been possible for gains to be obtained from trade in the manner described in the theory of comparative advantage.

Optimal Capacity. Refers to that output which corresponds to the minimum point of the average total cost schedule.

Optimal Distribution. The term used for the 'best' or most desirable distribution of (generally) income or wealth between the individuals composing a society or community.

Optimisation. A key concept in micro-economics; the consumer is assumed to maximum utility or satisfaction, subject to the costraints of income, while the producer is assumed to maximise profit and minimise costs, subject to the technological and legal constraints within which it operates.

Optimum. Means the 'best' situation of state of affairs. To achieve an optimum is to 'optimize' and a situation which is an optimum is said to be 'optimal'.

Optimum Firm. Means a firm in which the costs of production per unit of output have been at a minimum, having regard to the existing state of technical knowledge and managerial ability.

Optimum Plant Size. Refers to that size of plant at which long-run average costs have been at a minimum.

Optimum Tariff. Refers to the name given to the tariff which maximizes the welfare or utility enjoyed by a nation.

Option. A contract which allows the other party to buy or sell commodities or securities within a given time period at an agreed price.

Ordinalism. Refers to the doctrine which states that utility levels can only be ranked in ordinal terms.

Ordinal Utility. In an ordering of goods étc., that with the highest utility has been ranked above the good with the next highest utility and so on. This ranking or ordering will be ordinal as if it is not possible to say by how much utility differs between the first and second ranked good and, say, the second and third ranked good. Ordinal utility has been the cornerstone of neo-classical consumer demand theory.

Organisation. Organisation means the place where some economic process/activity-trade or industry has been carried on. Organising involves the establishment of an international structure of roles by indentifying the activities required to achieve the purpose of an enterprise, the grouping of these activities, the assignment of such the groups of activities to managers or workers, the delegations of authority to carry them out and provision for coordination of authority and communicational relationship up and down in the organisational structure.

Organisation of Petroleum Exporting Countries (O.P.E.C.). An association of countries formed in 1960 for the purpose of promoting the interests of the oil-exporting countries. The countries comprised Algeria, Bahrain, Brunei, Ecuador, Gabon, Indonesia, Iran, Iraq, Kuwait, Libya, Nigeria, Oman, Qatar, Saudi Arabia, Trinidad, and Tobago, the United Arab Emirates, and Venenzuela.

Out-of-the-Money. Refers to a put option whose strike price has been lower than the underlying futures price, of a call option whose strike price is higher than the underlying futures price.

Output. Refers to the end product of transforming inputs into goods. This transformation process is formalized by saying that out-put is a function of the various quantities and qualities of inputs used, which is a verbal expression of the production function.

Output Budgeting. Means a system of accounting which classifies costs according to the outputs in the production of which they are incurred rather than in terms of the inputs which are purchased.

Output Response Function. Refers to a hypothesis that if the aggregate effective demand for goods and services within an economic system steadily increases output will increase, but ultimately at a diminishing rate for response.

Outside Lag. Refers to the delay between implementation of a (macroeconomic) policy and its full or total effect. This normally takes the form of a distributed lag.

Outside Money. That money which is backed by assets which are not debts in that the assets do not represent a claim on individuals within the economy. Examples of outside money, fiat money, gold and foreign exchange reserves.

Overdraft. Refers to a system of bank lending by which the borrower is permitted to draw cheques beyond the credit balance in his account, up to an agreed limit, and to pay interest only on the daily amounts by which his account is overdrawn.

Over-Employed Workers. The workers who optimally would seek to work fewer hours than standard working work permits.

Overheads. Costs which are not directly chargeable to any unit produced. They include rent of premises, salaries of salesmen and research, salaries of directors, etc., and all other general expenses, as opposed to costs of raw materials, wages etc., the proportion of which that goes into each unit can be determined.

Overheating. A concept which is applicable to a situation of excessive demand for real resources in condition of full employment.

Overmanning. Refers to a situation in which the number of operators employed to operate a plant or production line or the number of workers in a term, is higher than that thought necessary as a result of work-study assessment or through comparisons with other factors at home or overseas, in consequence output per employee is below standard.

Overnight Money. Refers to money which is lent in one or other of the money markets, at the very shortest term of recall. From the lender's point of view it is money which he expects to require, if not the next day, then within two or three days at most.

Overpopulation. A subjective term used to describe a situation when the density of population in a defined area is regarded too high.

Overtime. Hours worked in excess of the standard working week. Such hours attract pay premium.

Overtrading. Means a situation in which a firm has little working capital.

Overvalued Currency. Means a currency whose exchange rate is fixed above the free market equilibrium rate.

P

Paasche Index. Means a type of index which is used for measuring changes, *e.g.* in prices. It uses current period weights, but since current year weights are seldom known, the index is difficult to construct. The index uses the following method:

$$\frac{\Sigma P_n q_n}{\Sigma P_n q_n}$$

where P_o = price in the base-year, P_n=price in the year under consideration; and q_n=quantity in the year under consideration. The index has the disadvantage that in times of generally rising prices it tends to underestimate prive increases.

Paid-up Capital. That part of the issued capital which is paid up by the shareholders.

Pan Ticket. A document which accompanies a grain sample of a commodity that is to be sold in the cash market, it lists official grade, test weight, moisture content, point of origin and other relevant information.

Paper Money. General terms which is used for money in the form of banknotes. Under a gold standard these are convertible into gold coin or bullion; otherwise thay are inconvertible.

Paper Entrepreneur. A business organiser who is applying the skills of the entrepreneur to the task of achieving short-term profits for the firm, not through new productive investment but through strategies involving simple the rearrangement of assest and the clever manipulation of rules and numbers, shrewd manoeuvring the transfer of losses from the firm to the public through a successful plea for public subsidies or tax concession, threats of legal actions and takeovers, and the finessing of accounts and taxation returns.

Paper Gold. Special drawing rights.

Paper Profit. If an asset increases in value in nominal terms, this is termed as paper profit; for example, if a house would sell now for a larger nominal sum than the price for which it was bought, a paper profit has been made. This may or may not be representing a real profit which depends on the rate of inflation.

Paradox of Thrift. Refers to a paradox that in certain economic circumstances the more frugal and thrifty are individuals and households, the lower will be the level of national income and factor employment; and the more prodigal and spendthrift are individuals and households, the higher the level of national income and factor employment. The latter statement means some unemployment of resouces, otherwise spending may simply result in inflation. Situations arise in which what is 'good' or the individual and house hold may be 'bad' for the nations.

Paradox of Value. Means a paradox in which an essential to life such as water is normally little valued, but a luxury, such as diamonds, carries a high price.

Paradox of Voting. Refers to the possibility that the system of simple majority rule voting may fail to provide an unambiguous choice between alternatives.

In the diagram below the preferences of A, B and C have been shown, the preferences of A and C have been single-peaked while B's preferences are not.

The paradox of voting has led to consideration of alternative to simple majority rule like approval voting, the Borda Count, exhaustive voting and point voting. In a majority rule system the problem of cycling may be overcome by logrolling or vote trading.

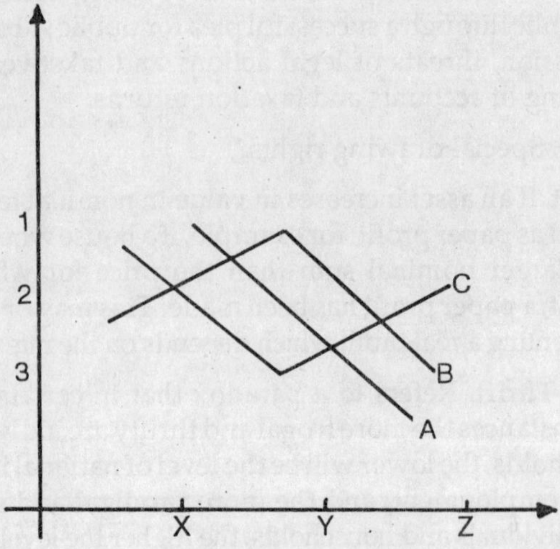

Paradox of Voting

Paretian Liberal, Impossibility of. The name assigned to a theorem which was presented by A.K.Sen. This theorem demonstrates that no social decision rule can simultaneously satisfy the Pareto Criterion and allow individuals to make decisions on certain 'personal' matters irrespective of the wishes of others (Personal Liberty).

Pareto Improvement. Refers to reallocation of resources which makes at least one person better of without making anyone worse off.

Pareto Non-Comparability. If when selecting between two states of society some individuals prefer one and some the other, the two states are considered to be Pareto non-comparable.

Pareto Optimality. Refers to any of a number of efficient states of economic affairs, from which it has been impossible to deviate so as to make one person or group worse off.

Pareto-Optimal Redistribution. Means the transfers of income or wealth from one individual to another which increases the utility or satisfaction of both donor and recipient, thus bringing about a Pareto improvement.

Pareto Optimum. If the economy's resources and output have been allocated in such a way that no reallocation can make anyone better off without making at least one other person worse off than a Pareto optimum is considered to exist. The concept was proposed by and is named after Vilfredo Pareto.

Pareto's Law. It is an empirical relationship which describes the number of persons whose income is x in a given population, advanced by Vilfredo Pareto (1848-1923). Italian economist and sociologist, Pareto concluded from his studies that national income had an inevitable tendency to be distributed in the same way regardless of social and poltical institutions and system of taxation. Subsequent studies have refuted both the universality and inevitability of Pareto's Law.

Par Rate of Exchange. Refers to the expression of exchange rates in terms of gold or dollars.

Partial Equilibrium. Refers to the study of a market for a commodity in isolation. Given the prices of all other commodities the conditions for equilibrium in a single market could be examined. This technique used by A. Marshall does not take into account the effects of changes in the price of a commodity on all other related market prices including the prices of factors of production.

Partial Equilibrium Analysis. Economic analysis of a small sector of an economy such as the market for a particular commodity, in which the prices of several or all other commodities are held fixed relative to one another, and spillovers between markets are largely ignored.

Participation Rate. Means the proportion of a population, of working age, in the labour force, whether employed or unemployed.

Par Value. Means the nominal or face value of a share or security. A share stands above par if its price on the stock exchange becomes greater than its nominal value.

Pay-Back Method. It is a method which is used for comparing the profitability of alternative projects, the object has been to determine over what period the net cash generated by an investment will repay the cost of the project.

$$\text{Pay-back period} = \frac{\text{Cost of Project}}{\text{Annual Increase in Income (after tax)}}$$

The most serious drawback of the pay-back method has been that it takes no account of the life of the investment and ignores the timing of proceeds.

Pay Ceiling. Refers to an effective upper-limit on the size of pay settlements. A pay ceiling may come to be considered as the norm or the going rate.

Payment-By-Results. The term used for systems of payment under which the worker is paid according to the volume of output he or the work group or plant of which he is part produces. It is also known as incentive payment systems.

Pay-Off. Refers to the net benefit that occurs when a particular course of action has been taken. The pay-off in a gambling situation has been obviously the sum won if the bet pays-off.

Payout Ratio. Means the percentage of the firm's net profit which is paid out as dividends.

Peak Period Labour Demand. Refers to the level of demand for labour at its highest point. This term usually refers to agricultural employment, which is cyclical by nature with peaks taking place especially at harvest time.

Pecuniary Culture. Refers to a social system in which the accumulation of physical wealth has been both acceptable to that society, and valued highly by that society.

Pecuniary Effects. Refers to the affects which are arising from changes in relative prices which only redistribute goods and services among people without affecting total production of consumption opportunities.

Pecuniary External Economy. The term used for a situation where the profits of a firm depend not on its own inputs and outputs but also on the imputs and outputs of other firms.

Penny Line. Descriptive of people waiting at the entrance of a work-site ascertain whether there is any work for them.

Pension. Pension schemes have been of two broad types; one, the capital-reserve system, involving redistribution over the lifetime of an individual, has been based on workers saving to accumulate capital which is then consumed during retirement, and the other, the pay-as-you-go system, involves redistribution at a point in time between individuals so that those still at work support the retired.

Per Capita. Per head, *e.g.*, per capita national income-the average level of national income for each member of the population.

Perfect Information. Means the possession by market participants in a competitive economy of complete knowledge and foresight with regard to the array of present and future prices as well as the location of goods and services. Any divergence from such circumstances can be considered to be as a state of imperfect information and has been commonly cited as a source of market failure.

Perfect Market. A concept sometimes used for the purpose of studying certain effects, in which it has been assumed that there occurs no transfer costs of goods from place to place so that uniform prices would be established everywhere, and that every seller has been in contact with every buyer and every buyer in contact with every seller.

Perfect Marketing Transparency. Means the objective of price information agreements; a market is said to be perfectly transparent for the sellers if all sellers know exactly the prices asked and obtained by their competitors, the terms of sale, the quality of their competitors' products and the names of their customers. The result could be conscious parallelism with regard to prices, particularly in an oligopoly paralysing price competition.

Permanent Income. It is also known as Normal Income and Average Expected Income. It is the average income that the individual or household is expected to receive over a period of years while retaining his wealth intact.

Permanent Income Hypothesis. The term used for a hypothesis that household consumption expenditures get related to permanent income and not affected by deviations from this amount.

Permanent-Income Theory of Consumption. A theory which was developed by Milton Friedman (b. 1912). According to this theory people gear their consumption behaviour to their permanent or long-term consumption opportunities, and not to their current level of income. In its simplest form this hypothesis of consumption behaviour may be put as follows:

$$C = cY^p$$

where Y^p denotes permanent disposable income, land C consumtion. Thus consumption varies in the same proportion as permanent income, a 10 per cent increase in permanent incomes raises consumption by 10 per cent. To the individual some increases in income appear of a permanent nature and influence the pattern of consumption whereas other increases are transitory and do not change the long-term pattern. The permanent-income hyothesis pays careful attention to the ways in which individuals form their expectations about their future incomes.

Personal Income. Refers to the flow of income that accrues to the individual or household. The income may occur as a result of the sale of his labour and/or his ownership of assets or it may take the form of a transfer income.

Personal Loan. Means the types of loan which is made by banks and certain other financial institutions to personal (i.e., non-business) borrowers, for the purchase of consumer goods, home improvements and so on, and repayable by regular amounts spread over a period.

Personal Saving. Refers to that part of personal income which is neither paid out in taxes nor spent on goods and services (a current consumption).

Perverse Migration. Means the migration of individuals particularly workers, from areas of relatively good economic performance to areas of poorer economic performance. Economics usually attempt to explain movement of workers from one area to another as a response to improved employment prospects or higher income level in the receiving areas. However, in reality a certain amount of movement is seen to take place from high to low income areas and from low to high unemployment areas. This is considered to be perverse migration. Such movement could be explained in terms of the influence of non-economic factors like physical environment.

Petty's Law. Refers to a statement of the tendency for the proportion of the working population engaged in service industry to increase with economic development. Sir William Petty (1623-1687) was the pioneer of numerical economics, has main interest being in public finance. He made significance contributions in respect of monetary theory and fiscal policy; his best-known work Political Arithmetic was published in 1691.

Phanthom Competition. The term used for the quotations by customers of other suppliers' prices at lower levels than the true ones.

Philips Curve. The statistical observation by A.W. Phillips (1958) that there occurred an inverse relationship between the rate of change of money wage rates and the unemployment rate in the UK over the period 1861-1957. That is,

$$\Delta W_t = f(U)_t$$

where ΔW denotes the change in money wage rates and U the employment rate in period *t*.

Prior to 1948 wages were flexible in both upward and downward direction and therefore the Phillips curve, illustrated below, intercepted the horizontal axis at a rate of unemployment in excess of 6 per cent. In the postwar period however money and wages proved to be inflexible in a downward direction and because of this the curve for this period lies above the horizontal axis. From the other axis it is evident that there will always be some rate of unemployment whatever the rate of wage inflation.

A theoretical underpinning for this statistical association was later given by Lipsey (1960) who postulated that the rate of money wage change would be a function of the degree of excess demand in the labour market, the unemployment rate was to be interpreted as a (negative) index of excess demand in the labour market. The Phillips curve was interpreted by many to mean that there occurred a long-run trade-off between the rate of wages inflation and the level of unemployment.

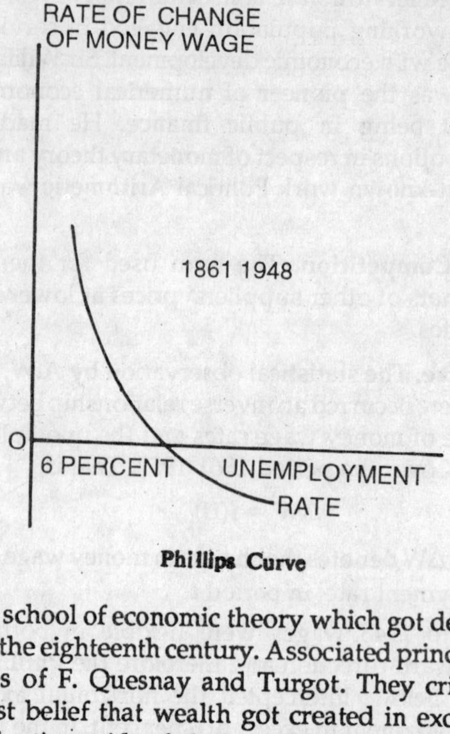

Phillips Curve

Physiocrats. A school of economic theory which got developed in France in the eighteenth century. Associated principally with the names of F. Quesnay and Turgot. They criticized the Merantilist belief that wealth got created in exchange and gave production pride of place in its creation. They identified the surplus over the resources used up in production as the source of accumulation. The surplus, or 'produit net' had been a surplus of material wealth produced by labour in conjunction with land.

Their analysis got limited by this concentration on agriculture which they identified as the source of all wealth. They had been proponents of laissez-faire and opposed all government intervention in industry especially taxation which was seen as an indirect (and therefore inefficient) tax on land. A single tax on land had been the practical policy guide of this school. The chief concept of their system was a belief that the natural order which incorporated natural laws embodying the right to enjoy the benefits of freedom to follow self-interest.

Pigou Effect or Real Balance Effect. Means a change in expenditure which is caused by a change in the value of money holdings that occurs as a consequence of changes in prices. Named after A.C. Pigou (1977-1959) a view that consumption has been not solely a function of income.

Pigovian Tax. Refers to a tax levied on the producer of an externality in such a way that after the tax has been introduced the private costs, as perceived by the externality-generating party, have been equal to the social costs of the activity.

Pivot Effect Hypothesis. Refers to the argument that incomes policy not only creates shift effects in the wage adjustment process but may also alter the slope of the Phillips curve or, more technically, the magnitude of response of the rate of change in wages to its determinants.

Planned Economy. Means an economy where crucial economic processes have determined to a large extent not by market force, but by an economic planning body which implements society's major economic goals. In such a system the greater part of production activity has been determined by obligatory input and output targets generated by vertical signals from an administrative hierarchical body.

Planning System. A term which has been used by Professor John Kenneth Galbraith in his Economics and the Public Purpose (1947) to describe that part of the national economy planned by its constituent firms. The concept has to be distinguished carefully from that of State planning systems, the more common use. The planning system is regarded the dominant part of the economy to which the market system has been subordinate; it supplies power, fuel, machinery, equipment, materials, transportation and communications -- a large share of the goods and services that firms in the market system must purchase.

Planometrics. A branch of economics which is specifically concerned with the construction of optimal macroeconomic plans L.V. Kantorovich is one of the pioneers in this area using sophisticated mathematical techniques to demonstrate the possibility of efficient central planning using programming prices of'objectively determined valuations'.

Plant Bargaining. Refers to collective bargaining between a single employer from a single plant and employees' representatives to establish rates to pay and conditions of work in that plant. Such agreements could either be a supplement to or a substitute for national bargaining.

Plant Mix. Means the proportion of different types of plant in a system, or contemplated for the future. In respect of electricity generating plant, the different types have been usually classified as coal, oil, natural gas, nuclear, hydro, pumped storage and gas turbine. The first four have been simply labelled by the fuels they use and are all steam-electric plants. Hydro plant means hydro-electric plant, in which the water used for electricity generation flows entirely via dams from natural catchment areas. In pumped storage schemes water has been pumped from a lower reservoir to a higher reservior, base-load electricity at off-peak times being used, and released from the upper reservoir to generate electricity at peak times. Gas turbine plant has been used for peak-load generation purposes.

Pinto (427-347 BC). A Greek philosopher. In reaction to the troubled times in which he lived, and for which he held economic growth to be partially responsible, he proposed that the ideal state should be a stationary one based on a caste system, with the ruling class practising a communistic way of life. His economic achievements got included an analysis of the division of labour and of the role of token money.

Point Utility Possibility Curve. It is possible to draw a point utility possibility curve for each bundle of goods. The curve reveals the combinations of individual utility levels by varying the distribution of the bundle of goods between the individuals. The possible distributions of two different bundles of goods have been depicted in the diagram.

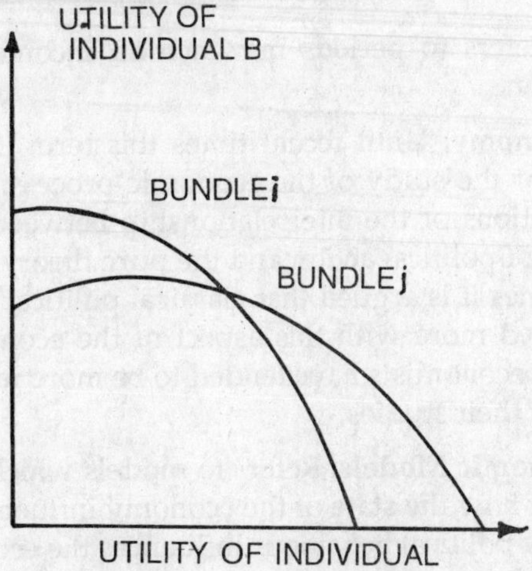

Point Utility Possibility Curve

Point Voting. Refers to a system of collective choice in which each individual starts with an equal number of 'points' which he is free to distribute in any way he chooses between the alternative choice on the various issues discussed. Hence an individual could be able to divide his points equally between all of the alternatives he favoured or concentrate his points on some highly important choice. This system bears some resemblance to the system of 'vote trading' known as logrolling.

Policy Instruments. Refers to economic and social variables which are manipulated by the government to influence policy variables. Frequently referred to solely as instruments it is possible to distinguish four main economic categories; fiscal policy, monetary policy, exchange rate policy and most recently the direct control of prices and incomes policy. It ought also to be noted that governments desire to influence policy variables by attempting social and institutional reforms. For example, they may try to reform the institution of wage bargaining believing that this may reduce wage inflation.

Policy-off. Refers to periods of free 'collective bargaining'. Periods in which no incomes are able to operate.

Policy-off. Refers to periods in which an incomes policy is in operation.

Political Economy. Until recent times this term is the common name for the study of the economic process. The term has connotations of the interrelationship between the practical aspects of political action and the pure theory of economics. Sometimes it is argued that classical political economy was concerned more with this aspect of the economy and that modern economists have tended to be more restricted in the range of their studies.

Politico-Economic Models. Refers to models which facilitate the study of how the state of the economy influences the policy and how political behaviour influences the economy.

Polluter Pays Principle. This principle states that the polluter should pay for polluting the environment. It was enunciated by the Organisation for Economic Co-operation and Development. The principle is consistent with (1) a Pigovian tax, (2) any tax or charge on polluters which encourages them to install measures to abate pollution, whether to the 'optimal' level or not. In narrower terms it has been usually thought of as a (Pigovian) tax which has been just equal to the marginal damage cost at the optimal level of pollution.

Pollution. The term used for an activity which impairs the quality of one or more receiving environment.

Polluting Rights. Mean the idea that certificates should be issued which provide the owner a 'right of pollute' in a given environment, say river.

Population Explosion. The term used for the ever increasing growth rates of population in the world, especially in developing countries.

Pork Barreling. Refers to the use of government funds as a source of political benefit; for example the channeling of funds into major public works like water supply projects, where they will be of most political benefit to those determining the priorities.

Portfolio. Means the set of assets held by an individual or institution. It generally refers to financial (including monetary) assets, but there has been in principle no need to regard it is excluding real assets.

Portfolio Balance Approach. The term used for an approach to monetary analysis which emphasizes the significance of decisions by asset-holders about the composition of their portfolios. One major variant of this approach is that while all holders need some diversity in their assets, they differ for personal or institutional reasons in their basic preferences between different types of assets--e.g., between long-term and short-term, fixed yield and variable yield assets.

Portfolio Theory. This was devised by Professor James Tobin (1981 Nobel Memorial prize in economics). This theory is a guide to the management of a portfolio ; it was based on his studies of how subjects actually behave when they acquire different assets and incur debts. The theory postulates that investors do not, and should not, seek only the highest average rate of return they can get from an investment portfolio. Rather, in order to avoid taking undue risks, investors both do and should pay attention to the 'variance' or instability of the stock or bonds or other assets held.

Position. Refers to an interest in a commodity market either long or short, in the form of open contracts which have not been liquidated.

Positional Goods. A term which was used by professor Fred Hirsch to emphasise the socially-influenced values attaching to the utility stemming from a given flow of goods and services. Many things valued in society possess hierarchical significance and personal satisfaction has been often derived from being top of the tree in one respect or another, or in enjoying a high status.

Positive Economics. Refers to that part of economic science which deals itself with statements that are capable of verification by reference to the facts. In Principle, all positive statements should be reducible to some from which is testable by reference to empirical evidence. As a doctrine, positivists would argue that economic science does not and should not encompass statements which involve value judgements, i.e., statements of the form 'X is good (bad).

Positivism. Refers to the philosophical doctrine that declares statements that are not verifiable by reference to empirical evidence to be at least inadmissible as part of science or, at an extreme, without meaning.

Potential Entry. For a particular industry, refers to the possibility of new competition from firms who are not currently producing competing products.

Potential Output. Refers to the maximum feasible output of a firm, industry, sector of an economy or economy as a whole, given its factor endowments. The difference between actual and potential output will therefore be excess capacity.

Potential Pareto Improvement. A potential Pareto improvement exists when the gainers from a change are hypothetically able to compensate those who lose, so that it becomes possible for no-one to be any worse off after the change and for at least one person to be better off.

Potential Real Gross National Product. Or potential output. Refers to an estimate of the level at which the gross national product would be if there were full employment of labour; the difference between potential G.N.P. and actual G.N.P. is called the G.N.P. gap; it serves as a measure of economic slack and of the waste of productive resources due to insufficiently high levels of employment.

Poverty. Poverty can be regarded as an absolute or a relative concept. The absolute poverty approach defines minimum levels of income needed to sustain life; for example, estimating minimum dietary requires and how these can be most cheaply met. The relative poverty approach defines poverty relative to appropriate comparator groups. Thus while an individual may have more than enough income to sustain life, if it is very low compared to the rest of the community the individual would be viewed as being in poverty. As a society grows richer so the income level defining poverty rises.

Prebisch Thesis. Refers to the proposition that technical progress in the developed countries results in higher wages and improvements in the standard of living for the work force but not in lower prices for the goods produced (some of which are exported to developing countries). In developing countries technical progress does not result in improved real wages but lower prices.

Precautionary Motive. Refers to one of the motives for the holding money, i.e., as a precaution against some unforeseen circumstance occurring which would otherwise necessitate transferring wealth from some non-liquid form that may incur high transaction costs or may take too long.

Predatory Pricing. Means the practice of driving prices down to unprofitable levels for a period so as to weaken or eliminate existing competitors.

Precautionary Unemployment. It is also known as 'wait unemployment'. An element of frictional unemployment, it has been suggested to arise if the nature of the job task or form to labour contract prevents an employee who takes a job taking advantage of another job at a higher rate of pay which comes along later. Under these circumstances employees may refuse the first job offer and wait for one at the expected wage.

Preference, Cardinality of. The view of utility which was held by many economists before the 1.30s, that the amount of utility gets related to the quantity of commodities already possessed and that changes in utility arising from change in the quantities possessed can be measured.

Preferential Hiring. Refers to an employer giving preference to the hiring of union members although he has not agreed to hire only union members or operate a closed shop.

Present Value. Means the worth of a future stream of returns or costs in terms of their value now. To get a present value a discount rate is used to discount these future returns and costs.

Present Worth. Refers to the capital sum, which, if invested at the time of the commissioning of a plant, would together with the interest earned suffice to pay the annual capital charges on the plant as they occur year by year.

If it has been necessary to calculate an average annual cost over the whole life of the plant, the total present worth may get converted to an equivalent average annual cost by multiplying by the appropriate annuity rate.

For a 12 per cent interest rate, the present worth factor is given by :

$$\frac{1}{1.12^{m}}$$

where m=years of life of the plant (assumed for depreciation purposes).

The present worth method provides a general and systematic approach to the problem of allocating a series of irregular cost to the units of a continuous output.

Price. Refers to the value of a commodity or service in terms of money; refers to an exchange ratio.

The terms 'price' has been used in relation to the exchange value of goods and some services; in respect of human services the equivalent terms 'wage','commission' or 'fee' are used. Again the price of borrowing money is called 'interest' and the price of hiring land or equipment 'rate'.

Price Control. Generally associated with the fixing of prices by government statutory order.

Price-Cost Margin. Refers to empirical measures of the profit margin where accounting date have been used and therefore the economic definition of profit cannot be directly observed.

Price Discovery. Discriptive of a process whereby price have been established on exchanges through a continuous auction process.

Price Discrimination. Refers to the charging of different prices to different groups of individuals for the same goods or services for reasons not associated with difference in costs. This may take place when there is a geographical separation of markets, the structure of demand in each market being different.

Price Effect. Means the change in the demand for a good that comes about because of a change in the price of that good. It has been composed of the income effect and the substitution effect.

Price Elasticity of Demand. Means the responsiveness of the quantity demanded of a good to its own price. In order to avoid the measure of elasticity being sensitive to the units in which quantities and prices have been measured, the elasticity of demand has been expressed as the percentage change in demand that takes place in response to a percentage change in price.
That is:

Price Elasticity of Demand =

$$= \frac{\frac{\Delta Qi}{Qi} . 100}{\frac{\Delta Qi}{Pi} . 100}$$

$$= \frac{\Delta Qi}{Qi} . \frac{Pi}{\Delta Pi}$$

where Δ denotes a symbol for 'change in', Pi and Qi denote the price and quantity of good *i*. If Δ is very small the resulting measure is termed as the point elasticity of demand. If Δ is significantly large the measure obtained has been one of the responsiveness of demand to this change in price and has been generally known as the are elasticity of demand.

Price Fixing Agreement. The term used for an agreement between two or more producers to sell at predetermined prices, generally for the purpose of exercising market power.

Prices Leadership. It is said to take place in an industry where one firm takes the initiative in marking price change and the other firms then follow. Three forms of price leadership have been identified; dominant firm, barometric and collusive price leadership.

Price Mechanism. System which is used in a competitive society for the distribution of scarce resources through the agency of price. If too little of commodity A and too much of commodity B has been produced, the demand price for A rises, and that for B falls. The signal is thereby given of the productive system to make the necessary adjustments. If competition were perfect, these adjustments would continue until marginal cost and price had become equal.

Price-Push. The name assigned to a type of inflation, similar to cost-push where entrepreneurs have been blamed for making inflation by charging unnecessarily high prices in order to make large profits.

Price Revolution. The name assigned to the influx of gold and silver from the newly discovered countries in America during the fifteenth and sixteenth centuries which made prices to quadruple. This is regarded to be one of the initial causes of the rise of capitalism and beginnings of the industrial revolution in the Western World as these high prices had been an incentive for speculation, accumulation of capital and establishment of new industries.

Price Setter. A firm operating in a non-competitive market faces a downward-sloping demand curve for its product and is thus having some discretion to select the price at which it sells rather than having to be a price taker.

Price Shading. Refers to the practice of selling below published prices.

Price-Specie-Flow Mechanism. The term used for the mechanism by which balance-of-payments disequilibria have been corrected under the gold standard. If Country A is importing more than it exports, it will pay for the extra imports in gold. This flow of gold will reduce the money supply in Country A and increase the money supply of its creditors. The change in money supply will decrease the price level in country A and increase the price levels in the creditor countries. These price changes will tend to correct the initial disequilibrium by making it cheaper to buy from Country A and more expensive to buy from its creditors.

Price Support Scheme. The term used for a method which is used for artificially raising the price of a good in the market. This will result in a situation in which supply exceeds demand and would therefore normally result in the government agency responsible for the support having to purchase the excess supplies itself. It is the simple explanation for 'commodity mountains', excess supplies of commodities (food, minerals etc.) which result from price support schemes.

Price Theory or Micro-Economic Theory. This theory is concerned with how the price system handles the problem of allocating scarce resources in a market economy. The price theory has been concerned with how relative prices are determined, not with how the general price level is determined. It is possible to divide price theory into five sub-sections : (a) the theory of demand and consumer behaviour, (b) the theory of business firm, (c) the theory of market organisation, (d) the theory of distribution, and (e) the theory of general equilibrium and welfare economics.

Primary Goods. As defined in the theory justice developed by John Rawls, these goods have been the basic rights, freedoms, income and wealth which are available for distribution in a society. Rawls' concept of distributive justice has been framed in terms of the distribution of these goods between individuals.

Primary Industry. A term sometimes used to include not only all types of rural industry but all types of mining and quarrying activities. Generally the term is restricted to rural industries only. In this latter sense, the term embraces the production of goods from agriculture, forestry and fishing.

Primary Market. The principle underlying market for a financial instrument or physical commodity.

Primary Money. Another name for base money or high powered money, i.e., the money which is issued by the monetary authorities.

Primary Workers. The term used for those individuals who remain in the labour force either as employed or unemployed irrespective of short-run change in wages and market conditions. Male heads of households have been the archetypal primary workers.

Prime Credits. Large financially strong corporations of excellent credit standing and able to sell commercial paper in the money markets.

Prime Rate. The lowest interest rate which is payable by borrowers having the highest credit rating.

Principal. Means the sum of money which is paid to the holder of a bond upon maturity to extinguish the liability.

Private Good. Means a good which displays rivalness in consumption and where exclusion may be practised by both producer and consumer.

Private Placing. Means the provision of business capital by a finance company, not by way of an ordinary loan but by the purchase of a new issue of debentures on shares.

Private Sector. The 'private sector' of the economy has been the combination of elements in the economy which have been not organs or agencies of central or local government and therefore includes the company sector and the personal sector.

Privatisation. Refers to the selling back to the private sector of government assets, like nationalised industries, share stakes owned or in private companies, testing stations, research centres, publicly-owned shopping centres and bus services.

Process. Refers to specific combination of inputs which can get altered in scale to produce higher levels of output. Thus, if it needs 2 units of capital and 1 of labour to produce 10 units of good X, the domination 2K+1L defines a point on a process, or as it is sometimes called, an activity ray. The point 4K+2L will then be able to difine another such point, and so on. In brief, each process reflects a specific capital labour ratio ϕ if the inputs in question are capital and labour. The number of processes available to produce a given output may get limited because of indivisibility in the inputs. The diagram below depicts a situation in which there are five such processes only. The linear segmented curves joining equal output points have been iso-product curves although they do not exhibit the familiar 'smoothness' and curvature of the typical textbook curve. This is since such smoothness can only come about by assuming that labour and capital can be substituted for each other in extremely divisible units. Once indivisibility exists the picture will look more like the one shown below. Points between processes and on iso-product curves are having and economic meaning. This is because it bonds possible to produce, say, the first 500 units of output with process C and the next with process B. This would in fact be illustrated by point G which lies on a 'facet' of the iso-product curve.

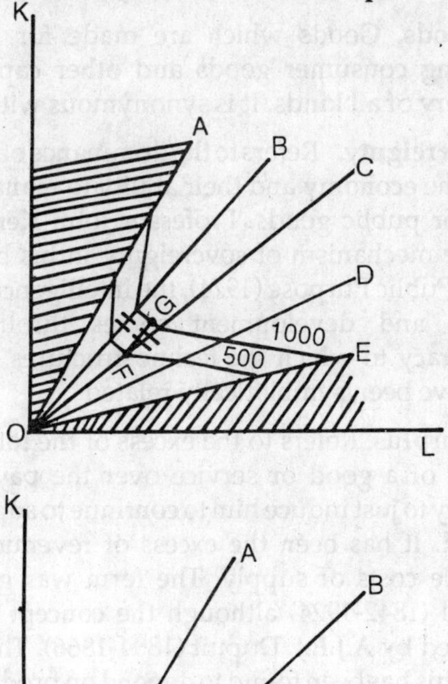

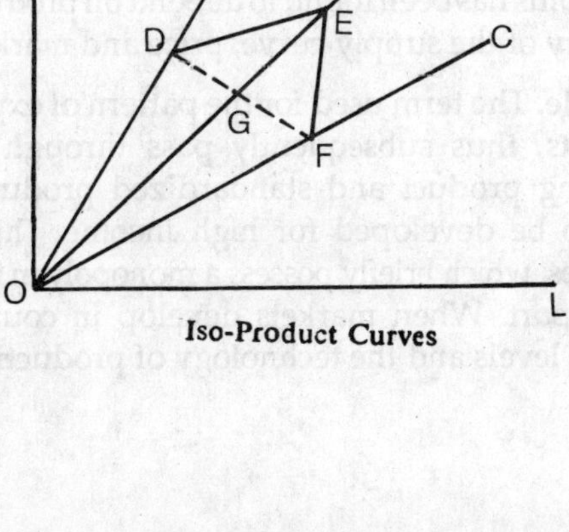

Iso-Product Curves

This analysis could also be used to indicate why an iso-product curve cannot bend outwards. Suppose it does, as in the second diagram, then, regarding only the three processes shown, points D,E and F all indicate combinations that would produce an equal output. But point E has been clearly inefficient since we can draw a facet from D to F and observe a point G on process B which uses less labour and capital than point E. Facets will therefore slope down from left to right for cases where some substitution has been possible, which establishes a prima facie case for the convexity of iso-product curves.

Producer Goods. Goods which are made for the purpose of producing consumer goods and other capital goods e.g., machinery of all kinds. It is synonymous with capital goods.

Producer Sovereignty. Refers to the dominance of large producers within the economy and their ability to manage the demand for major public goods. Professor John Kenneth Galbraith gave the mechanism of sovereignty in his book Economics and the Public Purpose (1974), the intelligence which justifies research and development comes through the public bureaucracy to which the technostructures of the weapons firms have been symbiotically related.

Producers' Surplus. Refers to the excess of the total earnings of a supplier of a good or service over the payment actually necessary to just induce him to continue to supply the amount involved. It has been the excess of revenue over the total avoidable costs of supply. The term was given by Alfred Marshall (1842-1924) although the concept had been well-developed by A.J.E.J. Dupuit (1804-1866). The magnitude of the surplus has been found to depend on production costs, the elasticity of the supply curve, price and market conditions.

Product Cycle. The term used for the pattern of experience of new products, thus subsequently pass through the phases of maturing product and standardized product. New goods have to be developed for high income, high labour-cost countries, which briefly possess a monopoly in their production and export. When markets develop in countries of lower income levels and the technology of production gets settled, the location of production gets moved to these countries to take advantage of lower labour costs and to meet the developing demand. If the product has become widely known throughout the world and its technology standardized, the location of production gets shifted to less developed countries to benefit from the low wage costs and be exported from there to the rest of the world. Such a cycle could be seen in synthetic fibres and semi-conductors.

Product Differentiation. Refers to attempts to create difference between products of a similar nature, e.g., breakfast cereals, by introducing distinct brand names, variations in preparation, and presentation and by skilful advertising. The object has to ensure that the product of any one firm is not considered as a perfect substitute, in the mind of the buyer, for the product of any other firm. If a product establishes itself in the public mind, it may then command a price somewhat higher than another product of similar qualities.

Production. Activities which are resulting in a supply of useful goods and services. These activities include mineral extraction, manufacturing, agriculture, transport and communication, wholesale and retail distribution and the work of civil servants and local government employees.

Production Coefficient. Refers to the quantity of productive services which are necessary to produce one unit of a commodity.

Production Frontier. It is also known as the production possibility curve or transformation function. This curve depicts the possibilities open for increasing the output of one good by reducing the output of another. In the diagram, resources have been considered to be limited so that if they are all devoted to the production of Y an amount Y_{max} could be produced. If they have been all devoted to X an amount X_{max} could be produced. Alternatively, by 'mixing' the allocation of resources to X and Y point such as A and B could be secured. Note that point D and any other point 'outside' the frontier are unobtainable.

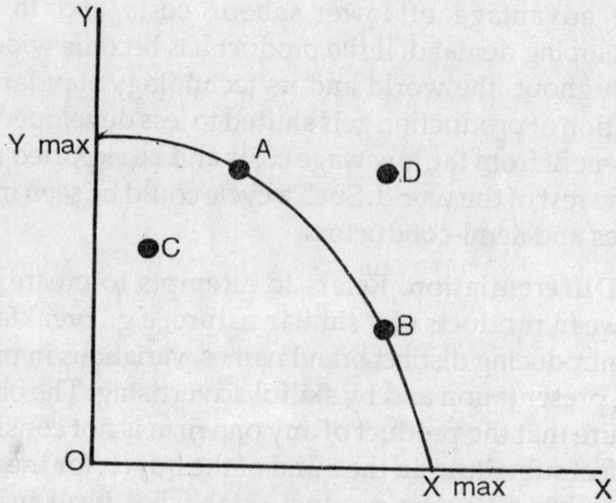

Production Frontier

A point like C, inside the frontier, could well get achieved. It would not represent an efficient use of resources however, because the resources available have been capable of reaching a point like A at which there is more of both X and Y. In short, C could only be realised by either not using all resources i.e., there would be unemployment--or by using the available resources inefficiently.

Production, Theory of. A branch of economics which is concerned with the study of alternative production methods and the consequences of decisions taken in respect of production methods. It also deals with the analysis of the determinants of a firm's choice of quantities of inputs, given its production function, the prices of the inputs, and level of output desired. Theory has been based on the hypothesis that the firm will wish to use that production function and set of quantities of the inputs which will minimise the overall costs of production for a given output. By varying the output, it then becomes possible to construct the output-cost relationships which have been the basis for much of the theory of the firm. Analysis in production theory forms the basis for the theory of marginal productivity, and the determination of factor prices.

Production, Time Structure of. Refers to the time interval between a decision to undertake production and the beginning of the outflow of the product. The more capitalistic or 'capital intensive' the method of production, the longer would be the time interval. In respect of a power station some 5/6 years may elapse between a decision to build and the initial flow of electricity into the Grid.

Productivity. Means output per unit of input employed. Increases in productivity come about from increased efficiency on the part of capital or labour.

Product Market. Means the market in which goods and services have been bought and sold in a private economy. The main sellers have been privately-owned and publicly-owned business firms and the main buyers are private consumers or householders. To be distinguished from the factor market.

Profit Constraint. A concept which is commonly used in managerial theory of the firm. It has been the minimum profit needed to ensure shareholder acquiescence towards company policy.

Profit Function. Means the specified relationship between profit and those variables like output and advertising which influence its size.

Profit Margin. Refers to profit per unit of output which is expressed as a percentage of price.

Profit Maximization. The term used for the hypothesis that firms aim to maximize profits. In the diagram profit has been defined as the difference between the total revenue received by the firm and total costs it incurs. The point of maximum difference has been seen to correspond to output level X* which is thus the profit maximising output. At this point the slopes of the two curves have been equal. The slopes of total revenue is marginal revenue (MR) and the slope of total cost curve is marginal cost (MC). Hence profit maximisation needs that

$$MC=MR$$

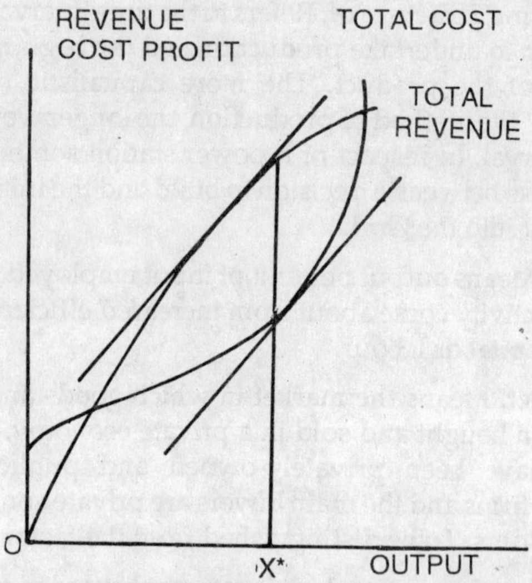

Profit Maximization

Profit Motive. Is considered to pertain where profit offers the spur which conditions firms' organization of production activities.

Profit Rate. Profit which is expressed as a proportion of the book value of capital assets.

Profits. Refers to the difference between the revenue generated from the sale of output and the full opportunity costs of the factors used in the production of that output. Included within costs have been the premium charge for risk taking and the costs of using the owner's capital. These have been not included as costs in the accountants' measure of profit which therefore does not correspond to this economic definition of profit.

Profits Push Inflation. Refers to a variant cost-push inflation, which attributes the origins of the inflationary process to capitalists who seek an enhanced share of national income. Prices have been thus said to be pushed up by oligopolistic producers who have a degree of market power that gives them considerable flexibility in the setting of prices, particularly in the short run.

Programming Methods. A generic name which is used for a set of optimization techniques and usually involving iterative solution methods. An example has been linear programming.

Progressive Tax. Generally refers to a situation where the proportion of income taken in tax (the tax rate) rises with income or spending power. Most income tax systems in Western countries have been progressive. Thus is achieved by a system of rising marginal rates of tax with increments of income.

Project Financing. A form of lending increasingly used for natural resource developments, where more emphasis has been placed on the borrower's future cash flow for repayments, rather than an immediate assets.

Proletariat. Refers to a class of persons which owns little or no property. The distinguishing characteristic of such a group has been the necessity for them to sell their labour services in return for wages. In Marxist theory the proletariat have been the exploited class which will eventually overthrow the capitalist bourgeoisie by social revolution and create a communist economy.

Promissory Note. Means a promise to pay a certain sum at a stated time, in documentary form. Depending upon its credit standing such a note has been negotiable.

Propensities to Consume and Save. Concepts which were developed by John Maynard Keynes (1883-1946). These represent the fractions of the total proceeds or income derived from employment which are, respectively consumed and invested. The amount which a community spends on consumption has been found to depend:

(a) partly on the amount of its income;

(b) partly on the other attendant circumstances;

(c) partly on the subjective needs and the psychological propensities and habits of the individuals composing it; and

(d) the principle on which the income is divided between them.

Property Rights. The rights which pertain to the permissible use of resources, goods and services. Ownership of an assets is having the following right : to use that asset, to change its form and substance and to transfer all rights through sale. Ownership of an asset has been not unfettered because some restrictions have been generally imposed by private contract or law

Proportional Tax. Refers to a situation where the proportion of income taken in tax stays the same as income increases. There is therefore a constant marginal rate of tax which equals the effective or average rate.

Propulsive Industries. A group of key industries whose interaction and expansion can offer a stimulus to growth in an economy. These industries are forming the nucleus of the growth pole concept introduced by the French economist Perroux.

Protection. Means the adoption by the State of special measures to protect an industry from competition.

Proxy Variable. Refers to the taking of unemployment or some other variable as a 'proxy' for demand, instead of directly measuring demand forces.

Proxy Variable. A variable which is used in regression analysis to replace or 'stand in for' another theoretically more satisfactory variable in cases where either data have been not available on the latter, or the latter is unobservable (e.g., 'desired' levels of consumption or permanent income).

Public Choice. A branch of economics which deals with the application of economics to the analysis of 'non-market' decision--making. It may also be considered as an economic analysis of politics.

Public Cognisance. A term which was used by Professor John Kenneth Galbraith in his Economics and the Public Purpose 1974 to describe the political recognition by the public of the basic divergence between the goals pursued by the planning system and the public interest.

Public Company. See Company.

Public Debt Ratio. Refers to the ratio of public money debt in a nation which is expressed as a ratio of gross national product (G.N.P.) O.E.C.D. studies reveal that the public debt/G.N.P. ratio is around 40 per cent in the United States of America, Japan, West Germany and Australia. In Britain, the ratio has been just over 50 per cent.

Public Expenditure. Broadly expenditures which are made by local and national government agencies as distinct from those of private individuals, organizations or firms.

Public Finance. Refers to the traditional name for the revenue and expenditure activities of government. Conventionally there have been at least three functions, namely the allocation function, distribution functions and stabilization function.

Public Good. Means a commodity or service which if supplied to one person can be made available to others at no extra cost.

Public Sector. The 'public sector' of the economy usually denotes the combination of the Central Government, the local authorities and the nationalised industries and other public corporations.

Public Sector Borrowing Requirement (PSBR). Refers to the amount by which the revenue of public sector organization falls short of expenditure.

Public Utility. Refers to a company or enterprise which has been the sole supplier of some essential good or service and is, in consequence, subject to some form of government control.

Purchasing Power Parity. Means of theory having little practical validity which considers the equilibrium exchange rate between two currencies to be when they have equivalent domestic purchasing power.

Purchasing Power Parity Theory. Refers to a theory which asserts that, left to the free play of market forces, the rates of exchange between currencies depend upon the relative purchasing power of the currencies in the country concerned.

Purchase Tax. A type of sales tax. It existed in the UK before the introduction of value-added tax in 1973.

Pure Competition. Refers to a large number of small firms selling a homogeneous product.

Pure Monopoly. Refers to a situation in which a single seller offers a product which has no close substitutes.

Put Option. The Buyer (taker) acquires the ratio to sell a futures contract at a basis (or strike) price agreed at the time of concluding the contract.

Pure Profit. Refers to a residual sum left over when we have subtracted from the revenue generated by some activity all of the opportunity costs of production, the normal profit needed to keep the producer in business.

Pushfulness. Refers to a propensity of unions to engage in a wage push, i.e., their mood for militant action.

Put, To. To sell.

Puts. A holder's option to sell.

Putty-Clay. Refers to an aspect of the production function which permits substitution of labour for capital and ***vice versa*** before actual investment is carried out but once machines are installed the capital-labour ratio cannot be varied. Thus tax ante capital has been 'putty' but ex post it becomes hard baked 'clay' Putty-clay models are seen as a compromise between perfect substitutability (putty-putty) and rigidly fixed proportions (clay-clay).

Putty-Putty. Means aspect of the production function in growth theory which allows capital to be continuously reshaped, both before (ex-ante) and after (ex post) investment has taken place. Thus capital is seen as 'putty' both before and after actual investment such that the capital-labour ratio may be continuously varied.

Pyraminding. If a tax is imposed at an early stage of production, the effect on the final price when a percentage increase is made at each successive stage of manufacture.

Pyramid Selling. Refers to a selling techniqe which involves a company selling the right to sell a product, or the right to sell a product. A pyramid company provides earnings to buyers of rights through the very act of selling more and more distributorship or franchises, and by charging participants for a place higher up the pyramid. Higher earnings are provided for selling franchises than for selling the product. The typical recruitment pattern involves each participant recruiting one person a week. The impracticability of this has resulted in many people losing heavily. The pyramid company has been outlawed in many American States. France, Canada, and several other countries.

Pyramid sub-Contracting. Refers to a system in which a subcontractor agrees to do a job for a fixed cash sum, this is then parcelled out in agreed cash amounts among 'self--employed' workers recuited to do the job.

Q

Q-Ratio. This term divided by Professor Japes Tobin (1981 Nobel Memorial Prize in economics). It is a ratio, derived empirically, which measures the relationship of the market value of physical capital (such as existing plant or other corporate asset) to its replacement cost. If the Q-ratio is low, corporations tend to acquire existing assets rather than build new plant and equipment. High interest rates may make existing assets look cheap and expense to replace.

Quality of Life. In current usage it is a phrase which covers a miscellany of desirable things not necessarily recognised or adequately recognised, in the market place. Some qualities of the life of a community which cannot readily be valued or measured have been such matters as civil liberties, compassion, justice, freedom and fair play.

Quangos. Quasi-autonomous non-government organisations which are created by governments for the purposes of delegating or avoiding responsibility. Quangos have been boards, commissions, authorities, and agencies which operate outside the normal departmental structure of government.

Quantity Theory of Money. A theory which was developed by the American economist Irving Fisher (1867-1947) the essentials of which have been contained in the equation.

$$MV = PT$$

where M=the amount of money (bank notes, etc. plus bank deposits), V=the velocity of circulation, P=a price index covering all transactions, and T=total volume of transactions per unit of time.

From this equation it follows that with V and T constants an increase in M must result in an increase in P. With V and P constants, an increase in M could be offset by an increase in T: with both P and T constant, a decrease in M could be offset by an increase in V. If T has been constant an increase in P must be due to an increase in M or V or both. The equation is useful in indicating the relationship between the four para meters. This suggests that inflation could be controlled by the monetary authorities through the regulation of the quantity of money in existence. If a certain growth in real income is anticipated, this can be realised without inflation by allowing the quantity of money in the economy to increase at the same rate.

Quasi-Rent. Means the return to a seller of a good or service over and above its opportunity cost when the good is temporarily in fixed supply. The concept was applied by Alfred Marshall to the determination of the price of capital in the short run when the supply of capital has been fixed. The owners of capital obtain a payment which is different from the opportunity cost of using that resource by the amount of Quasi-rent. In the long run when the factor can be augmented or depleted the equilibrium price will be reflecting the cost of alternative uses. Quasi-rent exists because prices in the short run have been not in equilibrium. Marshall used this concept as an element in his explanation of the rate of profit.

Quaternary Employment. Employment in educational establishments, research and development centres, and in providing consultant and specialist services, meeting the needs of the primary, secondary and tertiary sectors of the economy.

Queueing, Theory of. Theory dealing with the rates at which productive facilities and services should be provided so as to achieve optimum efficiency, i.e., to minimise `queues' or bottlenecks and synchronise better the supply of facilities or services with the demand for them. In management science, queueing theory tries to describe how customers arrive for a service, how that service meets their requirements in terms of average and variations in service time, how long a customer may have to wait and how long a service unit may be idle. The theory of queueing is also known as 'waiting line theory'.

Quick Assets (U.S.). Current assets which can be quickly converted into cash.

Quick Assets Ratio. Refers to the ratio of liquid assets to current liabilities. Liquid assets include cash, most term investments which can be quickly realized and accounts receivable where an allowance is made for bad debts. Stock is not included as it may not be readily realizable.

Quits. Employees who voluntarily leave their current employment either to change jobs or to leave the labour force.

Quota. Means an imposed limit on the quantity of goods which are produced or purchased. Import quotas might be used to restrict the purchase of goods from foreign origins, while export quotas have been used to stablize the export earnings of countries producing primary products by restricting supply, and thereby sustaining prices. Quotas may also refer to the minimum required level of production, especially in the context of planned economies.

Quoted companies. The term used for those companies whose share capital can be freely dealt on the stock exchange.

R

Radical Economics. The generic name which is used for writing in a socialist or Marxist tradition, relating in the main to Marxism but adopting and using other sources of ideas such as anarchism and libertarianism. The writers have been often referred to as 'The New Life.'

Raider Firm. The term used for a company which is having the potential to establish itself as a takeover threat to another company.

Rally. A brisk rise which follows a decline in the general price level of a security market, or of an individual stock or share.

R and D. Abbreviation of Research and Development.

Random Walk. An example of a time series model in which the current value of a variable has been equal to its most recent value plus a random element.

Range. Means the difference between the highest and the lowest price at which a given futures contract has traded during a particular period of time e.g., the period of the market, the closing period of the market, or any day, week, or month.

Range (of a Good). In regional or spatial economics, it refers to the maximum distance which people will travel for the purpose of buying a particular good. The range gives the outer limit of the area (known as the market area) within which a particular good will be offered from a given location. The range concept has been used, as part of central place theory, in explaining patterns of location of retail and service centres.

Rank Correlation. Refers to a measure of the degree to which two variables have been associated with each other, not necessarily in value, but in rank (or ordering). The measure involves the assigning of a rank to each of the observations on each of the variables according to decreasing value. Hence the highest observations for each variable would be assigned the number 1, the second highest 2 ect. The calculation of the rank correlation coefficient (sometimes called Spearman's rank correlation coefficient) involves computing

$$r_s = 1 - \frac{6 \sum_{i-1}^{N} D_i^2}{N(N^2-1)}$$

where D_t denotes the difference between the ranks assigned to the ^{i}th observation on each of the variables and N the sample size.

Rank of a Matrix. The term used for the maximum number of linearly independent rows of columns of the matrix.

Ratchet Theory of Pricing. This theory is a view that manufacturers tend to raise prices when costs rise, but do not reduce them when costs fall.

Rate of Interest, The. The term used for the price of money services While financial markets exhibit a range of rates of interest the theory of the rate of interest explains the determinants of the 'pure' rate of interest which has been the price that would have to be paid to borrow money so as to undertake a complete riskless enterprise. Keynes argued that the rate of interest had been monetary phenomenon reflecting the supply and demand for money.

Rate of Return. A general concept which refers to the earnings from the investment of capital, where the earnings have expressed as a proportion of the outlay. The term is applicable to a wide variety of situations in economics. It can refer to the earnings from the investment of physical capital, money capital and also to the return to investment in human capital. The term is most frequently applicable to the rewards from capital expenditure by businesses.

Rate of Surplus Value. In the Marxian scheme it refers to the ratio which surplus value bears to variable capital. Marx considered this as an expression for the degree of exploitation of labour by capital, for the rate of surplus value indicates how many hours the worker labours creating profit for the capitalist for every hour he labours creating the value equivalent of his own subsistence.

Rate Support Grant. The term used for a mechanism for transferring funds from the national government to local authorities.

Rational Expectations. Means the application of principal of rational maximizing behaviour to the acquisition and processing of information for the purpose of forming a view about the future. It indicates that individuals do not make systematic forecasting errors; on the contrary that their guesses about the future have been on average correct. Thus, the theory indicates that individuals use all the available and relevant information when taking a view about the future and at a minimum use information up to the point at which the marginal costs of acquiring and processing information equal to the marginal benefits derived from this activity. In the extreme where information has been complete and there exists no uncertainty, this hypothesis reduces to one of perfect foresight.

Rational Expectations School. This term used for a group of economists who, disenchanted with the failures of micro-economic policies in the 1970s.

The rational expectations school believes that there need be no involuntary unemployment, for anyone can find work by asking for it at a wage below the existing wage. The aim has been that markets should clear and that economic agents should set wages and prices so as to achieve full employment, maximise profits, and maximise economic welfare.

Rationality. The term used for the behaviour by an economic agent (consumer, producer, government etc.) which has been consistent with a set of rules governing preferences.

Rational Lags. Refers to a distributed lag formulation in which the weights on successive values of the lagged variable have been determined by the ratio of two polynomial lag schemes. This provides greater flexibility of lag structure than the simple use of the latter.

Rationing. The term used for any method of allocating a scarce product to service other than by means of the price mechanism. Rationing of some form must be undertaken if, within a market, price is artificially maintained at a level below equilibrium.

Rawlsian Justice. Refer to an approach to the issue of a just society, and in particular distributive justice, which has been postulated by the Harvard University philosopher John Rawls. In his book, A Theory of Justice, Rawls considered that a just arrangement of society is that which individuals would choose if they were uninfluenced by their own purely personal vested interests.

R, D and D. Research, Development and Demonstration.

Reaction Functions. Specifies for any one firm the optimum value for a choice variable given the value chosen by competitors. Reaction functions have been commonly used in oligopoloy theory, for instance, in a duopoly within which each firm chooses that output level which maximizes profit,. and considers the output level of the other to remain constant in response to that choice, the reaction function of the two firms permits us to trace the output path of the industry.

Real Balance Effect. Generally the term used to describe the situation where there exists a change in the demand for commodities because of a change in the quantity of real money balances.

Real Cost Approach to International Trade. The Ricardian theory of comparative advantage has been based on a real cost approach. Real cost was initially the exertion of labour in making a commodity, but it got subsequently extended to the use of capital, because the formation of capital involves abstinence from present consumption. The approach maintains that it is in differences in real costs which comparative advantage lies. Land, however, enters into the production of traded goods, but it has been not possible to regard the use of land as involving a real cost. Due to this deficiency the real cost approach is largely superseded by the opportunity cost approach to international trade.

Real Gross National Product. Refers to the value of the output of the national economy which is measured in the prices of some base year, allowing a true measure of the change in actual economic physical output.

Real Income. The term used for the value of goods and services produced within a given time period.The changes in real income over or between time periods have been computed by adjusting changes in nominal income arising from changes in the level of prices alone.

Real Interest Rate. An interest rate which is calculated by deflating nominal interest rate by the rate of inflation. If the inflation rate has been higher than interest rates, investors have been left with a negative real return if yields exceed the rate of increase in the consumer price index, the return has been positive.

Real Money Balances. Mean the quantity of goods and services which could be purchased from a given stock of money held by indivuduals. Changes in real-money balances could be computed by adjusting changes in the quantity of money held to take account of changes in the level of prices.

Real Money Balances. The value of money holdings which are measured in terms of the quantity of goods and services they command.

Real National Output. Means the values of total output--national income--measured in 'constant prices'--i.e., with the general rate of inflation deducted so as to record the real command over resources.

Real Wage Resistance. Description which was used by Sir John Hicks (b. 1904) to describe the reluctance of workers to accept a cut in their standard of living. An increase in prices consequently results in a price-induced rise in wages so as to maintain the standard of living.

Real Wage. Wage rates or wage earnings which could be measured in terms of the goods and services they can buy. Theoretically they could be measured by the slope of the budget constraint relating house of leisure to the amounts of market goods for which hours can be exchanged in the market. In practice, they could be obtained by dividing or 'deflating,' nominal wage rates or wage earnings by the retail price index.

Receiver. A receiver is a person who is appointed to take over the property of a debtor, and to receive the income from that property with a view to paying off the debt.

Recession. Means a significant reduction in employment and production, trade and investment. This term was defined by Arthur M. Okun (1928-1980) as two consecutive quarters of negative growth in the gross national Product.

Reciprocal Demand. Refers to the demand by one country, in terms of its own goods offered, for the goods of another. The concept was given by J.S. Mill to explain how the exact international terms of trade would be established between the two closed economy equilibrium price ratios between two commodities by using the strength of reciprocal demand in each country. This situation Mill described as the equation of international demand.

Recognition Lag. Means the period that elapses between the time an economic disturbance takes place and the time policy-makers and governments recognise that action is needed. The recognition lag may be negative, if a problem is foreseen and appropriate policy actions adopted before the event. Most lags are positive due partly to the difficulties of collecting appropriate data and partly as it is never certain what the consequences of a disturbance will be.

Recontract. Refers to an arrangement by which buyers or sellers are able to change the amount on offer if that particular set of price does not clear the market, the amount will then get changed according to whether there is an excess-demand or excess-supply situation.

Recursive Model. It is a model in which the current values of one set of variables could determine the current value of another, whereas previous (or lagged) values of the latter determine the current values of the former. A simple example of a recursive model is as follows:

$$Y_t = a + bX_t$$

$$X_t = c + dY_t$$

where X and Y have been variables and

a, *b*, *c* and *d* have been constants.

The Cobweb model in price theory is a recursive model.

Recycling. The term used for the process of returning the waste so that it can be re-used to manufacture the same product as before or some other product.

Redistribution. The term used for the process of altering the existing distribution of (usually) income or wealth in a society. Redistribution may occur as the result of a deliberate policy to transfer income between individuals or may be an 'accidental' effect of a policy.

Reduced Form (RF). The term used for the form of a set of simultaneous equations in which the endogenous variables have been expressed as functions of only exogenous variables, i.e., no endogenous variables appear on the right hand side of the equations.

Redundencies. Involuntary job losses which occur due to a reduction in manpower requirements on the part of firm.

Re-Export. A good which is imported from one country, and is not consumed within the importing country but is instead sent to a third country.

Reflection Effect or Full-Circle Effect. When for example an extension of aid overseas results in indirectly to an increase of exports as well. Suppose that out of S million aid to a country, half is spent on third country products, if part of this expenditure on third country products gets reflected back to the donor country as third-country imports, allowance should be made in assessing the cost of aid for this reflection effect.

Regional Assistance. Assistance by the Government to regions with special problems. A country is divided into special development areas, development areas (jointly known as the assisted areas), and enterprise zones.

Regional Development Grant. This term used for the payments made by the government to firms which are undertaking new manufacturing investment in those regions designated as Development Areas and Special Development Areas.

Regional Economics. That branch of economic analysis which deals with the spatial distribution of economic activity and spatial variation in levels of economic performance. The subject could be split in the usual way into macroeconomic and microeconomic topics.

Regional Multiplier. Refers to a version of the multiplier which is used in the analysis of regional economics. The regional multiplier has been used to predict the change in total income or employment in a region which gets resulted from an increase in some element of autonomous expenditures. The regional multiplier is somewhat similar to the usual multiplier used in macroeconomics in that an initial increase in demand is said to result in an even greater expansion of regional income as the income received from the initial injection of demand is spent and received from the initial injection of expenditure--the process coming to an end when the demand increase has been offset by leakages through saving, taxation and imports.

Regional Policy. Refers to a forms of government economic policy which has been aimed at altering the regional pattern of economic activity or economic performance.

Regional Wage Differentials. Refer to differences in the average levels of pay of groups of workers classified according to the region in which they are employed.

Regional Wage Structure. Refers to the ranking of the average of pay levels of different groups of workers classified in accordance to the region in which they are employed.

Registered Unemployed. In many countries such as U.S.A, U.K. etc., these comprise all persons who have been registered as seeking employment and who have been classified by the staff of the employment offices as capable of and available for work, whether they are entitled to unemployment benefit or not.

Regressand. Refers to the dependent variable in a regression analysis.

Regressive Tax. Normally the term is used to refer to a situation where the rate of tax falls as income rises. Most indirect taxes are generally considered to be regressive. With excise duties the same amount of tax has been paid per unit purchased. This represents a lower proportion of income the higher the latter becomes.

Regressor. An independent variable in a regression analysis.

Relative Deprivation. A concept which has been borrowed by institutional economists from sociology to offer a micro behavioural foundation of the allegedly non-market process whereby wages have been determined. Relative deprivation has been that feeling which is said to arise when individual/group *i* observes another group *r* (the referent group) experiencing something, like a higher wage than *i* currently has, and which *i* has been also desirous of obtaining and considers feasible. Perception of relative deprivation has been intimately related to the process of reference group comparisons and the choice of comparisons will dictate the magnitude of relative deprivation experienced by *i*.

Relative Income Hypothesis. According to this hypothesis, individual and/or household consumption has been a function both of income relative to that of other households or individuals and to the level of income in the immediately preceding periods. This two-part theory was postulated by J.Duesenberry (1949) to explain the conflicting long-run and short-run cross-section evidence on the specification of the consumption function.

Relativities. Refers to relationships between the average levels of workers and groups of workers in different pay negotiating units. Also, refer to the relationships between the average levels to pay of groups of workers in the same occupations but covered by different negotiating group. While frequently considered distinct from wage differential they have been essentially a specific sub-group of these.

Renewable Resource. The term used for any resource which is capable of being replenished, in part or whole, by 'natural' means. Examples include fish, timber, animal populations.

Rent. Economic Rent.

Rent Gradient. A relationship used in urban economics. It expresses the rent paid for of a unit of land as a function of distance from some reference point--generally the city or town centre.

Rentiers. Owners of capital who derive all or most of their income from this source, but who choose to exert no effective control over its use.

Rent, Ricardo's Theory of. It is a proposition which states that the rent of a piece of land has been the excess of the yield of that piece of land over that of the worst land in cultivation. Ricardo regarded that land at the margin of cultivation yielded no rent, indeed if rent was charged the land would not be cultivated. Farmers would have to pay more for the use of more fertile land, and the excess yield over that of 'no-rent' land would be its rent. Hence the net return to farmers on a unit of land of any given fertility would tend to be the same. Recardo regarded the rent of land as a surplus or economic rent.

Replacement of Cost Accounting. The term used for a method of accounting which adjusts for price changes by calculating profit as the difference between the selling price of a good and its replacement cost on date of sale.

Replacement Investment. Means the amount necessary for replacing that part of the capital stock which has been used up in the process of production.

Replacement Ratio. Refers to the ratio of total net resources (income plus benefits net of tax and housing outlays, allowing for rent and rate rebates) when unemployed to that when working.

This ratio may in certain cases become greater than unity and this possibility has led to a great deal of popular speculation about the disincentive effects of unemployment and other benefits available to the out cost of work.

Representative Firm. A firm which is characteristic of the industry or sector of the economy being analysed.

Repressed Inflation. Refers to a situation where a price freeze has been controlling the rate of change of prices without affecting the underlying inflationary tendencies.

Reproduction Costs. Costs which are involved to achieve a sustained level of production, such costs might be involved in conserving the natural environment or offering a training programme for recruits to the industry. Such costs, such as those incurred in a major reaforestation programme may yield no return in the short or medium-term.

Resale Price Maintenance. A trade practice which binds shopkeepers and dealers to sell goods at prices laid down by the manufacturer or other supplier. The main effect of resale price maintenance has been that it eliminates price competition between distributors of price-maintained goods.

Resale Price Maintenance. Refers to the agreement whereby manufacturers independently or collectively will specify minimum prices at which their products could be resold by wholesalers and retailers.

Research and Development (R and D). Activity which is denoted to increasing scientific or technical knowledge and applying that knowledge to the creation of new products and means of production as well as to the improvement of existing products and production processes. When research and development has been extended to the manufacture of a prototype commercial product, the term 'research development and demonstration' will be used to describe the whole sequence.

Reservation Wage. The worker searching the labour market for a job will be having some idea of the wage he desires or merits, based on his previous wage and wage offers that are known in some expectational sense. He can thus be viewed as setting a minimum standard for jobs he will find acceptable. This is termed as the reservation wage.

Reserve Base. The term used for the quantity in the financial system of those assets which, either practically or legally, may constitute the reserves of the banking system, and which in the traditional theory of the credit multiplier from the multiplicand on which that multiplier operates to find out the total quantity of bank deposit money.

Reserve Bank of India. Prior to the establishment of the Reserve Bank of India in 1935, the Imperial Bank of India, though primarily a commercial bank, carried out certain central banking functions and in particular acted as a banker to the Government.

The Reserve Bank was originally constituted as a shareholders institution with a share capital of Rs. 5 crores. The capital has remained unchanged to this day. The entire share capital was, in the beginning, owned by private shareholders with the exception of shares of the nominal value of Rs. 2.2 lakhs. which were given to the Central Government. Subsequently, the entire share capital of the Bank was acquired by the Central Government against compensation to the shareholders from 1st January, 1949, and it became a sates-owned institution.

The main function of the Bank has been to regulate the issue of bank notes and keep reserves for securing monetary stability. The Bank is the sole authority for the issue of currency in India other than one rupee coins/notes and subsidiary coins. As the agent of the Central Government, it undertakes the distribution of the one rupee notes and coins as well as small coins issued by the Government of India.

The Bank acts as banker to the Government of India, state governments, commercial banks and to some of the financial institutions including state co-operative banks. It formulates and administers monetary policy in order to influence the level of aggregate demand for goods and services by varying the cost and availability of credit. The Reserve Bank also plays vital role in the maintenance of the exchange value of the rupee, and acts as an agent of the government in respect of

India's membership of the International Monetary Fund. The Bank also undertakes a variety of developmental and promotional functions.

Reserve Currency. The name assigned to a foreign currency which a government is prepared to hold as parts of its foreign exchange reserves. It is used to finance international trade.

Reserve-Deposit Ratio. Refers to the ratio of reserves which are to be held with the Reserve Bank of certain countries by the commercial banks and the deposits held by the banks.

Reserve Requirements. Refers to the volume of reserves that member banks must hold with a central bank of certain country as a percentage against existing deposits. A reduction in the reserve requirement increases excess reserves and tends to stimulate the economy, whereas an increase tends to have the opposite effect.

Reserve Tranche. Formerly termed as the gold tranche. It is a credit line extended by the International Monetary Fund. The reserve tranchee is 25 per cent of a country's quota and may be borrowed automatically. In addition to the reserve tranche, there have been three credit tranches (each being 25 per cent of the quota) carrying progressively tougher terms.

Restricted Least Squares (Rls). A method which is used for estimating the parameters of an equation in which a prior information is taken into account. For example in a Cobb-Douglas production function we may desire to impose the restriction of constant returns to scale by constraining the sums of the estimates of the exponents of the factor inputs to be equal to one. The procedure has been based on ordinary least squares, but results in better estimates in the sense that their variances have been smaller than those which would be obtained by unrestricted techniques.

Restrictive Practice. (a) Any inefficient working method or system which has been difficult to alter, due to opposition from the management, the workers or both. The practice may be perhaps unnecessary overtime working, for which the management has been primarily responsible; or it may be a set of traditional working practices for which the unions are primarily responsible.

(b) Also, refers to a practice in restraint of trade or production. Among firms such practices as common prices, collusive tendering allotment of sales or output quotas, division of market exclusive dealing and loyalty rebates to customers may be used.

Restructuring. Means the reforming of the administrative and management structure of a company or the revising of its share capital structure; sometimes the term has been a euphemism for the dismissal of workers without any serious restructuring being involved.

Reswitching. (also known as double switching). In the capital controversy the notion that a technique of production abandoned when the rate of profits has been low may be introduced when the rate of profit rises to much higher levels with an alternative more profitable technique (or techniques) being used in the interim. It is a problem which is arising from heterogeneous capital. If the capital to output ratios in each technique have been not equal the factor price frontiers of the individual techniques exhibit varying degrees of curvature.

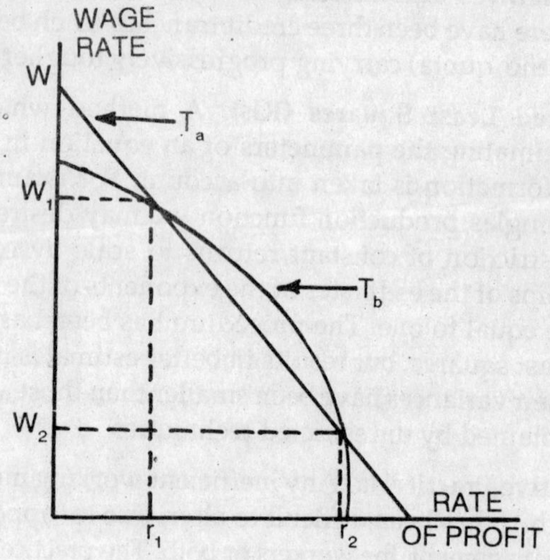

Factor Price Frontiers

This can be shown for two techniques with associated factor price frontiers T_a and T_b. For rates of profit r less than r_1 T_a has been more profitable. For $r_1 < r < r_2$, T_b has been more profitable, but for $r_1 > r_2$, it has been more profitable to readopt T_a which amounts to switching back to the technique abandoned who the rate of profit first rose above r_1. Hence the name 'reswitching'. The possibility of reswitching increases serious theortical problems for wide areas of neoclassical economics, especially the aggregate production and the marginal productivity theory of distribution.

Reswitching of Techniques. Refers to the possibility that a given manufacturing technique may be the most profitable one for business firms to adopt at two different rates of profit, while being unprofitable at rates between the two. For this reason, it has been not possible in general to draw a negatively inclined demand curve for capital as a function of the rate of profit or rate of return on capital.

Retail. The term used for the final stage in the chain of distribution from manufacturer to consumer. It is the outlet for goods and services purchased by consumers.

Retail Banking. The term is applicable to the traditional banking operations which are being conducted by the clearing banks and increasingly by the trustee savings banks and others, through their branch systems, with the general public.

Retail Price Index. An index number of prices of goods which has been often referred to as the 'cost of living index'. It is regarded as a measure of relative changes in the prices of a specified set of consumer goods which would be bought by the average household on a regular basis. The weights have been based on information from the government's survey of family expenditure to ensure that it relates to present day buying patterns. Goods representing larger proportions of expenditure will then be assigned more significant weights in the index.

Retention Ratio. Refers to the percentage of the available disposable income (i.e., earnings after tax and after fixed interest and dividend obligations have been met) retained within the firm.

The diagram below depicts iso-product curves and illustrates all three types of returns to scale. Each iso-product curve is representing an equal increment to production. Section ab illustrates increasing returns, *bc,* constant returns and *cd* decreasing returns.

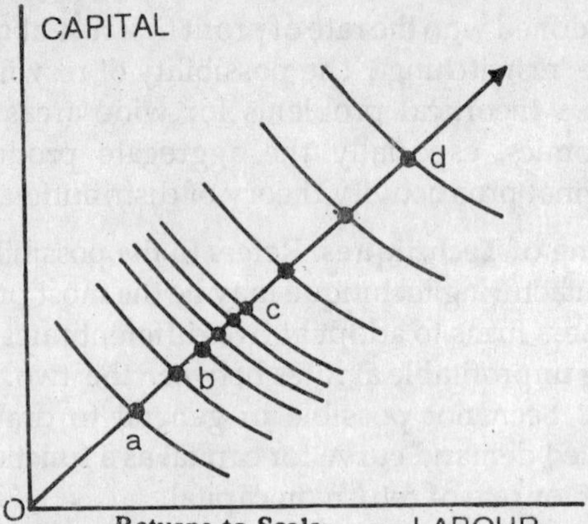

Returns to Scale

Resource Rent Tax. A tax which is based on profits in excess of a level necessary for the commencement or continuation of a project.

Revealed Preference Theory (R.P.T.). First formulated by Professor Paul A. Samuelson (b. 1915). It is a theory of consumer behaviour based solely on an analysis of choices actually made by the consumer in various price-income situations. A given income level and set of prices makes the consumer to select 'bundles' of goods he could purchase; the bundle selected is the revealed preference to all the other bundles that might have been purchased instead. Another income-price situation could reveal another bundle of goods as the revealed preference.

Reverse Dumping. Refers to the practice of selling a good abroad at a price higher than charged for the same good in the domestic market to take advantage of a monopoly position.

Revolving Credit Agreement. A written contractual agreement which is made between a commercial bank and a customer for the bank to offer short-term funds up to a specified limit for a stipulated period of time at an interest rate generally tied to the prime rate.

Right-to-Work Laws. In the US, where the term originated, the closed shop has been illegal and individual states have been free to prohibit the enforcement of a union shop clause. This prohibition is known as a right-to-work law. Such laws have nothing to do with the right to a job; rather they deal with the right nct to joins unions as a condition of employment.

Risk. Chance of injury or loss. There are two types of risk:

(a) insurable risk, e.g., fire, burglary etc.;

(b) non-insurable risk or uncertainty, e.g., the risk of loss through changes in the future demand for goods. This type of risk or uncertainty may be reduced by, inter alia, hedging.

Risk Capital. Capital subject to considerable risk. It is also called 'venture capital'.

Risk Management. The term dealswith the process of indentification, classification, measurement, and appropriate control of risks that threaten assets, both people and property, and the prospective earnings of a business or other enterprise. The costs of control and management of risks need to be weighed against the cost of insuring against risk, both elements being needed in most instances.

Risk Premium

1. An addition to the 'pure' discount rate so as to take account of the uncertainty associated with the future benefits or revenue from a project. Its use means that the risks involved increase at a compound rate with time, which has been unlikely to be the case. Only if risk consists solely of the probability of failure in different periods being equal and naturally independent, has been a risk premium appropriate.

2. In an uncertain world, refers to that part of the return to capital which compensates the owners of capital for the risk involved in its use in business ventures.

Rival. If one individual's consumption of a good reduce the quantity available to others then that good is considered to display rivalness or to be rival in consumption. Rivalness has been a characteristic of private goods which have been thus scarce and require a process of allocation. Examples of goods which are non-rival include the use of knowledge and sunshine.

Roosa Effect. Term which was formerly used for what is now more commonly called the 'locking in effect.' It was named after Robert V. Roosa, a US banker and economist who was an early proponent of its significance.

Rostow Model. One of the most famous historical theories of economic growth. It was suggested by Professor W.W. Rostow in 1961. He divides the growth process into five stages.

1. The Traditional Society
2. The Pre-conditions for take-off
3. The Take-off
4. The Drive to Maturity
5. The Stage of High Mass Consumption

Roundaboutness. The term which is used to define more time-consuming and usually more productive methods of production. Fish could be caught directly but inefficiently by hand. If a fisherman had to spend some time constructing a rod, he would be more successful in catching fish because of this roundabout process. A still greater time spent making a net, a yet more roundabout process, would make even greater catches. An increase in roundaboutness has been also described as a lengthening of the period of production.

RPI. Abbreviation of Retail Price Index.

Rule-of-Thumb. A simple formula or procedure which forms the basis for decision—making by economic agents. It can be argued that under conditions of imperfect information and uncertainty resort to rough and ready rules has been unavoidable.

Rybczynski Theorem. Theorem, developed by economist of that name, to the effect that if in the Heckscher-Ohlin framework one of the two factors of production gets increased, to maintain constant commodity and factor price it becomes necessary for the output of the good intensive in the use of the increased factor to expand and for the output of the other good intensive in the use of the constant.

S

Sackings. Mean discharges from employment for cause. Employees who have lost their job through some fault of their own. One element is labour turnover.

Salary. The term used for the remuneration of almost all non-manual and some manual employees in exchange for the supply of labour services.

Sales Tax. A tax which is levied on a market transaction. There have been many types of sales taxes but they may be divided between those which apply to a large range of expenditure and those which apply to sale of a specific good or service. Thus a value-added tax, a retail sales tax, a turnover tax and a comprehensive expenditure tax have been examples of general sales taxes. Customs, excise and protective duties have been examples of taxes on specific goods.

Salvage Value. When considering capital budgeting, the value of the capital assets at the end of the project life is to be taken into account. It is known as salvage value or scrap value.

Samural Bonds. Bonds denominated in yen, which are being issued in Japan by a foreign borrower.

Samuelson Test. According to the test one situation has been potentially superior in welfare terms to another if for every distribution of the commodity bundle in the first situation there exists some distribution of the second commodity bundle in which at least one person has been better-off and nobody is worse-off. This implies that the point utility possibility curve for the second bundle lies entirely outwith that of the first.

Satiation (Also known as Saturation). Refers to phenomenon of 'having enough' of a good. More formally, the utility attached to an extra unit of the good beyond its satiation level has been zero or negative, i.e., it creates zero utility or disutility.

Satisficing. It is an alternative theory of economic behaviour which was advanced by Herbert Simon in 1957. It has been a view that individuals and organisations have been not concerned with achieving the best possible or optimal results at all times, but only in maintaining certain satisfactory positions. As long as results take place above certain points then anything will do, and there will be no motivation to improve the situation further.

Satisficing Behaviour. Conduct which is aimed at achieving satisfactory aspiration levels of the objectives of decision-making and which may not therefore involve maximizing anything (e.g., profits). The concept of satisfying behaviour has been an integral feature of behavioural theories of the firm.

Saturation Point. Refers to a level beyond which the relative absorption of a product of service is not expected to increase. It is also defined in terms of a ratio; for example, ownership of refrigerators per household or per hundred persons. The saturation point once reached, the growth of demand slows down to levels determined by population growth and replacement.

Saving. That part of income which is not consumed; the withholding of money from expenditure on goods and service. The amount saved out of any given income has been found to depend upon the Propensities to Consume and Save and out of any addition to income on the marginal propensities to consume and save. In discussing the national economy, however, economists frequently use the term 'saving' for expenditure of a special kind–the employment of income in the creation of new capital. Thus saving has been identified with investment in real assets, and not with the "hoarding' of money which has been simply the non-expenditure of money held. Adopting this definition the saving and investment of a community can never diverge.

Saving Banks. Institutions which are aiming at encouraging and facilitating the small saver.

Saving Equal Investment. Refers to a maxim of Lord Keynes (1884-1946) who defined savings and expenditure on capital goods or investment as being of necessity equal to one another. The logic of his argument had been as follows:

Income = Expenditure on consumption goods and savings,

Output = Output of consumption goods and investment,
Since Total Income = Value of Total Output, and

Expenditure on consumption goods = Output of consumption goods.

Savings = Investment.

It has been the simplified (closed economy, no government) form of the basic Keynesian relationship. It really amounts to Injections = Withdrawals. It is both an identity and an equilibrium condition. In Keynesian theory, the relationship has been used to calculate the equilibrium level of income.

Savings Function, The. Refers to schedule detailing the relationship between aggregate saving (S) and income (Y), i.e., $S = S(Y)$. Savings could be related to either national of disposable income. The precise properties of the saving function have been the inverse of those of the consumption function, since $Y = C + S$.

Savings, Point of Zero. Refers to a level of disposable income at which it has been all consumed. Above this point, out of each additional unit of income a varying percentage will get devote to consumption and the remainder saved, below that point dissaving will take place, i.e. past savings will be used up and debts incurred.

Say's Law of Markets. A law which was formulated by the French economist J.B. Say. This law states that every increase in the supply of goods is a corresponding increase in the demand for goods so long as producers have directed their production in accordance with each other's wants. Hence, it was argued, a general over-production of goods cannot take place.

Scale Down. To buy at regular price intervals in a declining market, to scale up means to sell at regular price intervals as the market advances.

Scarcity. In economics, this term is usually reserved for situations in which the resources available for producing output have been insufficient to satisfy wants. This is different to saying that they have been insufficient to satisfy demand since demand relates to an expression of want backed by money. This concept of relative scarcity in relation to wants has been widely held to define the raison d'etre of economics because, otherwise, there would be no need to think about the 'best' allocation of resources.

Scarce Currency. Another name for hard currency.

Scatter. (also known as scatter diagram). Refer to a graphical representation of data in which the observed values of one variable have been plotted against those of another, without joining the points with intervening lines. A scatter diagram can provide useful pictorial information on the degree to which variables have been correlated with each other, and on the sort of mathematical relationship (liner, non-liner, etc.) which may exist between them.

Scientific Tariff. The term used for a tariff or tariff structure, which achieves the policy ends, often non-economic like national independence or military preparedness, at minimum cost to society. This is carried out by minimizing the cost of achieving each amount of benefit by adjusting the structure of tariff rates so as to equalize the ratio of marginal benefit to marginal cost in each industry protected and of maximizing the benefits of protection be selecting the general level of protection at which the marginal value of benefit equals the marginal cost of protection.

Scripophly. A term which was coined in the mid - 1970s to describe the hobby of collecting antique bonds, stocks, and other financial instruments.

SDR. Abbreviation of special Drawing Right.

Seasonal Adjustment. Refers to a name of any procedure by which seasonal influences have been taken into account, or (more usually) removed from data. The most common method involves the calculation of moving averages.

Seasonal Unemployment. Unemployment which results from the seasonal pattern of work in certain industries.

Secondary Banks. A term which is applied to a large group of deposit-taking financial institutions, many of them subsidiaries of, or associated with clearing, merchant and foreign banks. They competed vigorously for deposits, but also took up large sums in the newly developing money markets. They engaged in ordinary bank lending business, but also in the longer-term finance of expanding companies, frequently taking some equity interest. However many of them became heavily involved in lending for property development, and the property boom of the early 1970s. With tightening monetary conditions in 1973, and the collapse of the property boom in 1974, a number of these institutions got into difficulties. In this phase, known as the 'secondary banking crests', some houses collapsed, others were propped up by the 'lifeboat' operation initiated by the Bank of England. It should be noted that the term 'secondary bank' has been used differently to denote all recognized banks, other than the clearing and savings banks, operating in the U.K.

Secondar Industry or Manufacturing Industry. Refers to the processing of raw materials into finished products, including such activities as building and construction, and the supply of electricity and gas.

Secondary Market. It is a market for the resale and purchase of securities or other titles to property or commodities outside the organized exchange or primary markets. The secondary stock market deals in unquoted securities through private dealings amongst brokers, merchant banks and other person and institutions.

Secondary Workers. Refer to those groups whose attachment to the about force has been less permanent than those of primary workers. They include married women, teenagers and other workers (65 years of age or above).

Second Best, Theory of. Essentially, it is a theory which was first advanced by R.G.Lipsey and K. Lancaster. This theory states that if some part of the economy does not fulfil the Pareto optimal criterion it need not be optimal for any other sector of the economy to be expected to attain that position.

Secular Supply Curve. This curve relates changing levels of labour force participation to the phases of economic development, the latter variable being proxied by the real wage.

Secular Trend (also known as the Trend). The word 'secular' reveals that it is the trend computed for a long run of data.

Securities. A loose term which is embracing a wide range of financial assets, e.g., gilt-edged stock, equities and debentures. Short-term assets like bills have been sometimes included, but the word tends to refer to longer-term assets.

Securities are in two main forms:

(a) bonds, fully-paid stock, shares, stock units and un-numbered shares and

(b) partly-paid stock or shares.

Security Capital. Capital which is subject to a minimum amount of risk, as opposed to risk or venture capital.

Security Deposit, Initial. Synonymous with the term margin, a cash amount that must be deposited with the broker for each contract as a guarantee of fulfillment of the futures contract.

if the amount falls below a certain level, the broker may issue a call for an amount of money which will restore the customer's equity in the account to the original marginc level, this is termed as a security deposit (maintenance).

Self-Financing Ratio. Refers to amount of capital needed for new investment by an organisation obtained from its own earnings (i.e. from deprecation funds, profits and surpluses) expressed as a percentage of total capital requirements.

Self-Liquidating. Refers to a loan or other financial transaction which is having a low risk and a built-in procedure for ending the loan and clearing the debt, for example, hire purchase or bridging loans given by banks to make an individual to purchase a new house while in the process of selling the previous one.

Self-Liquidating Advances. Bank advances to customers which are for the purpose of trading over a temporary shortage of funds only e.g., when the farmer is faced with a heavy outlay of wages during the 'seed-time' to harvest period, the load repaid when the crop is sold.

Selling Hedge or Short Hedge. Selling futures contracts to provide protection against a possible decline in the prices of commodities.

Semi Log. Refers to a method of illustrating economic variables which change over time. For example if income growth has been constant, data may be plotted as a straight line on graph paper which has the logarithm of income on the vertical scale and time on the horizontal scale.

Seniority Practices. Refer to methods of regulating promotion., demotion and lay-off within a unit of a firm according to the seniority of the worker. Seniority rights could be viewed as beneficial to management and not simply to unions and workers.

Sensitivity Analysis. It involves changing the parameters of a decision problem and studying how this affects the outcome.

It has been particularly associated with cost benefit analysis, where the most common form has been the use of alternative discount rates. The purpose of the analysis has been to identify the important assumption upon which the analysis has been based those to which the outcome has been sensitive.

Serial Correlation. It is also known as autocorrelation. It is an econometric problem in which the current value of the error term in an equation gets correlated with its own past values, normally indicating that some systematic influence has been omitted from the equation. Nth order serial corrosion has been the correlation of the current value of the residual with its value N periods ago. First order serial correlation therefore means that the residual tends to follow a first order Markov Process of the form

$$e_t = pe_{t-1} + V_t$$

where e_t=damages the residual

v_t=damages a stochastic disturbance, and

p=damages the autocorrelation coefficient.

Service. In economic science it refers to a useful function fulfilled by a person, or organisation, and for the benefits of which consumers are prepared to pay a price. Payment, like service itself, may be direct or indirect.

Service of Debt. Refers to the payment of the interest due to on a debt.

Services. In an economic sense, they may be defined as any functions or tasks that are performed, for which there is has been a demand and hence a price determined in the relevant market. They are sometimes referred to as intangible goods, one of their characteristics being that in general they are 'consumed' at the point of production. They are generally non-transferable, thus preventing arbitrate, in the sense that the service cannot be purchased and then resold at a different type.

Severance Pay. Refers to a contractual method of ameliorating the economic costs of permanent layoff by giving compensation to workers made redundant. The aim of Severance pay has been to make job protection less necessary for the workers concerned and thereby to accommodate the process of economic change.

Shadow Price. Refers to a price or value which is imputed to unpriced social benefits or losses or to resources which are not satisfactorily priced in commercial markets. The concept has been much used in cost-benefit analysis. In evaluating any project, the economist may adjust a number of market prices and attribute prices to unpriced gains and losses likely to arise.

Shadow Price. Refers to an imputed valuation of a commodity service which does not have market price. Shadow prices have been used in cost-benefit analysis and in the application of mathematical programming to a planned economy. They represent the opportunity cost of producing or consuming a commodity which has been generally not traded in the economy.

Shadow Wage Rate. Refers to shadow price of labour.

Share. Refers to the individual portion of a company's capital which is owned by a shareholder. Shares are divided into different classes according to their terms of issue. Shares are brought and sold in multiples according to their price.

Sherman Act. One of the major foundation of antitrust law in the US, which was enacted in 1980. It was a response to public perceptions of earlier abuses by increasingly concentrated industries. The act forbids contracts, combinations and conspiracies in restraint of trade. In addition, monopolization and attempts to monopolize were prohibited. The maximum fine, originally $5,000. was raised to $50,000 in 1955, and to $1,000,000 for corporations in 1974.

Shift Effect Hypothesis. Refer to the argument that incomes policy might be having the effect of shifting the Phillips Curve to the left, thereby producing a lower rate of wage and/or price inflation for given values of their determinants--principally the level of unemployment. Tests of the hypothesis conventionally employ a simulation approach or shift dummy variables.

Shift-Share Analysis. A technique which is employed in the analysis of regional economic growth. This attempts to separate out that part of a region's growth which can be 'explained' by the mix of industries in the region ((its industrial structure) and that part which is to be explained in terms of particularly 'regional' influences.

Shop Steward. Refers to an appointed or elected representative of a workgroup who furthers the interests of employees in a plant or shop in matters like pay and conditions of employment.

Short Banking. The practice of not paying all monies received in business activities into the company's bank account.

Short End of the Treasury Security Market. A reference to short-term Treasury bills and notes with a duration of 90 days, 6 months, and up to 1 year, compared with notes and bonds with a duration in maturity of up to 30 years.

Short Run. Refers to the time period in the production process during which the fixed factors of production cannot get changed, but the level of utilization of variable factors can get altered. The concept was given by Alfred Marshall.

Short-Run Consumption Function. The term used for the functional relationship between consumption and income over the period of the trade cycle.

Short-Term Money Market. Refers to a market in which large borrowers and lenders of money and large buyers and sellers of securities come together to transact their daily business dealings.

Short-Time Working. Refers to workers who have been working fewer hours than the standard working week specified in their labour contract.

Side Payments. Those exchanges between individuals in a group made so as to induce allegiance to some common goals.

Sight Deposits. Refer to deposits held in banks and similar deposit-taking institutions which could be transferable by cheque or withdrawable in cash without notice.

Simulation. Refers to a form of forecasting which generates a range of alternative projections based on differing assumptions about future situations specifically to answer the question 'what would happen if?', rather than 'what will happen?'. In practice it is usually achieved through alterations to the values of exogenous variables and perhaps the parameters of economic models, and is often used to assess the likely impacts of various economic policies.

Sinking Fund. A fund which is built up by equal periodic instalments so as to accumulate a certain sum by a given date for some specific purpose, e.g., the replacement of a physical asset.

Sinners' Taxes. Taxes on alcohol, tobacco and betting.

Site Value Rating. The levying of local rates on owners of land rather than occupiers.

Situation Utility Possibility Frontier. Refers to the envelope of a set of point utility possibility curves. Sometimes it is known as the Welfare frontier. It is the locus of overall Pareto optima and shows the maximum possible level of utility for one individual for different given utility levels for other individuals.

Size Distribution of Firms. A frequency distribution where firms belonging to one industry or sector of the economy could be classified according to size. Size can be measured using a variety of indicators including sales, value-added, total assets and employment. Value-added has been generally thought of as the most appropriate measure to use.

Skewed Distribution. Refers to a distribution which is not symmetric around its mean value. A distribution which has a short left tail, and a long right one has been said to be skewed to the right, while a long left tail, and a short right one implies that the distribution has been skewed to the left. The degree of skewness could be calculated as the third moment of the sample or distribution about the mean.

Skill Differentials. Differences in the average levels of pay of groups of workers which are classified initially according to occupations which are subsequently assigned to broad skill groups.

Slack Plans. A notorious features of centrally planned economies has been the tendency for enterprises to strive for a plan which offers the production of less output than possible and/or the use of more inputs that necessary. This is carried out so as to enable the enterprise to meet plan targets by a comfortable margin.

Slump. Refers to a severe downturn phase or recession in the trade cycle. Any contactionary phase of the trade cycle could be termed as a slump but the term has been usually reserved for the most severe cases.

Slutsky Equation. Most simply defined as:

Price Effect = Income Effect

+ Substitution Effect

Named after E. Slutsky.

Snob Effect. The effect whereby as the price of a good falls and some sections of the community expand their demand for the good, other sections or individuals reduce their demand in order to differentiate themselves from the general trend. That is, they tend to do the opposite to the general trend. The effect is that the market demand curve may exhibit a seeper slope than would otherwise be predicted from a straightforward aggregation of individual demand curves.

Social Benefit. Refers to the sum of the gains of benefits deriving from an activity or project to whomsoever they accrue. These have been the relevant benefits for inclusion in cost-benefit analysis but should not include transfer payments.

Social Contract. Refers to a unanimous agreement (usually of a hypothetical or imaginary nature) between all of the individuals composing a society concerning the basic principles upon which that society will operate.

Social Cost. The sum of money which is just adequate when paid as compensation to restore to their original utility levels all who lose because of the production of the output. The social cost has been the opportunity cost to society (i.e., to all individuals in society) rather than just to one firm or individual.

Social Decision Rule. Refers to a procedure or method of making choices between alternatives which should be made by or on behalf of a group of individuals rather than a single individual.

Social Discount Rate. The rate used to discount collective or public investments.

Social Economics. Refers to the application of neo-classical economic theory to social policy. Where term 'social' has been interpreted as widely or as narrowly as the individual author chooses, although, most usually encompass health, education, crime, housing and welfare services. An alternative usage of the term has been that of certain radical economists who describe their work regardless of subject area as social economics.

Socialism. A term which is used to describe the general doctrine that the ownership and control of the means of production--capital and land should be held by the community as a whole and administered in the interests of all. For Karl Marx socialism has been an intermediate stage in the inevitable transformation of capitalism into communism. The socialist state has been characterized by the dictatorship of the proletariat and existence of scarcity.

Social Marginal Productivity Criterion, The. It states that the total net contributions of audit of investment to output should be regarded when allocating resources and not simply the part which accrues to private investors. The social marginal productivity of capital should be equated in its various possible uses if resources have to be allocated efficiently.

Social Optimum. Refers to that allocation of a society's resources, pattern of production and distribution of output which has been the 'best' attainable according to some stated set of objectives. The concept is most usually employed in welfare economics.

Social Relations of Production. The term which was used by Marx to define the social relationships between humans, which arise from a particular set of material forces of production. The most important relationship has been that among the classes following from ownership of the means of production and determining the division of the total product.

Social Returns to Education. Refers to the excess return on education over and above any extra earnings obtained from being educated.

Social Time Preference Rate. Society's rate of time preference represents the rate at which society has been willing to trade consumption between different time periods..

Social Welfare Function. Refers to a statement of a society's objectives in which the level of social welfare of well-being has been represented as a function of the way in which resources have been allocated. In the form in which this concept was introduced by A. Bergson, social welfare has been generally made a function of the levels of utility of the individuals forming the society.

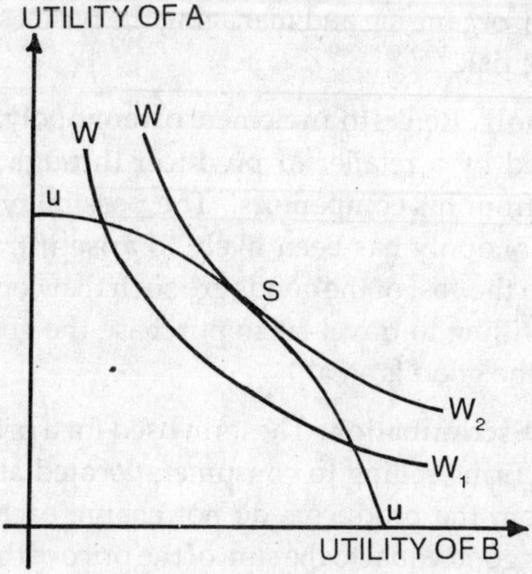

Social Welfare Function

Soft Commodities. Commodities such as coffee, cola, sugar and tea; hence the term 'soft commodities futures markets'.

Soft Company. A company which is engaged in analysis and consultancy, as distinct from the actual development, production and marketing of a range of products. Some soft companies develop to a point where they become major product companies, i.e., hard companies. Soft companies need low capital and management expertise; hard companies require major up-front investments in manufacturing equipment and distribution before the first sales are made, and depend on venture capital.

Soft Currency. A currency which is having a falling exchange rate due to continuing balance of payments deficits. Such a currency would not be held by other countries as part of their exchange reserves.

Soft Loan. A loan having no rate of interest or one below the cost of the capital being lent.

Sole Proprietor, The. Refers to the commonest type of business unit in which a single person has been responsible for raising the capital, organising and managing the business, and undertaking the risk.

Spatial Monopoly. Refers to an element of monopoly power which is obtained by a retailer or producer through locating at a distance from his competitors. The possibility of obtaining such a monopoly has been likely to arise if transport costs relative to the cost of the goods are such that consumers have been unwilling to travel far to purchase the good (*i.e.*, if the range of the good is small).

Spatial Price Discrimination. The term used for a pricing strategy in which firms selling to consumers located at various distances from the producers do not charge each consumer a price for a good equal to the sum of the price of the good 'at the factory gate' (the f.o.b. price) and the true transfer corts of delivering the good.

Special Drawing Rights (S.D.Rs). An international reserve currency system which was created by the International Monetary Fund in October, 1969. It provides for a new type of money (known as 'paper gold') to serve by agreement of the free world nations as the first international legal tender. S.D.Rs are used along with gold and dollars as monetary reserves; they are not held by individuals or private businesses but used in transactions between governments and central banks.

The first allocation of S.D.Rs by the International Monetary Fund took place on 1 January 1970. S.D.Rs as international assets, can be used between central banks in cases of balance-of-payments difficulties, S.D.Rs bear interest and have a gold value guarantee.

While originally the S.D.R. was fixed to the official price of gold, from 1 July 1974, it became a composite unit reflecting the value of 16 major currencies, weighted by their relative importance in international transactions. The currencies in the 'basket' valuation are those of countries with a share in world exports of goods and services in excess of 1 per cent.

The complexity of S.D.Rs has been reduced; from January, 1981, the system became based on five instead of sixteen currencies. However. S.D.Rs still amount to only 5 per cent of the world total.

Specialisation. Concentrating activity in those lines of production in which the individual or firms has some natural or acquired advantage. Specialization accompanied by trade will increase the living standards in all regions beyond those which would have been achieved had every region been self sufficient. The gains from specialization have been illustrated within the static theories of absolute advantage and comparative advantage but there by also be dynamic elements as the theories of the virtuous circle and productivity growth illustrate.

Specialisation, Coefficient of. A statistic calculated to indicate the degree to which the economy of a region has been specialized in certain economic activities. 'Specialization' is interpreted to mean that the regional economy under investigation has a mix of industry which differs from that of the nation of which it forms a part. The coefficient is expressed as follows :

$$\Sigma | S_{aj} - S_{an} |$$

(the two vertical lines indicate absolute values i.e., ignoring positive or negative signs) where $S_a j$ denotes the share of industry a in total industrial activity of region *j*, while S_{an} denotes the share of industry a in total national industrial activity.

Specie. Precious metal in cointed form.

Specie Flow Mechanism. According to the traditional theory of the operation of the gold standard, a corrective mechanism by whish deficits and surplus in balance of payments would tend to be eliminated by included flows of gold.

Specie Points. Refer to those levels of the exchange rate of a currency which is on a gold standard at which it becomes profitable to move gold into or out of the country.

Specification Error. Refers to an econometric problem in which the form of the relationship to be estimated has been wrongly specified, either through an incorrect form of function (e.g., linear instead of non-linear) or through the omission of relevant variables, or inclusion of irrelevant variables. If the specification error involves anything other than the inclusion of irrelevant variables, all estimation techniques will give rise to biased parameter estimate.

Specific Tax. Generally, a tax which is imposed on each unit of output of a good and not on the value of output.

Speculation. Refers to the practice of buying or selling with the motive of then selling or buying and thereby making a profit if prices or exchange rates have changed.

Speculative Boom. Refers to investment in highly risky projects but with high expected rates of return or capital gain in a period of rapid economic expansion or boom.

Speculative Demand. Refers to the demand for money for the purchase of financial assets, as distinct from the transactions demand for money. The two financial variables, the transactions and speculative demand for money, have been influenced by income and interest rates respectively. Higher interest rates imply a higher return on holding bonds, and a larger opportunity cost against holding cash or interest fires bank deposits.

Speculative Unemployment. Refers to an element of frictional unemployment. More accurately described as speculative underemployment, it is suggested it arises because of a fall in the real wage which is regarded as temporary. This will make some workers to reduce their present supply of hours in favour of offering more hours at the higher rate expected to govern in the future.

Spillover Hypothesis. Refers to the notion that important wage settlements set a pattern which has been followed by or at least significantly influences subsequent settlements. Such spillover effects have been stressed by the who emphasize the role of comparability and institutional forces in wage determination.

Split Pricing. Refers to the practice of selling a product uniform in quality and other characteristics at different prices, because it has been branded or packed differently, or distributed through different channels, or both.

Spite Effect. The imposition of a tax may give a feeling of anger on those on whom it has been levied and in consequence there may be a desire to hit back and inflict losses on the government. With an income tax this may result in reduced work effort. The tax base and so income tax payments have been also reduced. The satisfaction of revenge may compensate the taxpayer for his own losses.

Spread Effects. Beneficial effects of the growth of a regional economy on the economies of other regions.

Stability. Refers to the extent to which an equilibrium price or set of prices will be secured despite any 'shocks' to the system which temporarily move price away from its equilibrium level.

Stabilization. Refers to a normative approach to fluctuations in the level of economic activity. The implicit assumption has been that cycles or other irregularities in the time path of economic variables should be smoothed out, by the use of policy instruments to achieve desirable values of policy targets.

Stabilization Function. Refers to the role of government in manipulating fiscal and monetary policies for the purpose of maintaining a high and even level of economic activity.

Stackelberg's Duopoly Model. A model of a two firm market developed by H. von Stackelberg. It has been an extension of the Cournot duopoly model incorporating the idea of a 'sophisticated' duoplist who recognizes that the competitor is acting on the Cournot assumptions. The 'sophisticated' duopolist will act like a monopolist incorporating the rival's predicted decisions into its considerations, and in effect becoming a price leader choosing the price which maximizes profits subject to the known reaction of the rival firm. Stable equilibrium will be realised as in the Cournot model except that the 'sophisticated' duopolist will possess higher profits and the 'native' duopolist will have lower profits. If both firms become 'sophisticated' then disequilibrium will result with the necessity for collusion if a price war, damaging to the profits of each duopolist, has to be avoided.

Stagflation. The terms used for the periods of recession and rising unemployment coupled with positive rates of price inflaction.

Standard Commodity. It is a composite commodity which is constructed such that its price does not change when there are changes in the distribution of income. It represents Sraffa's solution to the problems of an invariable measure of value which plagued the classical school and particularly D. Ricardo.

Standard of Living. It is also referred to as the level of economic welfare, utility or real income. It refers to the level of material well-being of an individual or household. In economic analysis, the standard of living has been usually held to be determined by the quantities of goods and services (including leisure) consumed.

Stationary State. An economy in a stationary state functions as if output in every period has been consumed in the same period. The stock of consumer goods gets used up through the period, but it has been always exactly replaced at the end. The idea of a stationary state was an important ingredient in the wage fund doctrine. The growth theory of classical economics may be essentially considered as a progression towards the situation of a stationary state or zero economic growth.

Steady-State Growth. In growth theory it refers to a dynamic condition of an economy where all real variables have been growing at a constant proportional rate (which may be zero or negative).

Stereotypes. Refers to a possible source of discrimination that arises from information imperfections within the labour market. When employers cannot readily assess the quality of job applicants, they may use sex or colour characteristics as a supplementary, inexpensive test. Although such characteristics or stereotypes have nothing to do with productivity they have been nonetheless correlated with productivity.

Sterling Area. It has a group of countries and territories which, because of their strong trade and financial connections with the UK tended to stabilize the exchange rate of their currencies with sterling, and to hold all or a large part of their external reserves in sterling.

Stock. The issued capital of a company, or a particular issue of securities, e.g., *by* a government, which has been in a consolidated form so that it can be held or transferred in any amounts.

Stock - Adjustment Demand Function. A demand function where demand in any one period reflects the difference between actual possessions and some 'optimal' desired stock of consumer durables.

Stock Appreciation. Refers to an increase in the nominal value of inventories because of a rise in prices during the period in question.

Stolper -- Samuelson Theorem. Using the Heckscher -- Ohlin framework, Stolper and Samuelson showed that on certain restrictive assumptions international trade necessarily lowers the real wage of the scarce factor of production without it being necessary to specify its pattern of consumption. A corollary to this proposition has been that protection necessarily raises the real wage of the scarce factor.

'Stop-Go'. Refers to action on the part of the government to curtail aggregate demand due to (say) a balance of payments deficit, which is soon followed by action with opposite effect to ameliorate the rise in unemployment caused by the first policy intervention.

Stop Limit Order. A stop order which becomes a limit order after the specified stop price has been reached.

Store of Value. One of the functions of money has been that unlike a barter situation, it makes wealth, or value to be stored.

Straddle Option. A combination of a 'put' option and a 'call' option which may be exercised in both respects at a common specified price before the expiry date.

Strike Insurance. In some countries it is a form of mutual aid used by a variety of industrial concerns to protect themselves against the selective strike tactic.

Strikes. Withdrawals of labour which is associated with an impasse in the collective bargaining process, either with regard to the negotiation of a new contract of employment or over the interpretation of an existing agreement.

Structural Unemployment. On a Keynesian view this form of unemployment is resulted from the coexistence but mismatching of the unemployed and existing job vacancies. The unemployed have neither the right skills nor live in the right places to fill the existing job vacancies. It is therefore often thought of as a more extreme form of frictional unemployment which can only get eliminated by retraining workers or by a change in the location of either industry or the unemployed.

Structure-Conduct-Performance Framework. It is both a means of classification and a framework for analysis in industrial economics. The conventional approach is to identify and specify the causal chains linking aspects of market structure, like concentration and barriers to entry, with elements of business conduct e.g., advertising and research and development --- and industrial performance. Examples of the last would be profitability and innovation. The direction of causation is generally presumed to run from structure through conduct to performance, as with concentration and profitability for instance.

Structure of Taxes. Every country is having a range of different types of taxes. The structure of the tax system refers to this mix.

Subsidy. A payment which is made by the government (or possibly by private individuals) which forms a wedge between the price consumers pay and the costs incurred by producers, such that price has been less than marginal cost.

Subsistence. Refers to the minimum level of consumption necessary for existence. The concept had been used by the classical economists to explain the long run level of wages. Wages were constrained to be at subsistence level by population growth.

Subsistence Expenditures. A level of expenditure which is necessary to sustain a subsistence or 'survival' standard of living. In linear expenditure systems it refers to some minimum quantity of each separate set of goods (between which sets there is no substitutability) which will be bought regardless of price.

Substitute. Means a good which can be susbtituted for another good, or an input that could be substituted for another input. In neo-classical theory substitution possibilities have been generally assumed to exist, accounting for the 'smoothness' of indifference curves and ISO products curves.

Substitution Effect. Refers to the effect on the demand for a good of a change in price of that good assuming real income has been held constant. The meaning of 'real income' varies according to which measures of the substitution effect is chosen. According to J R Hicks constant real income means that the consumer stays on the same indifference curve.

According to Slutsky, real income is constant if the consumer can buy his original combination of goods before the price change occurred. The difference has been shown in the diagram.

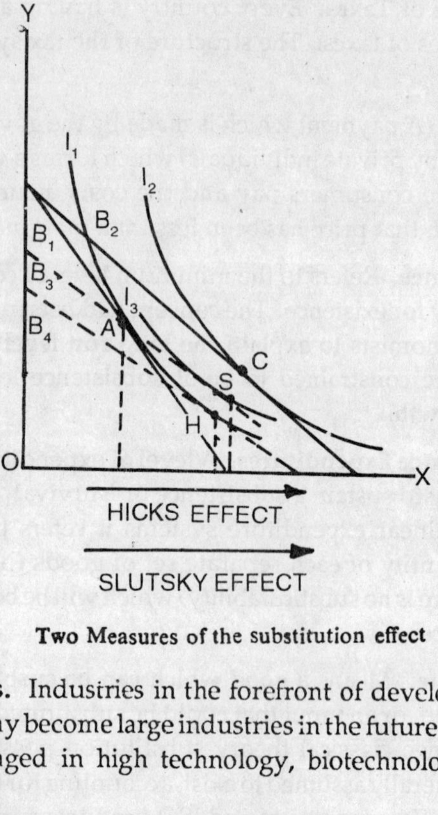

Two Measures of the substitution effect

Sunrise Industries. Industries in the forefront of developments and which may become large industries in the future, e.g., industries engaged in high technology, biotechnology, and solar energy.

Super-Environment. Those factors which are outside the control of the 'representative' firm in the long-term. This has been a concept used in growth theories of the firm and has been treated as exogenously determined.

Super-Neutrality Money is considered to have this property if a change in the rate of growth of the supply of money does not have any effect on the rate of growth of real output in the long-run. It means that the level of output associated with the natural rate of unemployment has been independent of the inflation rate, and of any past disequilibrium in the economy.

Supernumerary Expenditure. Refers to expenditure on a good or group of goods over and above some minimum or subsistence expenditure.

Supplementary Financing Facility. A facility which is extended by the International Monetary Fund utilising funds obtained from some oil producers and industrial countries. It is also known as the 'Witteveen facility'.

Supply. Means the amount of a commodity or service which will be offered for sale at a given price per unit of time.

Supply and Demand Curves. A graphical presentation of supply and demand functions, showing on the one hand how much of a commodity will be supplied per unit of time at any given price, and on the other how much of a commodity will be bought per unit of time at any given price; the equilibrium price is the price at which there will be just sufficient demand to take the whole of the supply of the market.

Supply and Demand, Laws of. In respect of goods and services:

(a) If, at the price ruling, demand exceeds supply, the price tends to rise; conversely, when supply exceeds demand the price tends to fall.

(b) A rise in price tends to contract demand and expand supply; conversely, a fall in price tends to expand demand and to contract supply.

(c) Price tends to a level at which the demand is equal to the supply, i.e., to an 'equilibrium price'.

(d) The greater the increase in price, the greater the expansion in supply.

(e) For any given price increase, the expansion in the quantity supplied will be greater, the longer the time the market is allowed to adjust.

Supply Curve. The term used for a graphical representation of the relationship between the supply of a commodity and its price (usually with price on the vertical axis, and quantity supplied measured along the horizontal axis). The positive relationship between these two variables has been reflected by the fact that the supply curve slopes upwards from left to right.

Supply Side Economics. The forces considered by many economists to determine output; the availability or supply of capital and labour, and the state of technology. Hence the volume of money should grow in line with the growth of output generated by capital accumulation and labour force growth.

Supply-Side Economics. Refers to a body of thought which emphasize that the principal determinant of the rate of growth of national output in both the short and long-run has been the allocation and efficient use of the labour and capital in an economy.

Surplus Units. Any economic unit whose assets become greater than its liabilities, and has been therefore willing to lend money, extend credit, or purchase financial instruments.

Survivor Technique. Refers to a statistical method of identifying the minimum efficient scale of plant or firm. It is based on the rationale that in competitive markets those plant/firms which survive the best in the market place are those with minimum costs.

Swap Arrangements. A method of improving liquidity arrangements which was developed in the 1960s by swapping currencies. The central banks of two countries would credit each other with an equivalent amount of the other's currency such that either government could draw on this extra foreign exchange reserve if necessary. It has been usually for a specified period of time, after which the transactions would be reversed at the original rate of exchange.

Swiss Numbered Accounts. Anonymous accounts permitted in the banking system of Switzerland; secrecy is protected not only by civil but also by the criminal law. The identity of clients is known only to selected members of the bank's management.

Switch Dealer. A dealer who disposes to others goods that one trading party does not wish to receive from another trading party under, say, a bilateral trade agreement. The activities of these dealers injects some flexibility into bilateral trade agreements which oblige trading printers to keep their trade with each other in approximate balance.

Switch Selling. Advertising one model and trying to sell a more expensive one. The offer or advertisement of a 'cheap' commodity has been used to arouse consumer interest; persuasive salesmen then concentrate on selling dealer models to customers who have shown interest.

Syndicated Loans. Refer to loans which are involving several banks joining together to raise massive sums (say $ 1 billion or more) for a single borrower.

T

Take-Over. Means the acquisition by a 'raider' company of more than 51 per cent of the voting shares of another company.

Taker. Refers to the buyer or purchaser of an action.

Tangible Assets. Then term used for physical assets such as plant and machinery, which are distinguished from intangible assets like as the value of a patent or a firm's goodwill.

Tap Issue. Means the issue of bills and securities by the Treasury direct to Government Departments and other buyers at a special price, without going through the market.

Tare. Means the weight of the packing or container of an article. This must be deducted from the gross weight to find the actual or net weight of the article.

Target Return Pricing. Refers to the setting of prices at a level which will ensure an adequate return on investment by a company, if achieved.

Targets (also known as policy targets). These refer to a set of quantitatively fixed objectives of economic polity, to be achieved by a choice of values for policy instruments. This approach to macro economics in particular was advocated by the Dutch economist Jan Tinbergen in the 1950s and was extended by Henri theil in the late 1950s and early 1960s. They altered Tinbergen's approach in three ways :

1. he replaced targets with a welfare function or los function to be optimized ;

2. the instruments themselves entered the function to be optimized, reflecting the costs associated with the use of different instruments;
3. uncertainty was permitted for by the use of certainty equivalence.

Further developments which followed this pragmatic approach use the methods of control theory which allows for non-linearity of the functions etc.

Tariff De Combat. A tariff which is used as a bargaining counter in attempting to secure trade advantages.

Tariff. (a) It is a duty or tax which is charged by a country on its imports from other countries ; a customs duty. The duty may be imposed on an 'ad valorem' basis, as a percentage of the value of the goods, or by way of a specific amount per unit of weight or volume. The tariff could be used to protect home industries from the competition of foreign producers, or it may be adopted to reduce the total imports bill a country has to pay. (b) It also refers to a method of charging for services, e.g., supplies of gas or electricity.

'Tariff Factory'. Means a change in the location of production of a good from a low cost situation to a higher cost location in another country, where the inability to sell in the latter country, over a high tariff wall, makes necessary the creation of a 'tariff factory' for supplying the market in that country.

Tariff Structure. The term used for the overall pattern of tariff rates. Tariffs are not usually applicable to all imports at a uniform rate. A typical structure may permit duty-free entry to raw materials, a positive tariff on semi-manufactures and a still higher rate on finished goods. Such a structure gives rise to an effective rate of protection in excess of the nominal rate.

Taxable Income. Gross income minus allowances and expenses. In theory taxable income should include all accretions to spending power within the taxable period (usually one year). The concept of total accretion (consumption plus increase in net worth) is accepted by many economists as a sound basis for defining taxable income. This definition would include all factor earnings and all gifts and windfall gains. They are included whether they are realized or not. All reductions in wealth like capital losses and wear and teat are allowed for.

Taxation. Compulsory levies on private individuals and organizations which are made by government to raise revenue to finance expenditure on public goods and services, and to control the volume of private expenditure in the economy. Taxes are classified in various ways. Some are termed as direct taxes, examples of which are income tax and wealth tax. Others have been called indirect taxes. These are taxes on transactions especially expenditure. Examples have been excise duties and value-added tax.

Taxation Adam Smith's Canons Of. Smith's canons of taxation were as follows :

(a) the amounts people paid in taxes should be equal, i.e., proportional to their incomes;

(b) there should be certainty with regard to the amount to be paid;

(c) there should be convenience of payment and collection;

(d) economy should be observed so that taxes should not be imposed of a kind where the cost of collection was excessive.

Taxation Purposes Of. The purposes of direct and indirect taxation have been broadly :

(a) To provide the public authorities with the revenue needed for meeting the cost of defence, social services, interest payments on the national debt municipal services, etc.

(b) To give effect to economic policy, the objects of which may be as follows:

(i) increasing the economic welfare of the community as a whole by reducing the inequality of income;

(ii) reducing or increasing purchasing power through increasing or reducing purchase taxes;

(iii) checking the imports of a commodity from abroad in order to help to correct and adverse balance of payments;

(iv) influencing the rate of economic growth of the nation;

(v) to reduce or increase the money supply.

Taxation Schemes, Fraudulent. Schemes which are designed to minimise or avoid the payment of taxes using illegal means and procedures. Schemes may involve simply the concealment of income, or they may involve ways of 'annihilating' income by the creation of fictitious debts.

Taxes. Refer to compulsory financial contribution by a person or body of persons towards the expenditure of a public authority. Taxes on income (i.e., on wages, salaries, profits; dividends, rent and interest) and on capital have been known as 'direct' taxes.

Taxes on commodities or services are known as 'indirect' taxes. Other indirect taxes include purchase taxes, entertainment taxes and import duties.

Tax Avoidance Scheme. A business scheme which seeks to avoid or minimise the payment of tax; it has been basically lawful and conducted within the framework of existing legislation however deficient or inadequate that legislation may be.

Tax Break. A situation which is providing some relief from tax, in whole or part.

Tax Credit. A credit which is given directly against a tax ; the tax payable gets reduced by the amount of the credit. It can apply in several different situations. In some countries for example Kenya) personal income tax credit have been given instead of personal allowances against gross income. When an income tax credit has been raised all taxpayers benefit equally unlike the situation with personal allowances under a progressive income tax system where an increase would benefit high income earners and tax payers more than those in low tax-paying positions. Another example relates to value-added tax. Under the system employed in the EEC a tax-paying organization has been liable for VAT on the selling price but has been allowed as a tax credit the amount of VAT which has been paid on purchases of inputs. A common case arises with multinational companies.

Tax Credit Scheme. Refers to an income maintenance programme in which everyone has been guaranteed a minimum income, while income above that level is taxed. When a certain income level is reached, the tax paid will be just equal to the guaranteed payment this is the 'break-even' income level. This type of programme has been formally identical with the negative income tax though there are differences of emphasis in presentation. Both types of scheme have been characterized by (1) a minimum guaranteed income, (2) a 'break-even' income level, (3) a tax rate, if any two of these are known, the third element may be calculated (so long as we confine ourselves to a single proportional tax rate).

Tax Disincentive. An income tax may make work effort to get reduced. Its existence makes leisure relatively more attractive, as it is not subject to taxation. It is termed as the substitution effect of the tax. The will also encourage someone to work longer hours to obtain a higher gross income so that his net income is not reduced so much because of the tax. This is termed the income effect of the tax. The two effects thus pull in different directions. In general it may be argued that the substitution effect operates more strongly the higher the marginal rates of tax and the income effect may operate more strongly with high average rates.

Tax Evasion Scheme. A business scheme which helped to avoid or minimise the payment of tax; it is basically unlawful infringing the framework and principles of existing legislation.

Tax Expenditure. A term which is used describe the various allowances which may be used to reduce tax liability -- generally liability to income tax.

Tax Haven. A country which is offering special opportunities for minimisation by way of free zones, cash grants, and tax incentives, so as to obtain additional employment and gain votes. All havens have been not equally useful to all users or tax refugees. Countries which have reputations for offering special advantages to investors or immigrants are France, Monaco, Italy, Spain, the Channel Island, Malta, the Caribbean, Latin America, the Bajamas, Bermuda, Cayman Islands, Hong-Kong Liechtenstein, Luxembourg, the Isle of Man, the Netherlands, Antilles, Panama, Switzerland, Vanuatu and the British Virgin Islands.

Tax, Marginal Rate of. Means the amount of tax a person pays on the last unit or increment of income received.

Tax, Regressive. Means a tax which takes a larger percentage of income from people the smaller their income.

Tax-Rort Account. False bank accounts, which may be opened for the purposes of tax evasion; a financial institution may open such false bank accounts with money on deposit from the public. The accounts are opened in false names by bank officer, or employees of other financial institution.

Tax Sharing. Proposals that a federal or central government share some part of its tax collection with state and local governments.

Tax Shelter. A medium or process which is intended to reduce or eliminate the tax burden of the individual.

Tax Shifting. Refers to the phenomenon whereby those on whom taxes are levied are able to pass the burden either partly or fully on the others.

Tax Yield. The revenue which is collected from a tax.

Technical Progress. A central element in economic growth which makes more output to get produced for unchanged quantities of the inputs of labour and capital to the production process.

Technological Dualism. Refers to the process of combining capital intensive heavy industry with labour-intensive methods elsewhere to utilize the excess labour. The heavy industry makes the move towards modernization and the other projects employ the excess labour while the basic capital infrastructure gets built up.

Technological Effects or 'Real' Effects. Effects which after the total production possibilities or the total welfare opportunities for consumers in the economy. The effects are described as economise when they gave been favourable, and diseconomies when they have been unfavourable.

Technological External Effects. An alternative name for externalities. The adjective 'technological' and been included originally to differentiate such effects from pecuniary external economies.

Technological Progress. Progress which is characterised by (a) improvements in the methods of production, achieved through more effective management, more advanced specialisation, better utilisation of labour, equipment and materials and in the rationalisation of productive process in general; (b) improvements in the quality of resources in the form of more highly skilled labour and functional differentiation of capital; (c) improvements in the quality of products; and (d) a rising capital-labour ratio, i.e., an increasing amount of productive fixed capital per worker.

Technology. Means a body of information and techniques, and of skills and experience, developed for the production and used of goods and services.

Technostructure. Refers to the managerial class and their technical and planning expertise which modern industrial production needs. The concept has been an important feature of J.K. Galbraith's thesis that corporations within modern capitalist economies have established sovereignty in product markets.

Temporary Layoffs. Employees who are discharged by their employer but knowing that they might return to that same employment at sometime in the near future.

Tenders. These are the offers made to supply at a fixed price. A discount house, for example, tendering for an issue of Treasury Bills, will offer to take up so many bills at a certain prices.

Tender to Contract Cover (T.T.C). Refers to an option which allows exporters to fix forward exchange rates on which to base their tender prices. If an exporter wins a contract, the deal must proceed at the agreed price; if not, these is nothing lost save the fee. In this way, the customer only enters into a commitment of trade at the agreed rates if a contract has been awarded.

Term Assurance. Refers to a form of insurance life cover; the life office agrees to insure the policyholder's life for a fixed term for a fixed annual premium; if the policyholder outlives the term of the policy, nothing is payable.

Term Loan. A bank loan made for a fixed term of years, at a fixed rate of interest, and normally repayable by installments spread over a period.

Terms of Trade. The term used for the relationship between the prices of exporters and imports. It may be expressed as an index.

$$\text{Index of Terms of Trade} = \frac{\text{Price Index of Exports}}{\text{Price Index of Imports}}$$

The price index of exports measures the change in the aggregate value of a representative selection of exports as compared with the corresponding value in a base year; similarly the price index of imports measures the change in the aggregate value of a representative selection of imports as compared with the corresponding value for the same base year. If the prices of imports rise in relation to the price of exports, then the terms of trade have move against the exporter.

Term Structure of Interest Rates. Refers to the structure of relationship between interest rates, or more strictly the redemption yields, on securities of different terms to maturity (i.e., repayment).

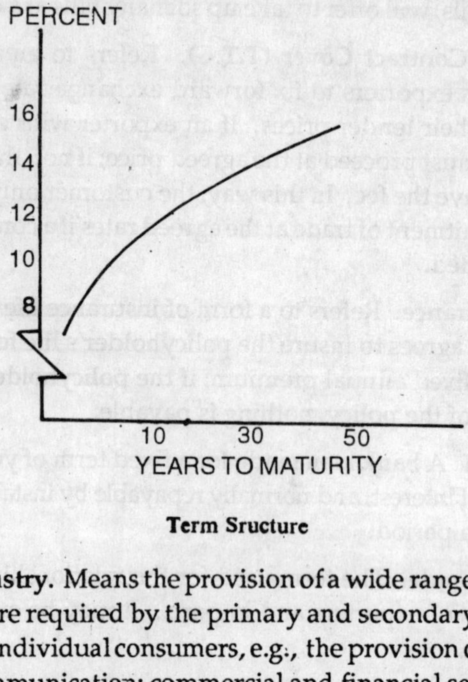

Term Sructure

Tertiary Industry. Means the provision of a wide range of services which are required by the primary and secondary industries and by individual consumers, e.g., the provision of transport and communication; commercial and financial services such as insurance and banking; the provision of health, legal and educational services; and the wholesale and retail trade.

Threshold. The point beyond which there occurs some change in the behaviour of the economic agent i.e., a threshold on price expectations implies that expectations are not revised constantly in the light of accumulating evidence of price changes but are revised at intervals once the rate of price change gets exceeded a certain point.

Threshold Analysis. A technique which is used in physical planning in determining the desirable size of communities and the provision of public services. The analysis rests on the idea that there have been indivisibilities in the provision of public services such that there exists a given minimum and maximum population for which the provision of some public or communal service is viab.'

Threshold Effect. Means an increase in the level of taxation which a community is said to be willing to pay resulting from some crisis or national emergency.

Threshold of a Good. In regional or spatial economics, it refers to the minimum population which can provide a market for some good or service. If the population of an area (such as a town) is below the threshold, demand for the good will be so low that its provision is not economically viable. The concept is relevant where there are economies of scale in the provision of a good; thus the average cost of the goods falls as sales rise.

Thrifts. Financial institutions such as savings and loans associations, mutual saving banks, and credit unions.

Throughput Economy. Type of an economy in which resources are continuously used up without replacement or recycling.

Tight Money. A monetary policy which is regarded as retarding economic activity. opposite of easy money.

Time Deposit. Means an interest-bearing deposit for a fixed period of time.

Time Sharing. Refers to an arrangement in which the financial contribution towards the purchase of an asset has been related to the use of that asset in terms of time, thus a group of purchasers may share the cost of a 'second home', each enjoying the right to occupy it for a prescribed period of the year.

To-Arrive Contracts. The term used for contracts for cash grain or other commodity which allow for shipment or arrival at some specified time in the future. These contracts should specify amount, grade, price and origin of the commodity.

Token Money. Reffers to any form of money the value or which as means of payment rests on legal enactment, e.g., legal tender, or on conventional acceptability, and which bears no relation to its intrinsic commodity value.

Total Cost. Refers to the total cost of producing any given level of output. In the short-run total costs could be divided into two parts, fixed costs, i.e., those costs which do not vary with output (sometimes referred to as overhead costs), and variable costs, i.e., those costs which vary directly with output.

Total Remuneration. Means the total pecuniary benefits a worker receive from his employment. Most frequently the term is used to refer to the salary and fringe benefits of white-collar workers.

Total Revenue. Refers to the total receipts from sales of a product or series of products produced by a single firm or industry.

Trade. Means the exchange of commodities between individuals or groups either directly through barter or indirectly through a medium such as money.

Trade Barrier. This is a general term to cover any government limitation on the free international exchange of merchandise. These barriers may take the form of tariffs, quotas, import deposits, restrictions on the grant of import licences or strict regulations pertaining to health and/or safety standards.

Trade Bill. A commercial bill which is used in transactions actually involving goods. A trade bill has been drawn by the seller and accepted by the buyer and has been payable on a set date in respect of goods purchased. It can be offered for discount to a discount house or to the seller's own bank. The rate of discount charged depends upon the credit standing of the traders and occasionally upon the goods concerned. Trade bills guaranteed by a credit insurance company will command a finer rate of discount.

Trade Credit. Credit which is extended by a trader or producer to his customers through terms of sale which permit payment at sometime after the actual transfer of the goods.

Trade Cycle. Alternating periods of trade boom and depression, especially characteristic of 19th century business activity when cycles of this nature occurred at fairly regular intervals. Lord Beveridge in his Full Employment in a Free Society (1944) examined the cycles of business activity from 1792 to 1913 revealing intervals of from 5-11 years between one boom and the next, with an average of 8 years. During boom periods employment, wages, prices, profits and production rise together, only to decline during the ensuring slump. While all, or nearly all, industries are simultaneously prosperous or depressed, fluctuations occur most sharply in the production of capital goods. The long drawn out depression from 1920-39, between the two World Wars, differed in character from previous periods. A short period of boom after the First World War was followed by acute depression. Unemployment in the years 1920-28 averaged 1.5 million. Superimposed on this came the Great Depression of 1929-35 in which unemployment rose to the unprecedented heights of almost 3 million, declining only slowly. By 1939 unemployment had decreased to about 1.5 million. The Great Depression was more severe and more worldwide than any other. All capitalist countries were affected. In very marked contrast, the period following the Second World War was for many years one a boom, unemployment in Britain rarely exceeded 500,000 or 2 per cent of the working population.

Trade Cycle, Theories of The. Theories adduced by economists to explain fluctuations in trade have included :

(a) 'Real causes' theories. (i) Attempts to explain the trade cycle in terms of harvest fluctuations attributable to the weather. One of the most famous of these theories was the 'sunspot' theory of William Stanley Jevons (1835-1882). Jevons traced cyclical trade fluctuations to cycles in harvest yields; in turn he correlated the harvest fluctuations with the appearance of spots on the face of the sun, it being argued that sunspots influence the weather and hence harvest yields. This and other climatic theories are no longer accepted as primary explanations of trade movements. (ii) Theories that fluctuations in capital - producing industries are due to the fact that the demand for their products is a derived demand.

(b) Psychological theories. Theories that business persons are influenced alternately by waves of optimism and pessimism. When trade is good people are optimistic, buying more while prices rise and production is stimulated. When trade is poor pessimism prevails buying is reduced prices fall and production is depressed. The importance of these theories lies in the light they throw on the forces which tend to accentuate fluctuations, even if they do not themselves produce them. John Maynard Keynes (1883-19946) attached great importance to the psychological influences affecting the propensities to consume and save.

(c) Monetary theories. Theories that stress the role of the quantity of money and credit, and the rate of interest, in influencing business activity. The view that the trade cycle is a purely monetary phenomenon has been held by Ralph G Hawtrey (1879-1975) who regarded the Bank Rate as the mainspring of cyclical change. A reduction in Bank Rate and other short-term interest rate encouraged merchants to carry larger stocks of goods and stimulates trade generally; an increase in interest rates had the reverse effect. Hawtrey argued that by raising the Bank Rate a stop could be put to any boom, and by reducing the Bank Rate we could end nearly all depressions. The first proposition finds agreement in the Government White Paper on Employment Policy of 1944, although the Paper expressed doubt that changes in the rate of interest at the bottom of a depression will have any decisive effect on the course of trade.

(d) Over-production and under-consumption theories. Numerous and divers theories but all may be described as theories of the deficiency of effective demand. John A. Hobson (1858-1940) argued that in good times profits increase without a corresponding increase in the wages level and the purchasing power in the hands of the general public. Surplus profits are invested and productive capacity is greatly enlarged; but there is no market to carry off the increased supply of consumers' goods and a crisis persists until the surplus of stocks is worked off.

(e) Saving-investment theory. A theory that consumption depends on the level of income, and that this in turn depends on real investment. Now saving, i.e., the abstention from the purchase of consumers' goods, is a prerequisite for investment. Thus saving, consumption and investment depend on one another, together determining the level of total income. For full employment of resources to be maintained it is essential that the effective demand for goods and services should be sufficient to absorb all the output of the economic system. When saving is not translated into investment, the demand for goods is insufficient to cover all that is being produced; output falls and unemployment results. Between the two World Wars saving tended to exceed investment with adverse effects on employment. In these circumstances, incomes tend to fall until savings is once more brought into equality with investment. This may be at a level which is socially unacceptable. The solution lies in stimulating investment and hence incomes and effective demand.

Trader. An individual who buys and sells for his own account on an Exchange for short-term profit, also an employee of a broker or financial institution who specialises in handling purchases and sales of securities for the firm or its clients.

Trade Unions. Combination of workers which are formed for the purpose of taking collective, as distinct from individual, action against their employers for the improvement of pay and other working conditions. Most unions also develop 'friendly society' activities offering their members additional insurance against sickness and accident. There are two types of union; (a) craft unions, members of which are all engaged in the same--or one or two closely associated--occupations; (b) industrial unions, members of which come from branches of a particular industry.

Transaction Costs. Refer to those costs other than price which have been incurred in trading goods and services. These costs can be substantial particularly in markets where the good being traded is durable and complex.

Transactions Demand. Means the demand for money that people require to have available for spending, as distinct from the speculative demand for money. For convenience, people require cash and a bank account, to meet living expenses as they arise and occasional emergencies. The two financial variables, the transactions and speculative demand for money, are influenced by income and interest rates respectively.

Transactions Approach. The name assigned to Newcomb and Fisher's version of the classical quantity theory of money; MV = PT. It differs from the Cambridge version M = kPT in that the velocity of circulation -- V is included directly as opposed to its reciprocal k which appears on the right-hand side in the Cambridge equation.

Transactions Demand for Money. Refers to a motive for demanding money for the purpose of transactions, i.e., of payments and receipts, using money in its function as a medium of exchange. The amount demanded has been a function of the volume of economic activity.

Transfer Costs. The costs which are involved in moving some object between two points. The costs will include not only the direct costs of movement which will vary with distance moved (and thus may be called 'distance costs'), but also all the costs of loading, unloading, handling and administration at each end of the journey. This later set of costs are termed as terminal costs.

Transfer Incomes. Income which cannot be considered as payment for current service to production and which therefore do not enter national income.

Transfer Payments. Payments made by public authorities which are not made in consideration of goods and services currently produced, e.g., national assistance payments, unemployment benefit, grants to students, family allowances, interest paid on the national debt.

Transfer Pricing. The pricing of goods and services which are merely being transferred from one part to another part of the same organisation, e.g., movements, including international movements, of goods and services within a multinational corporation.

Transformation Problem. Refers to the problem in Marxian economies of deriving a unique set of prices from values, i.e., labour inputs.

Transitory Consumption. Refers to an unanticipated rise or fall in consumption.

Transitory Income. Unanticipated income. A windfall gain or windfalls loss.

Trans-Shipment Points. Means the locations at which transport changes from one type or mode to another (e.g., at a sea port there is a change between land or river transport and sea transport). These locations are also known as point of model interchange.

Treasury Bond Tender. The term used for a method of sale of government treasury bonds, adopted by some governments. A tender usually makes provision for two types of bidders -- 'competitive' and 'non-competitive'. The return on such an investment is called the 'yield', this being determined by the outcome of competitive bids in the tender.

Trend (also known as time trend)

1. An underlying, long-run component in time-series data, which is often calculated to display the long-run direction of movement of a variable. There have been various methods by which the trend can be established, including regression analysis and moving averages.
2. A measure of the average level of an economic magnitude (such as income) at a particular point in time. Cycles may occur around the trend level, which may not be a constant but may grow at a variable or a constant rat. If the growth rate has been constant then the trend may be plotted on a semi-long diagram.

Trust. Refers to various legally defined and regulated arrangements under which assets belonging to an individual or a group are placed in the custody of trustees who, depending on the type of trust, may actually manage them for the benefit of the owners. For various reasons, including tax advantages, trust arrangements are widely used by private individuals and by institutions.

T-Statistic. A statistic following the t-distribution, t-statistics are commonly used in hypothesis tests to determine the statistical significance of the parameters of econometric models, and are calculated as the ratio of the estimated parameter value to its standard error.

Turning Point. Refers to the point in the business cycle when an expansionary phase of the business cycle is replaced by a contractionary, phase or *vice-versa*. Peaks and troughs are termed as turning points.

Turnpike Theorems. A class of propositions in growth theory which is concerned with the closeness of optimal growth paths to balanced growth at the highest rate. The name 'turnpike theorem' was given by R. Dorfman, P. Samuelson and R. Solow in Linear Programming and Economic Analysis.

Two Sector Growth Model. A model which is used in growth theory where the fundamental differences between consumption and capital goods have been reorganized, with one sector concerned with each of the two goods. Example include the models of J.E. Meade, and H. Uzawa.

Tying Contract. Refers to a condition of sale needing the buyer of a given product to purchase another (different) product, usually complementary to the first product. For example, a seller of stapling machines might needs buyers to purchase his staples as a condition of buying the machines. The contract may be the seller's means of leveraging his monopoly of the first product; of exploiting the interdependence of the two products' demand functions; of applying price discrimination among buyers with different intensities of demand; if ensuring that the reputation of the desired product has been not damaged by buyers; use of inferior copies of the product not desired; and of avoiding the effects of price control on the desired product (assuming no control on the product not desired). These agreements may be illegal.

U

U-Form Enterprise. Refers to a company in which decision-making has been centralized around a top board of executive whose functional responsibilities are applied to all company products. This form of organization has been common to small and medium-sized firms : large firms adopting the U-form organization tend to suffer control loss.

Unanimity Rule. The term used for a procedure for collective choice which needs that before a policy can be adopted it must be approved by all of the members of the community affected by the decision. If this rule has been adopted we can be sure that any policy adopted will be a Pareto improvement.

Unanticipated Inflation. Refers to that proportion of the actual level of inflation which people did not expect : actual minus expected inflation. If people expect the rate of inflation to be 5 per cent per annum but in fact inflation is 10 over that period the unanticipated inflation rate would be 5 per cent.

Uncertainty. Refers to a situation in which the likelihood of an event occurring is not known at all. That is, no probability distribution could be attached to the outcomes. If the event in question is an investment in a project, uncertain returns would imply that the conceivable returns will be known but their probability of occurrence will not be known. In such circumstances it becomes necessary to resort to some rule based on the investor's attitude to the balance of gains and losses in the event that a particular choice has been taken and a particular set of circumstances occur.

UNCTAD. Abbreviation of United Nations Conference on Trade and Development.

Under Developed Countries. A term which is being used for developing countries. This term is now used infrequently, in favour of less perjorative terms.

Underemployment Workers. The underemployed worker is one whose marginal rate of substitution of income for leisure is less. An underemployed worker would prefer to work a larger number of hours than that offered to him by the standard working week.

Underemployment. According to the dual labour market hypothesis, the secondary labour market is having many workers who either already have skills that would enable them to function satisfactorily within the primary market or who could be trained for skilled jobs at no more than the usual costs. Given the barriers to entering the primary sector, however, they have been forced to take-up unskilled secondary sector jobs and are in this sense underemployed.

Undervalued Currency. Refers to a currency which, due generally to be a balance of payments surplus has been below its free market equilibrium level. To correct this, revaluation becomes necessary.

Underwriter. One who agrees to bear a risk, or some part of it, in return for a payment known as an insurance premium. Issuing houses also underwrite new issues of shares such that if the whole issue has been not taken up by the public, the underwriters will be left to take up the remainder of the issue.

Unearned Income. Any type of non-wage income which could be in the form of profits, interest or rent. It is differentiated usually for taxation purposes as most 'earned' income i.e., wage income has been taxed at source, but unearned income often has to be declared and taxed separately.

Unemployment. Means of all those individuals who have been not in employment and who have been either in the process of moving to a new job or who have been unable to find work at the prevailing real wage rate.

Unemployment Benefit. In many countries, it refers to a payment which is made to an individual who is unemployed. These payments are made from the 'National Insurance Fund and are related to the level of national insurance contributions made by the individual, prior to unemployment. There have been other forms of transfer payment made if an individual has been not eligible for unemployment benefit. The purpose of such payments has been to ensure incomes do no fall below subsistence level during periods of unemployment.

Unemployment, Cost Of. Mean the direct and indirect economic and social costs to society of unemployment of labour; these include (a) the cost to the nation in unemployment pay and subsistences, allowances, (b) the loss to the nation of tax revenue, both by way of income tax and indirect taxes; (c) the loss in output due directly to the waste of resources; (d) the adverse effect on health and the consequent additional burden on the health services; and (e) the social, family, and individual impacts which are serious yet incalculable.

Unemployment Rate. Refers to the number of persons who are capable of working and willing to work but unable to find suitable employment. It is expressed as a percentage of the total number of persons available for employment at any time. The rate of unemployment could be calculated.

$$\frac{u}{e+u} \times 100$$

where

u=numbers unemployed
e=numbers employed
e+u= labour force.

Unemployment Rate. Refers to an index of the supply of labour at the prevailing wage rate.

Unemployment Trap. Refers to a situation in which middle and older aged persons retrenched during a recession have been passed over during the subsequent economic recovery, employers tending to hire the younger short-term unemployed and new job seekers; the predicament of those caught in the unemployment trap worsens notwithstanding considerable experience and competence previously greatly valued.

Unequal Exchange. In its strict Marxian form it refers to the exchange of the products of developed economies at prices above their labour values for the products of less developed economies at prices below their labour values.

UNIDO Guidelines. Refers to a technique of appraising projects in developing countries and an alternative to the Little Mirrlees method. It has been essentially a cost benefit analysis where the numeraire is present consumption.

Unintended Inventory Disinvestment. Means rundown of stocks due to an unexpected rise in sales or fall in production.

Unintended Inventory Investment. The term used for the Stocks resulting from the failure of expected orders to materialize.

Union Density. Means the proportion of the labour force that is unionized. Union density varies widely across industries and the key factors appear to be average establishment size, the degree of product market concentration, and the wage rate.

Union Market Power. The market power of trade unions has been a function of the elasticity of derived demand for union labour.

Union/Non-Union Differential. Means the extent to which unions have raised the wage of their membership relative to equivalent non-union labour.

Union Political Power. Means the influence that unions exert, directly and indirectly, on the political process.

Union Security. Collective bargaining issues, like check-off and closed-shop, in which the employer helps the union organize and maintain the workforce.

Union Shop. The term used for an arrangement whereby a worker must join the union within a specified period of time after beginning employment. The employer thus has complete discretion in his choice of labour.

Uniqueness. When used in the context of general equilibrium theory it refers to the existence of a unique set of market clearing prices.

United Nations Capital Development Fund. A special body which was created by the United Nations General Assembly in 1966 to facilitate economic growth in developing countries by supplementing existing sources of capital assistance with grants and loans: generally earmarked to finance small scale rural development projects which have been not able to generate alternative financing due to insufficient collateral or credit worthiness on the part of the applicant.

United Nations Conference on Trade and Development (U.N.C.T.D). An organisation set up by the United Nations to assist the less developed nations, defined as those countries with a gross national product per head of less than $600 a year. It seeks to accelerate the growth rate of the less developed countries to not less than 5 per cent per annum. The Conference endeavours to do this by arranging aid and finance, and by promoting trade. In respect of finance, special drawing rights have been made available at the International Monetary Fund to assist the less developed countries when faced with an unexpected slump in their export receipts. The first U.N.C.T.D. meeting was held in Geneva on 1964. The sixth meeting was held in 1983. By the, virtually all industrial nations and Third World nations considered that the organisation had become an indispensable forum for North-South dialogue. However, the sixth conference was considered to have achieved little beyond emphasising the need for a stronger commitment to overcoming protectionism and for continuing financial flows to the south, the Action Plan of 1981 was, however, re-affirmed. It was recognised by many that only an increase in the value of exports from debt-ridden countries could ease the basic problems.

United Nations Development Programme (UNDP). The World Bank established its programme to finance sector and feasibility studies in 1961. Already in 1959 the United Nations has created the Special Fund, now the United Nations Development Programme (UNDP) to undertake pre-investment work. It was, and it continues to be, the Bank's policy to refer all requests for financial assistance for sector and feasibility studies to the UNDP. Only studies that the UNDP is not able to or prepared to handle on a time schedule appropriate to the requirements of the project have been organised by the Bank and financed out of its own resources. On many occasions, the UNDP has financed a study and asked the Bank to execute it. Whatever the source of financing, the Bank almost always employs consultnats for the actual carrying out of the studies. However, the Bank, in cooperation with the government concerned prepares terms of reference for the consultants, supervise their work, and carefully evaluates their final report.

United Nations Industrial Development Organisations. It was established in 1966 as a United Nations special body following a resolution of the United Nations General Assembly. The organisation offers technical assistance designed to accelerate the industrialisation of developing countries. It helps countries in executing industrial surveys, formulating industrial development policies, conducting project evaluations and assessing plant or industry productivity and marketing strategies.

Unit Trust. In many countries, it is a method of investment by which money subscribed by many people is invested on their behalf by a management company; the investment and management has been subject to the strict legal provisions of a trust deed. The investments acquired are held by a trustee which may be a bank of an insurance company. The management company and the trustee have been parties to the trust deed which defines their respective responsibilities and contains the rules for the operation of the trust.

Unsecured Credition. Persons to whom debt has been owing, but who have been uncovered or unprotected by prior claims on land, property, and other assets. In the event of a business failure, an unsecured creditor many expect a return of funds in whole or part when all prior clams have been met; hence an unsecured creditor might be able to lose all.

Unvalidated Inflation. Means an inflation rate which has been not accompanied by a similar rate of increase in the money supply.

Up-Market. Refers to that part of a market which caters for the demands of the higher socio-economic groups.

Urban Economics. Means that branch of economics which is able to apply the tools of economic reasoning to the analysis of economic activity in and the economic problems of, cities and towns.

Urbanization Economics. Refers to cost saving which arise when economic activities have been concentrated in urban areas. These economics, also known as economies of urban concentration, have been a particular form of agglomeration economies. The existence of urbanization economies helps to account for the growth of urban industrial and commercial centres.

User Cost

(a) A term which was introduced by Lord Keynes to describe the reduction in the value of capital equipment due to its being used as compared with its not being used.

(b) In cost-benefit analysis it refers to the total costs incurred by users in their use of a facility, including social as well as private cost, e.g., the cost of using alternative road systems including such factors as the costs of petrol, wear-and tear on vehicles, time, pollution, and social intrusion.

User Cost of Capital. Revers to the implicit rental value of capital services, or the price a firm should itself pay for the use of the capital stock it owns or is considering acquiring.

Usurious Loans. Loans at exorbitant rates of interest.

Utilitarianism. Philosophical and political term which is used to describe the doctrines of Beatham and his followers, who look as their criterion for judging actions the principle of the greatest happiness of the greatest number.

Utility. The capacity of a good or service to satisfy a human want. Utility cannot be measured in any definite quantitative form; it is sufficient to be able to say, however, that the utility of commodity A>B>C, and so on.

Utility Function. A function which states that an individual's utility has been dependent upon the goods he consumes and their amounts. More formally written as

$$U = U(X,Y,Z.....)$$

where X, Y and Z are the amounts of the goods in question.

Utility, Ordinal. A concept of utility which is based on the idea of a preference ordering, it has been assumed that a consumer compares alternative bundles of goods deciding whether he prefers one to others, or is indifferent between them.

V

Vacancies. Employer's unsatisfied demands for additional employees.

Vacancy Rate. Refers to an index of the demand for labour at the prevailing wage rate.

Validated Inflation. Refers to inflation which is permitted to persist because the government permits the money supply to expand at the same rate as inflation.

Valuation Ratio. The stock-market valuation of a firm's ordinary shares as a ratio of the book value of assets due to ordinary shareholders.

Value. To an economist this term refers to the 'exchange value' or price of a commodity or service, i.e., the power it possesses of acquiring other goods or services by means of exchange.

Value Added. Refers to the value added to a commodity at each stage of its manufacturer; for example, the value added by a flour miller to the final value of the flour, minus the cost of the wheat. The value added at each stage of processing will be equal the final value of the bread sold.

Value-Added Tax. Refers to tax levied on net business turnover. It differs from a turnover tax in eliminating from the taxable 'base' the cost of inputs such as material and labour, it is a tax on the'value added' to a group of inputs by the operations of the firm. This 'value added' is the difference between the untaxed selling price of an article or service and the unit cost of production.

Value, Money, a Standard of. One of the functions of money is that it acts as a store of value.

Value of Service Principle. Refers to a basis for charging for services which may be adopted by a monopolist who enjoys the power to discriminate between markets. A monopolist adopting this principle will divide the total market served by him into a number of minor markets, exacting the maximum gain from each market.

Value Theories of. Theories devised to explain the exchange value or price of commodities and services. These have included:

(a) *Labour theory of value.* A theory which states commodities are sold in ratios determined by the amount of labour expended on producing them.

(b) *Cost of production theory of value.* A theory which states that the value of a commodity is governed by the cost of the various factors employed in its production. This theory will be simply a restatement of the labour theory of value expressed in monetary terms.

(c) *Marginal theory of value.* A theory which states that the value of any commodity or service is determined by its marginal utility for any particular purpose. Thus value depends on relative scarcity, or on demand in relation to supply.

Vanilla Product. A standard product, e.g., a straightforward Eurobond fixed-interest issue, without the sophistication of options or swaps.

Variable Capital. In the Marxian scheme refers to that part of capital, represented by labour power, which undergoes an alternation of value in the production process.

Variable Costs. Refers to costs which very directly with variations in the volume of output. The major variable costs involved have been those of labour and material. Also known as 'prime costs'.

Variable Labour Costs. Mean the costs of employment that very proportionately or more than proportionately with hours worked. The principle examples have been hourly wage rates and overtime/premium-time pay. But various non-wage labour costs will also offer have a variable as a will as a fixed cost component.

Variable Proportions, Law of. This law states that if the quantity of one productive service gets increased by equal increments, from zero, the quantities of the other essential productive services remaining fixed, the resulting increments of product will increase for a period, then become constant, and then decrease.

Veblen Effect. Refers to the phenomenon whereby as the price of a good falls some consumers construe this as a reduction in the quality of the good and cease to buy it. The result will be that the market demand curve will exhibit a steeper slope than would otherwise be predicted. It could even slope upwards in contradiction of the law of demand. The phenomenon is termed after Thorstein Veblen.

Velocity of Circulation. Refers to the average number of times that each unit of money (whether in the from of coins, notes or bank deposits) changes hands in the course of a year. In other words;

$$\text{Average velocity of circulation} = \frac{\text{Volume of spending per year}}{\text{Total volume of money}}$$

The velocity of circulation has been taken into account in the Quantity Theory of Money. In the 'equation of exchange' MV=PT, where M denotes the quantity of money. V the velocity of circulation, P the price level, and T the total volume of transaction. With T constant, an increase in the quantity of money will not raise the price level proportionately if V falls. The velocity of circulation has been not constant, changing in boom and depression.

Vehicle Currency. In the major foreign exchange trading centres most business is generally carried out in a few major currencies, holders of other currencies converting them into one or other of these major currencies for carrying out their transactions. Such major currencies are called vehicle currencies, and while a number of them are in active use, the US dollar is still the world's principal vehicle currency.

Velocity of Circulation. Means the speed at which a given sum of money circulates in the economy -- i.e., the average number of times a unit of money changes hands in a specified time periods. One version of the equation of exchange has been as follows:

$$MV=PT$$

where M denotes the money flow, V the velocity of circulation, P the general price level and T the level of transactions. On rearrangement it becomes as follows:

$$V=\frac{PT}{M}$$

Vertical Disintegration. An opposing trend to vertical integration. It is a situation in which an isolated process has an optimum scale of operation much greater than that required by the other processes of manufacturer and, therefore, tends to be undertaken by a specialist firm which supplies a number of firms in the main industry.

Vertical Integration. Refers to the amalgamation of firms engaged in the different stages of production of the same commodity to achieve greater economic strength and profitability. Although the units may be far apart, geographically, both the sources of rawmaterials and the outlets for the products have been assured.

Vertical Merger. Means the amalgamation of two firms who produce products that are belonging belong to different stage of the same production process.

Vertical Phillips Curve. The hypothesis that in the long-run there occurs on trade-off between the rate of money wage change and the level of unemployment as the Phillips curve originally suggested. In contrast to Phillips' original hypothesis, Friedman (1868) has postulated that is the real wage, not the money wage which is the focus of the wage bargain.

The hypothesis states that workers are concerned to protect the real value of their wages and will therefore demand money wage increases which compensate for the expected rate of inflation. That is:

$$\Delta W = F(U)_t + \lambda \Delta P_t^e$$

Δ = W denotes the change in money wage rates.

U = denotes the unemployment rate, and

ΔP^e denotes the expected change in prices, all in period t.

This is illustrated below. Starting from equilibrium point A at the natural rate of unemployment the government expands aggregate demand in an attempt to reduce unemployment. As demand rises, employers hire more labour and unemployment declines. Of course, employers can only hire more labour by offering higher wages and therefore we move up the short-run Phillips curve to B, but now assuming zero productivity growth prices rise, real wages fall and unemployment falls back to C. Now there exists a positive rate of inflation at the natural rate, for those who remain in employment formulate their expectations of future price rises on the basis of the past behaviour of prices and demand higher money wages to compensate for the positive rate of inflation. If no further action is taken by government this equilibrium rate of inflation will continue.

However, if the government again tries to reduce unemployment below the natural rate we shall move up a second short-run Phillips curve to first, point D then E, Points A, C and E will be on a vertical Phillips curve. The system tends towards the natural rate.

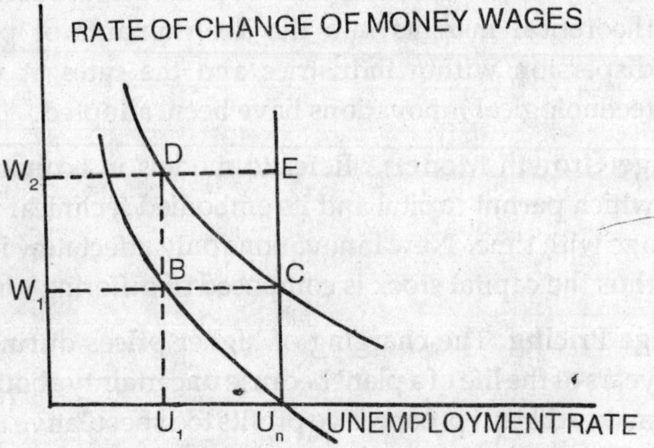

Vertical Phillips Curve

Verical Supply Curve. Means market situation in which output cannot be permanently expanded by a fiscal or monetary expansion of demand. for total output cannot be expanded without improvements in productivity.

Vicious Circles. This term refers to developing countries. This implies that a subsistence economy will remain as such because total output is low, having little or no reserve stocks. Hence, after consumption occurs place there is no surplus for capital accumulation without which there is little hope of increasing output. The key to breaking the vicious circle has been capital accumulation. If a country succeeds in breaking out of the vicious circle, then the opposite effects may happen, in fact a virtuous circle, once capital accumulation begins, outputs rises, and then income rises, giving a larger surplus from which more savings can contribute towards investment and capital accumulation.

Victim Company. A firm which is the subject of a takeover bid.

Vintage Capital Models. These are models of economic growth in which capital is not treated as one homogeneous stock, but as a series of layers of past investment, each layer having its own unique characteristics and representing a more efficient technology then its predecessors. Such models are able to provide theoretical insights into the determinants of productivity dispersion within industries and the rates at which new technological innovations have been adopted.

Vintage Growth Models. Refer to models in economic growth which permit capital and its embodied technical progress to age with time. New innovations only affect new investment, thus the capital stock is composed of differing vintages.

Vintage Pricing. The charging of higher prices during the early years of the life of a plant because uncertainty about the figure makes distant prospective profits too speculative to count on; because of uncertainty, short pay-off periods' are adopted and the price level in the early years reflects this. On the whole, the more dynamic an industry, the shorter the pay-off periods and the higher the price.

Visibility Hypothesis. Incomes policy tends to rely heavily on techniques of publicity and censure. These exposure effects possess their strongest impact upon those wage settlements which are most in the public eye, i.e., which are most 'visible'.

Visible Balance. Means that part of the current of a balance of payments statement, which gives the relationship between the value of physical goods exported and those imported. The other component of the current account has been invisibles e.g., trade in services such as insurance, transport, tourism.

Voluntary-Exchange Model. Refers to an approach to the analysis of the provision of public goods which seeks to establish conditions under which these goods can be provided on the basis of unanimous agreement -- i.e., without coercion. The voluntary approach was first advanced by Knut Wicksell who argued that (1) each public good should be financed by a separate, identifiable tax. (2) that the unanimous agreement of all members of society would be required to decide on the amount (if any) of the good to be supplied. The analysis was extended by E. Lindahl, who presented a model in which both the share of taxes and the amount of good were open to debate. In Lindahl's model, equilibrium needs each individual to pay a tax rate just equal to the individual's marginal utility from the goods. This can be illustrated for a two-person community (consisting of A and B) in the diagram below which has the quantity of the good along the horizontal axis and the share of tax paid by A and B along the vertical axis. A's tax share increases from the bottom up and B's share (corresponding) increase from the top down. The schedule D_A reveals the amount of the good A will wish to produce at different levels of his tax share.

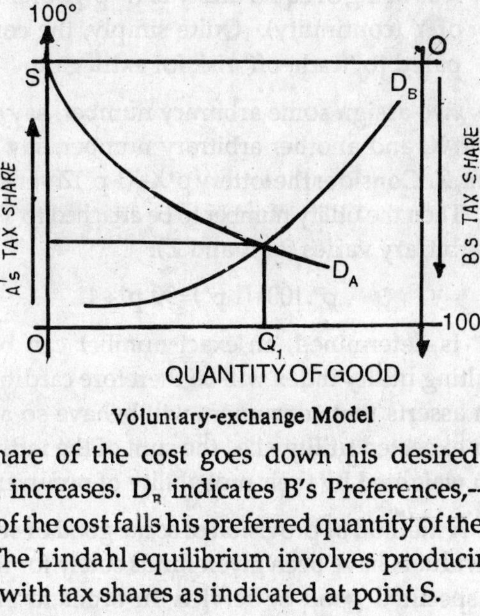

Voluntary-exchange Model

As his share of the cost goes down his desired level of provision increases. D_B indicates B's Preferences,--again as his share of the cost falls his preferred quantity of the good increases. The Lindahl equilibrium involves producing Q 1 of the good with tax shares as indicated at point S.

Voluntary Unemployment. Refers to that unemployment which results from the process of job search and speculative and precautionary unemployment.

Von Neumann -- Morgenstern Utility. Named after J. von Neumann ((1903-57) and O. Morgenstern (1902-77). It is an approach to demand theory which is held to be applicable to risk situations. Among the axioms are:

1. that all alternatives have been subject to the preference or indifference relationship (completeness).
2. transitivity of preferences.
3. if X possesses probability of p and D possesses a probability of (l--p) then if X is preferred to Y when both are certain events, then the lottery of p. X+(l--p)D is preferred to p.Y+(l--p)D.
4. if X has been preferred to Y and Y to Z then some probability p*, exist such that the consumer regards p*. X as being of equal utility to (l--p*)Z and to the certainty of Y (continuity). Quite simply, the consumer if prepared to 'trade-off' risk for extra gain.

Now, we assign some arbitrary number, say 100 to the best event, X, and another arbitrary number, say l, to the worst event, Z. Consider the lottery p*X+(l-p*)Z versus the certainty of Y. Then the utility number to be attached to Y is (substituting the arbitrary varies for X and Z):

$$p^*.100+(l-p^*)=99.p^*+1.$$

If p* is determined, an exact number can be found. The resulting utility index will be therefore cardinal. The theory then asserts that consumers will behave so as to maximize their expected utility - i.e., the sum of the individual utilities each weighted by their probability of occurrence.

Voucher. A method of provision of some good or service in which individuals have been given funds solely for the purchase of the specified good or service. In order to ensure that the money provided has been spent for the specified purpose, a coupon or 'voucher' is given which can only be exchanged for the specified good.

Voucher Schemes. Vouchers have been a means of in-kind redistribution. They transfer purchasing power while restricting the individual's spending decision, for example, education vouchers must be spent on education.

W

Wage Contour. Refers to a set of key rates across several different international labour markets. Contours could be bounded by the specific product market in which the firms populating the contour operate or they may be confined to a specific labour market or sphere of influence of a trade union. Across the contour wage settlements will exhibited a marked degree of uniformity.

Wage Contracts. Refer to the formal and informal agreements between employers and either employees or their representatives about the number of hours to be worked, the quality of work, and the remuneration that is to be received in return.

Wage Differentials. Refer to differences in the average levels of pay of groups of workers which are classified according to the industry or location in which they work or according to the occupational or racial group to which they belong. In its narrower sense this term is applicable to differences in the pay of group of employees in a single negotiating group.

Wage Drift. The term used for the gap between nationally-negotiated wage-rates and actual earnings which tend to be higher. This difference occurs due to overtime payments, bonuses and other incentives. In view of the significance of the trends in wage-rates and actual earnings in the national economy, variations have been often expressed in percentage form. This is calculated :

$$\left(\frac{E}{M} - 1 \right) X\,100$$

where E=ratio of average earnings at end of period to those at the beginning, and M=corresponding ratio in respect of wage-rates.

Wage Fund. A fund which is available for the payment of wages.

Wage Fund Theory. Adam Smith took over from the phsysiocrats the idea that wages are advanced to the workers in expectation of the sale of their output. Wages could not be raised unless the capital earmarked to pay them was also raised. Capital, in turn, was determined by savings. The classical school, developed its theory of wages around these ideas. In the short run, there was a given number of workers and a given among of savings to pay their wages. The two together decided the average wage. In the long-run, the supply of labour was related to the minimum subsistence needed to sustain the labour force.

Wage Indexation. Means the adjustment of wages in line with changes in the cost-of-living. In this way real incomes can be maintained during inflationary periods.

Wage Inflation. Means a rise in money wages over time. It may be due, but need not, be to wage-push inflation.

Wage Leadership. Refers to a characteristic of industries in which productivity has been rising and firms find it easier for a variety of reasons to concede demands for wage increases than to reduce prices; the wage increase gained in one trade or industry tend to stimulated pressures for similar increases in other branches.

Wage-Price Spiral. Refers to the notion that wage increase cause price increases, via the increase in production costs, which in turn feed through into wages, as worker seek to preserve the purchasing power of their wages, and so on. The interpretation of the wage-price spiral as a mechanical sequence has been intimately linked to the cost-push view of inflation.

Wage-Push Inflation. Refers to a variant of cost-push which attributes the origins of the inflationary process to trade union pressure in the labour market.

Wage Rates. The term used for the rate of payment an individual receives for the supply of each of the minimum number of hours specified in the wage contract. Often referred to as basic hourly wage rates, they are able to specify some minimum level or remuneration the individual can expect for each hour of the standard working week.

Wage Round. Refers to the hypothesis the substantial linkages exist between the settlements of all negotiating groups in the economy and that in consequence wage settlements conform to certain patterns each year.

Wage Structure. Refers to the ranking of pay levels of different groups of workers classified according to the industry or location in which they work or according to the occupational or racial group to which they belong.

Wage, Theories Of. Theories seeking to account for the level of wages in a community. The main theories which have been advanced are as follows :

(a) *Subsistence theory*. This theory states that if wages rose above subsistence level an increase in population would inevitably follow, thus forcing wages down again to subsistence level. In many parts of the world, in which the standard of living is very low, this problem persists; nevertheless the advanced industrial countries have demonstrated that this 'law' is not inevitable and that rising wages can get associated with a falling birth rate.

(b) *Wage-fund theory*. A theory which states that the amount available for wages is limited by the amount of capital; thus there is a definite 'fund' from which wages are paid, and if some get more, others get less. Wages depend, therefore, upon the proportion that the working population bears to capital.

(c) *Marginal productivity theory.* A current theory which states that wages tend to be equal to the value of the marginal product of labour. The marginal product has been the additional income that would accrue to an organisation from the employment of one extra person (of alternatively the decline in total income from the dismissal of one person).

The neoclassical theory of the demand for labour relates labour demand only to the real wage, given the quantity of other factors the firm is using. Competitive firms that are able to change the quantity of labour they employ, costlessly and immediately, will hire labour up to the point where the real wage is equal to the marginal product of labour.

Wagner's Law. A hypothesis, advanced by a German economist Adolph Wagner which stated that the development of an industrialized economy would be accompanied by a rising share of Public Expenditure in Gross National Product. Wagner identified three main reasons of this expenditure growth.

1. A relative increase in the costs of public administration, law and order and the regulation of economic activity as a society got developed.
2. 'Cultural' and 'welfare' activities offered by the state were said to have an income elasticity of demand greater than one — that is as incomes rose the demand for these services would increase more than in proportion.
3. Economic development would get accompanied by a rise of industrial monopolies which would need state control.

Walras Law. This law states that given *n* markets if *n*-l markets are in equilibrium then the last one must also be in equilibrium because there cannot be a net excess of demand or supply for goods (including money).

Want Creation. Means the identification by firms of latent consumer needs and their conversion into conscious wants, by the active marketing of products so designed to meet the identified intent needs.

Warrant. Means the buying of an agreement which offers the owner the opportunity to purchase equity capital.

Warranted Rate of Growth. Means the rate of economic growth at which desired saving has been equal to required investment. A concept developed by Sir Roy Harrod in his Economic Dynamics by using the equation.

$$G_w = \frac{S_d}{C_r}$$

where

G_w = warranted growth rate;

S_d = fraction of income representing the amount of saving that people currently want to make;

C_r = fraction in which the values of the numerator and denominator are such that people find that the amount of capital goods on hand, fixed and circulating, is just what required.

Waste. An inevitable by-product of economic activity.

Wealth. Goods and other assets in existence at any time which command a market value (i.e., price) if offered for sale. It implies that such assets have utility and scarcity value, and that it becomes possible to transfer their ownership from one person or body to another. Economic science is concerned with the production and distribution of wealth defined in this way and not with assets which have value in the mind of the owner only. Wealth is a fund of goods which can be consumed; it represents stored up facilities for the satisfaction of future wants.

Wealth Effect. Refers to an increase in aggregate expenditure due to a fall in the price level and interest rates. Any fall in aggregate demand by the induced effects of falls in the price level and interest rates will get reversed.

Wealth Tax. A tax which is levied on net wealth and is normally levied at regular intervals — usually one year — on the net assets of individuals though in some countries such as Norway it is payable by companies as well.

Welfare Economics. A branch of economics which deals with studying the extend to which economic activity maximises human welfare, and the evaluation of public policies relating to the economy designed to achieve that end.

Welfare Frontier. A concept which represents the maximum well-being any person can enjoy, given the levels of welfare enjoyed by the remaining members of the community. Given the state of the arts, there is no position within the frontier which can be regarded as one of maximum social welfare; conversely there is no point outside the frontier attainable by society.

Welfare State. Refers to a nation that provides minimum standards in respect of education, health, housing, pensions and other social benefits, etc. when the individual means of certain sections of the population may be inadequate to provide these standards.

Well-Behaved. Refers to a property of production (and utility) functions. It needs that production (utility) is zero if one of the inputs (commodities) is zero, that the marginal product (utility) is always positive, but diminishes smoothly with increasing amounts of a given factor (commodity). This notion is playing a crucial role in the neo-classical theories of growth and distribution.

Whipsawing. A technique which is used by some unions to extract a concession from an employer by threatening to strike whereas his competitors continue to operate, and, after he has conceded to attempt to force a second employer to grant the same or even enhanced terms and conditions of employment or face a strike. Employers could be able to meet this tactic by co-ordinating their collective bargaining activities and perhaps by negotiating as a single group.

White Collar Workers. Employees and employers who are not engaged in physical work and who undertake duties which appear to be functionally related to authority.

Wholesale. The term used for the intermediate stage in the chain of distribution. Wholesalers specialize in the process of distribution, purchasing the output of firms for re-sale and distribution to retailers.

Wicksell Effects. The Wicksell effect shows that contrary to the marginal productivity theory of capital the real rate of interest in the economy may be different from the aggregate marginal product of capital. Wicksell argued that an increase in the supply of capital (investment) affects not only the price of new capital, but also changes the units in which the existing stock of capital is valued. He argued that the net effect of a rise in wages and a fall in the rate of interest has been to raise the value of existing capital. It means that the value of capital in two economies may differ according to the level of wages and the rate of interest although the stock of real capital is identical and the techniques in use are the same. This effect is known as the Price Wicksell effect. The Real Wicksell effect refers to a change in techniques consequent upon a change in the rate of interest.

Wieser's Law of Costs. A law formulated by Friedrich von Weiser (1851-1926), an Austrian economist. It states that the cost of a commodity is the alternative foregone in producing it.

Wildcat Strike. A strike which is called by local groups of union members, ostensibly without the authorization of the official union leadership and in contravention of established procedures.

Willingness to Pay. Means the valuation placed by individual on a good or service in terms of money. Its used as an indicator of valuation has been controversial in two respects. First, it will be constrained by ability to pay so that those with higher incomes will appear to value goods more highly than those with lower incomes. This may contradict some concept of fairness or justice. Secondly, it has been open to moral objection when the good in question has been the removal of a nuisance such as noise or pollution, since it might be argued that the monetary transfer should be half to the sufferer in the form of compensation.

Windfall Gain. Refers to a unanticipated addition to income.

Windfall Loss. Refers to unanticipated reduction in income.

Winding Up. See Liquidation, Receivers.

Windows. Opportunities for profitable investment in markets or transfers between markets; for raising capital in different markets; or for profitable arbitrage taking advantage of fluctuations in interest rates and exchange rates.

Wire House. A business house operating a private wire to its own branch wire to its own branch officers, or to other firms.

Withdrawals (also known as leakages). Any income which is not passed on in the circular flow of income, and therefore has been not available for spending on currently produced goods and services.

Withholding Tax. Generally a tax which is levied on dividends and interest made by a company to an overseas destination. Most Western countries have such a tax.

Workable Competition. A concept which was first put forward by Professor J.M. Clark (1884-1863) in 1940. He asserted the widespread existence of competition notwithstanding equally widespread monopoly elements in the real world. Even within what appeared to be monopolistic or oligopolistic market structures, important elements of competition may be found. The emphasis should not therefore be on structure or even on conduct but on actual performance in respect of price, profits, products, and technical progress. Hence, the more workably competitive an industry, it may be argued, the more prices will approach those which would rule in conditions of perfect competition permitting for the fact that internal economies of scale might make perfect competition impossible.

Working Capital. Refers to the amount of current assets which has been financed from long-term sources of finance. Gross working capital has been alternatively defined as the sum of all current assets while net working capital is the amount by which current assets exceed current liabilities. The size of working capital has been an indicator of the liquidity and solvency of a company particularly when related to other financial indicators in the form of financial ratios.

Working Capital Ratio. This is calculated by dividing current liabilities into current assets. It has been a measure of a firm's liquidity.

Working Control. The control over a corporation or company comprises, theoretically, ownership of at least 51 per cent of the total voting shares; however, effective control can sometimes be exercised through ownership, individually or by a group acting in concert, of less than 50 per cent of the shares.

Working Population. Refer to all those who are willing and able to work and either in employment or registered as unemployed.

Work in Progress. Means production which remains uncompleted at the end of the accounting period.

Work-Leisure Model. It is an application of the theory of consumer behaviour to the allocation of time question. The individual worker has been assumed to devote time both to market work and to non-marketable activities called leisure. He maximizes his utility by choosing combinations of goods (obtained by working) and leisure hours subject to time and price constraints, which could be combined into a single budget or income constraint, the slope of which measures the wage rate. Equilibrium will exist where the marginal rate of substitution of leisure for goods in consumption has been equal to the slope of the budget line (the wage rate). The effect of a rise in the wage rate can be decomposed into income and substitution effects although the direction of the total effect cannot be determined a priori but depends on whether the negative income effect (assumpting leisure to be a normal good) outweight the positive substitution effect.

Work Sharing. Refers to a means of maintaining employment levels by reducing hours of work per employee.

Work to Rule. A partial form of strike, which results in a slowdown of production rather than complete cessation. Workers insist on producing only according to the strict rules of some written job description or departmental rule and can usually manage seriously to impair productive efficiency. Adherence to some written rules could be able to avoid the application of sanctions by employers.

World Bank. A group of three institutions; the International Bank of Reconstruction and Development, the International Development Association and the International Finance Corporation. The common objective of these institutions is to help raise standards of living in developing countries by channelling financial resources from developed countries to the developing world. The Bank was established in December, 1945.

In 1946, the World Bank had 38 members; in 1960, 68 members; in 1970, 113 members; and in 1982, 143 members. The members range from the Seychelles (population 67,000) to China (population 1 billion). Lending has expanded from $3.4 billion in 1972-73 to $13 billion in 1981-82, a increase in real terms about 6 per cent per annum. In 1982, the Bank had a staff of 2,600; the headquarters is in Washington. D.C. Despite many criticisms, the World bank has been the largest single source of development funds for the world's poorer nations.

'World Development Report'. An annual publication of the World Bank. Its publication began in 1978. The report surveys the state of the world in terms of poverty and wealth, health general well-being, and describes the nature and character of the projects supported in whole or part by the Bank

X

X. cp. Abbreviation of ex-capitalisation.

X. d. Abbreviation of ex-devidend.

X-Efficiency. A situation in which a firm's total costs are not minimized because the actual output from given inputs is less than the maximum feasible level. This outcome is also termed a situation of 'technical inefficiency'. X-efficiency is a direct function of monopoly of market power in which competitive pressures are weakened. The term was originally applied to the manager-worker relationship but can be extended to deal with the manager-owner relationship.

Xu. A fractional unit of currency of Vietnam. 100 Xu being in value to a dong.

Y

Y-Efficiency. Means the effectiveness with which existing profitable market opportunities are exploited.

Yen. The currency unit of Japan divided into 100 sen.

Yield. The return on a security based on its current earnings in relation to its current price on the stock exchange.

Yield Gap. The difference between an average yield on equities and a corresponding yield on long-dated fixed-interest securities.

Yuan. Also known as renminbi. It is the monetary unit of China. It is subdivided into 10 Chiao, the chiao being again subdivided into 10 fen.

Z

Zaire. It is the standard unit of the currency of the Zaire Republic.

Z-Chart. A chart which relates to the output of a firm. It shows graph of monthly totals, the cumulative monthly total and the moving annual these three graphs together taking the shape of a letter Z.

Zloty. It is the standard currency unit of Poland. It is divided into 100 grosze.

Zoning. A term used in town and country planning for areas set aside for particular purposes as, for example, light or heavy industry and green belts.

ZPG. Abbreviation of zero population growth. It is an American term for a rate of growth giving a stable population.

Zurish. The financial centre of Switzerland.